METER

| 0 | 1/2 | 1 MILE |

National
Assembly

RAJAVITHI ROAD

Chitra Lada
Palace

RAMA V

ROAD

Royal Turf Club

Government
House

RD'PITSANULOKE
ROAD

RD

NG

ROAD

SAWANKALOKE RD.

SRI

AYUTHAYA

PETCHABURI

Klong

Maha

Nok

ROAD

ROAD

RAMA I

ROAD

Don Muang
Airport

Victory
Monument

Klong

Samsen

ROAD

KRUNG

KASEM

ROAD

RAMA VI

ROAD

Chulalongkorn
University

PHYATHAI

SOI CHULA

SANAM-MA

ROAD

ROAD

RAMA IV

ROAD

SIPHYA

ROAD

ROAD

Lumpini
Park

KROEN

KRUNG ROAD

SURIWONGSE

ROAD

ROAD

SILOM

S.

SATH

Klong Sathorn

Sam! H. Bryant

DATE DUE			
AUG 2 5 '7			

Alec Waugh
has written more than forty books.
Among them are the following:

Novels

THE LOOM OF YOUTH (1917)
KEPT (1925)
THE BALLIOLS (1934)
NO TRUCE WITH TIME (1941)
ISLAND IN THE SUN (1956)
FUEL FOR THE FLAME (1960)
THE MULE ON THE MINARET (1965)
A SPY IN THE FAMILY (1970)

Travel

HOT COUNTRIES (1930)
LOVE AND THE CARIBBEAN (1959)

Autobiography

THE EARLY YEARS OF ALEC WAUGH (1963)

Biography

MY BROTHER EVELYN AND OTHER PORTRAITS (1968)

Miscellaneous

IN PRAISE OF WINE (1959)
A FAMILY OF ISLANDS (1964)
WINES AND SPIRITS
(Time-Life Books. Foods of the World Series, 1968)

BANGKOK

The Story of a City

BANGKOK

The Story of a City

by Alec Waugh

LITTLE, BROWN AND COMPANY

BOSTON / TORONTO

LIBRARY OF CONGRESS CATALOG CARD NO. 77–121426

FIRST EDITION

T06/71

Published simultaneously in Canada
by Little, Brown & Company (Canada) Limited

PRINTED IN THE UNITED STATES OF AMERICA

TO MAUDIE ISRANKUL

One of my very first Thai friends and still one of my dearest, who as much as anyone has helped me to understand why I love so dearly the city where she was born.

Acknowledgment

I wish to express my gratitude to those who have helped me with this book; to the officials of the Library of Congress at Washington, D.C., who greatly assisted me in my researches; to H.H. Prince Prem of Purachatra and Prince Piya Rangsit who with their friendship and hospitality have enlightened for me so many aspects of Thai life and customs; to Captain Bisdar Chulasewok, the custodian of Prince Chula's Palace; to St. Clair McKelway, who was an editor in Bangkok at the time of the first coup d'etat. But most of all I am indebted to the writings of the late H.R.H. Prince Chula Chakrabongse, in particular to his *Lords of Life*, which is the basic indispensable authority for every student of the country's history. I am most grateful to his widow for having graciously allowed me to reproduce some of the photographs that illustrate it.

Contents

Illustrations

BANGKOK
The Story of a City

1

How It All Began

I T began with a quarrel about white elephants; at least that is
what they believe on the banks of the Menam River.

In the middle of the fifteenth century the king of Burma
asked the king of Siam to give him one of his white elephants.
The king of Siam, although he had seven of his own, refused
this neighborly request; that was the start of three hundred
years of warfare. At the end of it, in 1767, Burmese forces captured and sacked the Siamese capital of Ayudhya. Which is
why they say that but for a quarrel about white elephants, the
city of Bangkok would not exist.

At the start of the final campaign, the site of the present city
was a collection of huts forty miles south along the river. On
the west bank of the river was a fort that could mount eighty
guns and that had originally been founded by the French a
hundred years before, when Louis XIV had territorial ambitions in Southeast Asia. It was called Dhonburi. On the east
bank of the river was a colony of Chinese traders; they called it
Bangkok — The Village of the Wild Plum — and in the days of
good King Narai it was of value as a trading post. When
Ayudhya fell, one of the few survivors was a general who had
left the city in a mood of pique because the king would not

allow him to fire his gun without express permission. With only five followers he cut his way through the Burmese lines, to establish at Dhonburi the base of a resistance movement that would, he hoped, oust the Burmese. His name was Taksin.

The people to whom he addressed his appeal had originally migrated from southern China, fleeing before Kublai Khan in the middle of the thirteenth century. They were a small, dark brown race with delicate features. They were gay, pleasure-loving, avid for freedom, proud of themselves and of their independence. They were imitative, absorbing the national characteristics that appealed to them during their slow trek southwards. Through the Chinese they had become animists as well as Buddhists. In Thailand today you are unlikely to see a garden or a building which is not decorated with its own spirit house, where the local deity is appeased with offerings of food and flowers. Their animism is fortified with a belief in the tenets of astrology. No Thai would make any important movement until an astrologer had pronounced that the day intended was propitious.

On their way south, where they contributed their labor to the construction of Angkor Wat, they were deeply influenced by the Khmers, their Buddhism being colored and informed by the Brahminism that justified their need for pomp and ceremony. Buddhism with its negations would never have completely satisfied their exotic nature; it might be said that in mingling the two strands of secondhand indic culture, they rejected extremism and retained happiness.

By the middle of the fourteenth century their wanderings were finished; they had reached their frontier, and in 1350 they founded their capital of Ayudhya — which they called the divine blessed city — on the banks of the Menam, in the center of the rich plain that was enriched by the waters of the Himalayan snows. Not only was the countryside capable of producing enough rice to feed a considerable population, but Siam was admirably placed to conduct a two-way traffic with India and China. When the Portuguese arrived in 1500 it was to find a city of a million inhabitants, resplendent with monasteries and temples.

During the next hundred and fifty years Ayudhya's prosperity increased. It was the *entrepôt* for the trade between India and China. The journey around the Straits of Malacca was long and dangerous. On the west coast of Siam on the Bay of Bengal was the port of Mergui, which at that time was owned by the kings of Siam. From it the river Little Tenasserim ran into the long leg of the Malay Peninsula. This part of the journey was pleasant enough, but it was followed by a rough passage through the jungle. Finally the traveler had to proceed on foot, with carts carrying the cargo. It was a highly uncomfortable trip, but even so it was preferable to the journey around the Straits, and Indian traders were able to collect, in Ayudhya, Chinese and Japanese silks, tea, porcelain and copper goods, in return for scented woods, pepper and hides. Geographically the city could not have been better placed. Yet it was open to attack by the Burmese both from the west and from the north. It was highly vulnerable.

Of the city's million inhabitants, barely ten thousand were left when the sacking of the city was complete in 1767; those who were not slaughtered on the spot were taken into captivity. The king himself, though he sought refuge in a temple, was put to death. Everything of value was removed. The Burmese had no intention of occupying the city they had captured. They were concerned with loot and with revenge. They destroyed everything that did not seem worth carrying home. Nearly all the records were burned. Yet even so, General Taksin did not feel that the task of recovery was beyond his power.

It is surprising that he should have done so, in view of the particular and peculiar structure of the people to which he issued his appeal. There was no country of Siam in the sense that we understand the term. The kings were known as kings of Ayudhya. And the kings themselves owned the country and the complete allegiance of the inhabitants. They could claim their services, either as soldiers or as workmen. They were known as "The Lords of Life." Yet at the same time their kingdom was not defined. They had claims on Cambodia and on parts of the Malay Peninsula, though it was not clear what those rights were. They were entitled to tribute, though the amount was not specified and they did not always get it. They claimed a voice in the election to the Cambodian throne. Yet there were provinces in their own north over which their authority was dubious. You will hear it said that Paris is not France, that London is not England, that New York is not America; but Siam on the other hand was Ayudhya, just as later it was to be Bangkok. When Ayudhya was destroyed, and its royal family liquidated, you would have assumed that was the end of the country. Yet that did not happen. Taksin's appeal to the various local leaders was effective. He soon had an army and luck was on his side. Burma suddenly found itself involved in a war with China, and was not able to do more than leave a certain number of garrisons scattered about the country. These Taksin was able to destroy, one by one; finally within a year and a half in a single main battle near Ayudhya, he broke the effective power of the Burmese army, and was able to have himself proclaimed king.

We know very little for certain about King Taksin; his reign was to last for fifteen years, but for most of this period he was engaged in military campaigns. The Burmese returned to the attack and had to be beaten back. There were other campaigns on the northern frontier. He had no time to devote to the building of his new capital. He allowed the future city of Bangkok to remain across the river, a collection of Chinese tradesmen. His chief lieutenants during these campaigns were two brothers, whose father had been an official in the old regime. They were called Thong Duang and Boonma; and there is every reason for believing that their mother was a Chinese lady. Each rose quickly in rank and prominence — the elder one being elevated to the rank of Chao Phya Chakri, the other as Chao Phya Surasih. Nomenclature in Thailand is very difficult to understand. Until 1917 what we call surnames did not exist. One was known by what passport authorities call a given name. Often a man was known by the rank he held. The word Chakri meant commander in chief; so Thong Duang became known as General Chakri, and in this way the long succession of kings that was to ensue became known as the Chakri dynasty.

General Chakri was highly effective in the field; he repelled four Burmese invasions and brought to heel two Laotian principalities; in the course of his operations he brought from Vientiane the Emerald Buddha, which is today the most important object of worship in the capital. No one knows how old it is. Prince Chula Chakrabongse states in his book *Lords of Life: A History of the Kings of Thailand* his belief that it was carved in northern India by the Greeks. He considers that the original nephrite stone came from the Caucasus, and that its journey through Ceylon and Burma to Siam must have taken a thousand years. No one has ever doubted that if a man swears falsely by the image, the grisliest fate will in the end befall him.

Traditionally Cambodia had been a vassal state of the kings of Ayudhya, and Taksin, elated by his successes, was resolved to reassert his rights and assure that its throne was occupied by a monarch who had been approved by himself. He felt however that he was too old, too exhausted by many wars to undertake a new campaign, so he entrusted its conduct to General Chakri, while he himself remaining in Dhonburi would devote his energies to the interior organization of his kingdom. This in view of the country's interests was no doubt a prudent decision; it was less fortunate for his own. Apparently the years of battle, followed by seven years of absolute rule, had corroded his stability. Military men are not always successful as politicians. The techniques of the guardroom and the formulas of military discipline are not easily transferred to the deliberations of the council chamber. Men who have obeyed and issued orders as soldiers — in the confidence of instantaneous obedience — feel that treachery is afoot when their opinions are debated by a cabinet. Taksin, as a king, became hysterically distrustful of his advisers. His reprisals were fierce and frequent. He tortured his wife, his sons, and a number of high officials in an attempt to make them confess to crimes they had not committed. He began to suspect that his courtiers were carrying on illicit trade, thus robbing him of the revenues to which he was entitled. He accepted as evidence the sworn testimony of a single individual, and unscrupulous informers grew rich on the fines which they extorted from their neighbors.

It has also been noted that soldiers in their declining years tend to become fanatically religious. This happened to Taksin. He imagined himself a reincarnation of the Buddha. He fasted in the belief that thus he would acquire the power to fly and he flogged the monks who refused to worship him. He became in fact insane. It was not long before the city was in revolt with a General Sanka restoring order at the head of a military junta.

The news of this confusion reached General Chakri in Cambodia. He immediately abandoned his campaign and hurried home. He was welcomed on all sides, General Sanka meeting him outside the city walls to make obeisance. The officers of state followed, and on April 6, 1782, offered Chakri the throne,

An aerial shot of the Grand Boulevard showing the ·Monument to
Democracy

which he accepted. It was a bloodless revolution. There was no fighting.

Taksin surrendered without a protest, and with the request that he be allowed to live out his days in a Buddhist monastery. Chakri had been his favorite general. They had fought side by side; they had never quarreled. Taksin might well have hoped that this wish would be conceded him. But it is not expedient to have a deposed king living even as a priest within the confines of the country over which he once ruled; and it must be remembered that a priest can leave a monastery any time he likes. It would be equally impractical to have him living outside the country, where he might become the center of a conspiracy against the state. There was no alternative to his execution. He apparently bore no ill will, and on his way to the scaffold asked if he might be able to take his leave personally of his old brother-in-arms. It is reported that Chakri could not trust himself to speak; he was in tears and waved the messenger away.

In Siam the blood of a royal person may not be shed; the execution of such a one is performed by a blow on the back of the neck with a scented sandalwood club. Prince Chula has written that death was instantaneous and that it was as merciful as the guillotine. On the other hand there are reports that the victim was placed in a velvet sack and beaten to death — which must have been a lengthy process. The last prince to be executed in this way was Prince Raksanaret in 1848. But when Prince Chula in 1931 asked whether there still remained on the staff a man trained to perform an execution in the traditional manner, he was assured there was.

History is replete with the stories of men, honorable enough, patriotic enough, astute politically, responsive to self-interest, who in the fog of revolutionary partisanship have backed the wrong horse — or the right horse at the wrong time — and faced a firing squad. At a first glance it would seem that General Sanka was one of the lucky few who spotted the winner at the start. He had headed a revolt that had become inevitable; he had restored order to the capital, without any intention of taking over the supreme authority himself. When the ideal leader appeared at the gates with his elephants and troops, he recognized the man of destiny who would save the hour and paid him homage. Surely he had deserved well of the state in general and of Chakri in particular. Surely he could expect quick promotion? In any other country, yes, but not in Siam.

Treachery was the greatest crime a Thai could commit. It is not surprising that it should have been — it was endemic in the country. Of the thirty-three kings who ruled in Ayudhya during the four centuries of its existence, a third were murdered or reached the throne through murder. To plot against a king was the greatest of all crimes and Sanka had conspired against Taksin. Chakri was innocent. He did not usurp a throne. He occupied an empty one. But Sanka was a criminal. He must pay the penalty. He was executed not with a sandalwood club but with a sword.

In this way the reign of the Chakri dynasty began with an episode that is curiously revealing, curiously interpretive of the Thai mentality, of the Thai regard for tradition, for the exact letter of the law, for refusing to let the end justify the means. Only in Siam could the general who had enabled a brother officer to ascend a throne have been rewarded for his services by decapitation. It is an episode to remember whenever one finds oneself puzzled by the apparent contradictoriness of Thai policy and conduct in private as in public matters.

2

The First of the Chakris

THE accession of Chakri to the throne marked the beginning not only of modern Thailand but of the city whose life story this book will describe. Chakri's first act was to move his capital across the river from Dhonburi to Bangkok. He made this decision on military grounds. The land at Dhonburi was slightly higher, but Bangkok was protected by water against the attack which he anticipated through the west. The site that he chose for his royal palace was at that time occupied by a colony of Chinese tradesmen, but he was able to persuade them with the aid of appropriate compensation to move a little farther to the south and east. The area to which they moved, which is known as Sampeng, is still Chinatown. On the lots that the Chinese had abandoned, Chakri was able to run up a collection of wooden pavilions with such speed that his coronation took place before the end of June. The first king of Ayudhya had been called Rama Tibodi, and as this was one of the many titles that Chakri assumed, he has become known to *farangs* — as foreigners are called — as Rama I; and indeed that title was conferred on him many years later by his great-great-grandson. The Thais refer to the dynasty in terms of reigns: first reign, second reign. The Thai word for reign is *rajakala* so the kings are known as RI, RII, and so on through the dynasty. Consequently *farangs* and Thais find themselves able to understand to which king the other is referring.

It was Rama I's plan to reproduce opposite Dhonburi a city resembling as far as possible the destroyed Ayudhya. In the Rijksmuseum, in Amsterdam, there is a painting of that city as a Dutchman saw it at the start of the seventeenth century. It was unquestionably a very lovely city. The directors of the East India Company compared it with London. In the middle of the century a Dutchman described it as being six miles around, stone-walled, with canals running down one side of its broad streets. The king's palace was a town apart; much of it was gilded. At the close of the century a Frenchman described it as larger than Paris, with poor houses and magnificent pagodas. Maurice Collis evokes its grandeur in his *Siamese White*. He quotes from the Abbé de Choisy's journal of a voyage to Siam published in Paris in 1687. "We went for a walk outside the town. I stood frequently in admiration of the strong great city, seated upon an island round which flowed a river three times the size of the Seine. There rode ships from France, England, Holland, China and Japan while innumerable boats and gilded barges rowed by sixty men plied to and fro. No less extraordinary were the camps or villages outside the walls inhabited by the different nations who come trading there, with all the wooden houses standing on posts over the water; the bulls, cows and pigs are on dry land. The streets, stretching out of sight, are alleys of clear running water. Under the great green trees and in the little houses crowd the people. Beyond these camps of the nations are the wide rice fields. The horizon is tall trees, above which are visible the sparkling towers and pyramids of the pagodas."

In a later passage he describes how "we rowed down the long canals under the green of the trees while the birds sang and passed between rows of wooden houses perched on posts, very shabby-looking outside but we were to find them clean within. We entered one of them prepared to see the peasants in rags, but all was spick and span. The floor covered with mats, Japanese coffers and screens everywhere. Hardly inside the door, they offered us tea in porcelain cups."

This was the city that Rama I proposed to reconstruct on the curve of the Menam, forty miles nearer to the sea. But that was not all he planned. He did not want only to recreate the fabric of a gutted city; he wanted to revive in exact detail the life that had been lived within those walls — a life which, though he himself cannot have known it, had no counterpart upon the globe; a way of life that was created by an accident of history, of geography, of the racial streams that combined with history and geography to produce the Thais themselves.

The most widely loved and admired people in Europe today are the Danes and the Thais have been called the Danes of Asia, not only because Bangkok is built as Copenhagen is — upon a series of canals — but because of their temperamental resemblances: their gaiety, their sunniness, their independence, their love of beauty, their frivolity. Today, as the popularity of the package tour mounts every year, Bangkok is increasingly overrun with tourists. It is the "must" city for every tour to the Far East. And it is a "must" city because it was built in terms of that essential frivolous gaiety that distinguishes the Thais from other races. Bangkok is an expression of themselves, of their religion, of their beliefs.

Basically the country is Buddhist and every rich man's house has its own Buddha room. The monastery was in early days the educational center of Thai life, and though there is now a highly evolved secular education system, most professional men serve in the priesthood for three months before marriage. Even the present king put on the saffron robe and went round in

The Monument to Democracy

the morning with his begging bowl. That is essential Buddhism, but it is the Brahminism that the Thais acquired from the Khmers in Cambodia that gave the glow and glitter to the pageantry of the city's life.

At the base of everything the Thais believed in early days was the supremacy of the king himself. He was distant and divine, the Lord of Life — restrained only by the ten virtues: charity, moral living, support for religion, honesty, compassion, freedom from wrongful ambition, freedom from thoughts of revenge, loving the people as their father, moderate with punishment, constant care for the people's welfare and happiness. He was answerable to no one but himself. Yet it was not the king but the monarchy that was divine. And there were no rules to decide the succession to the throne. The king was chosen by an electoral council so that this high position went to the man best fitted to fill it. Elaborate ceremony and pomp enhanced and protected his presence. The ministers who approached him had to do so prostrate; the populace could not look at him; nobody could touch him. The members of the royal family were similarly guarded. When Chulalongkorn's wife and daughter fell into the river they had to be left to drown, because the boatmen were not allowed to touch them. Rama III was a heavy sleeper, but the page who was instructed to wake him at seven was not allowed to touch him. He had to shout the time into the monarch's ear and sometimes it was not until eight o'clock that he was ready to get up.

The Abbé de Choisy has described how in Ayudhya the streets would be lined with soldiers when the king on his elephant made his afternoon procession through the streets. The chief ministers proceeded and followed him with their ceremonial hats, shaped like pyramids and circled with gold rings indicative of rank. The soldiers in spite of the heat wore helmets and cuirasses and carried gilded shields. The atmosphere of pomp was such as the Pharoahs once enjoyed. Yet the populace was not allowed to benefit from the spectacle. Not only were the streets cleared, but bamboo screens were set in front of the houses. A special language was used when royalty was addressed. The rules of procedure had been laid down by King Trailok in the Palace Law of 1450, and they had been maintained unaltered. No one had any wish to alter them. The Thais did not feel themselves demeaned by prostrating themselves in the royal presence. On the contrary, they took a pride in subjecting themselves to divinity. Once one of the royal boatmen ran his lord's barge aground. According to King Trailok, death was the penalty for such a misdemeanor. The king was fond of his old servant and wanted to spare his life; but the boatman refused. His pardon would have diminished the dignity of his calling. He was proud to make amends for his mistake.

It was for this reason that Rama I was so anxious to make Bangkok as like as possible to Ayudhya; he wanted to restore to the Thai people the inheritance of faith that was the backbone of their lives. They were lost without it. He summoned experts who could recall the details of the old city and reproduce what had been destroyed. Such buildings as still remained were pulled apart and the bricks were brought down the river. Because Ayudhya had been surrounded by water, he cut canals so that Bangkok too should have a river cast around it like a moat. And he insisted that one of these canals should be wide enough for the boat racing that had been so popular in Ayudhya. And to the north, as a defense against invasion, he converted a section of lowland into a swamp, which later, when the fear of invasion was past, was converted into orchards. He was resolved that Bangkok should not be subjected to the same fate as Ayudhya.

Rama I ruled for twenty-seven years. He was crowned at the age of thirty-two. It is astonishing how much he accomplished. He was a man who knew how to put first things first. And his first project was the building of the Grand Palace which was to be the symbol of his authority. The palace was far more than just his home; his secretariat was there, the court of justice, the ministries, the treasury, the regiment of guards, the regiment of artillery, the stables for the horses and the elephants, the art studios and school. These were known as "the outside." Then, a city within a city, was "the inside" which no man but the king could enter, except his young sons and relatives. An official anxious to transact urgent business could enter only with the king's permission. The police who guarded him were female. Here were his private residence, his flower gardens, the home of his queens and their children and the vast concourse of attendant girls and women who fulfilled various duties. The area of the palace was one square mile. It was later to be surrounded by a thick white crenelated wall so that it could serve as a fortress in case of need.

The building was begun in 1783, and within two years very substantial progress had been made. At last there was a home worthy of the Emerald Buddha, and the world has never ceased to be enchanted by the lofty oblong building in the palace grounds, with its red and gold ceilings, the gold mosaic of its walls, the roofs with their blue and orange tiles, the carved gold gables surmounted by the sacred snakes — the nagas. Gold bells with pendants hung from the eaves. In a rich procession the image was brought from Dhonburi and placed on a canopied throne above a high set altar. The compound of the temple was filled with small temples linked by cloisters.

By the end of the next year the palace was practically finished and the king felt that he would be justified in staging a public blessing of the city which was now roughly organized into a housed and operative community. He also decreed that he himself should be recrowned, since at his coronation the appropriate ceremonies had not been carried out. Experts now assembled the details of the original services. The crown and the regalia had been lost. No record existed of the coronation of King Taksin and no trace of his crown was found. But replacements were made, which Brahmin priests handed to the king. The high officers of state then presented him with symbols of the royal possessions — gold coaches, arms and weapons, the palace buildings, finally the countryside itself, its forests, rice fields — and of all these the king was the owner. Symbolically he returned them to his ministers. He adjured them to take good care of them. He vowed that he and they would defend both the Buddhist religion and the kingdom. It was on this occasion that he rechristened The Village of the Wild Plum, calling it "Jewel Abode of the God Indra" — *Ratanakosindra*. He chose this name because legend claimed that a deva had carved it for Indra, and for a time the Brahmins had accepted Buddha as the ninth avatar of Vishnu, and the superior of Indra. Many of Rama I's architectural achievements still remain — the Amarindra group, the Dusit Maka Prasat, the Wat Sutat and the Wat Po. Many of these buildings were embellished with frescoes and wood carving.

It may seem that it was extraordinary that so much could have been achieved in so short a time but royalty at that time had the resources of a conscript labor. Thai peasants paid practically no taxes, but they were liable to be taken for three months a year from their homes and fields to work for the government. They seemed to accept these conditions without discontent. It was part of the Thai way of life and they liked the Thai way of life.

Rama I had not only to rebuild a city; he had to revise the Buddhist canon; only a small part of the written legislation had survived and he had to get the laws of the land codified and arranged. At the same time he was still threatened by the Burmese. Four invasions were launched during his reign. Each one was beaten off. And very often the king was in command of his own armies. There can be little doubt that he was an astute tactician.

Practically the entire royal family at Ayudhya was wiped out by the Burmese, so that the new dynasty dates back to General Chakri through whose veins flowed no royal blood whatever. Polygamy was practiced generally at this time. There was usually a first wife, then there were a number of companion wives or Royal Lady Companions (Chao Choms). Rama I had in all twenty-eight such minor wives who produced twenty-five daughters and seventeen sons. Many of these ladies were the daughters of notables who were anxious to have a blood relationship with the royal family; it was convenient for the king to be surrounded by wives instead of servants. But the fact that, among the minor wives, the average was one child to one mother does not suggest that these ladies received a great deal of the royal solicitude. Rama I's first wife Amarindra had nine children, all of whom had been born before her husband was crowned. Five of them were already dead at the time of the coronation, and the four survivors became automatically celestial princes and princesses. Their mother was never ennobled, until her son on his succession raised her to queendom. Rama I, however, raised to the celestial ranks his brother, two sisters and eleven nephews and nieces. The children of minor wives were known as Phra Ong Chao or royal body prince.

There is an old saying: "If you throw a stone in Bangkok, you will hit a prince, a priest, or a dog." In order to keep down the number of princes, there was a dropping of rank with each generation, so that in five generations a title disappeared. It could always be renewed however by a fresh gift of rank by the king; ennoblement was the privilege of the throne.

In addition, there was the rank of Krom, which still exists. Prince Chula provides the following explanation: "In those days of simultaneous military-civil service, some of the senior princes had command of their regiments-departments which could be used by the king in war or peace; they were called Kroms. The majordomo of a prince acted as the chief of staff or adjutant and he was given the title of Khun, Luang, Phra according to the importance of the Krom. Instead of the Krom being known by the name of the prince, it was known by the title of the majordomo. Thus if the majordomo was Phra Supat, the Krom would be known as Krom Phra Supat. It was the custom amongst the Thais not to call their superiors by name, so the prince himself would be called by his Krom, e.g., Krom Phra Supat, and he became associated with it as if he had been given a dukedom. In later years, when princes no longer commanded their individual regiments-departments, the bestowal of a Krom became an additional way of giving a prince further honor. But a prince of high rank who was not a Krom would still remain higher than one of the lower rank who was a Krom. Furthermore it must be remembered that being a Krom was not a hereditary honor, although one of his sons might become worthy of being a Krom and would get the same title by the king's choice."

The absence of names and hereditary titles makes the nomenclature of Thailand almost impossible for a *farang* to follow. There was, probably owing to the proliferation of princes, no system of inheritance by primogeniture. This caused complications where the succession to the throne was concerned. There existed in early days the position of deputy king (Uparaja). This title was not usually given to the eldest son, but to the prince who was best fitted by age and by achievement to occupy the post. Rama I for instance chose his only brother, Boonma. There was only one example of a deputy king ascending the throne during the Chakri dynasty. The existence of a deputy king affected the atmosphere of the court and no doubt had a beneficial effect on the conduct of the eldest celestial son, who knew that he would not inherit unless he had deserved the honor.

It was not only through the buildings he erected that Rama I left his imprint on the life of the city that he founded. He inaugurated many ceremonies, and in particular enlarged the Kathin festival, which is still observed. During the wet season the monks were forced to remain in their monasteries and when the young temporary monks went into residence, it was the custom for the people to take presents to the temples. The king himself always made gifts to the monasteries in which he had a special interest, but in 1807 he decided to make a gala of the occasion, and he invited the nobles to join him in an elaborate but informal procession by boat around the city, with the boats decorated, each to represent some kind of fish. It was a great success. Rama I had always seen the river as the heart stream of the city. Whereas his predecessors in Ayudhya had kept themselves hidden from the public gaze, Rama I wanted the public to feel itself a part of the royal pageantry. It was he who built the magnificent scarlet and gold barges that were shown in the film *Around the World in 80 Days,* and are included today in every sightseeing tour of the city.

For the last years of King Rama's life the country was at peace, and able to profit to the full from its rich soil and its fortunate geographical position in terms of trade. Mergui had been captured by the Burmese in 1767 — later in 1824 it was to be taken over by the British — so that Siam could no longer serve as an *entrepôt* for the trade between India and the Far

East, but its direct junk trade with China was considerable. It was on this trade that the country's economy was built. The population of the country was now about four million and was mainly agricultural. The peasants were self-supporting. They paid no direct taxes but instead supplied conscript *corvée* work. The taxes on alcohol and gambling dens did not bring in much revenue. But every junk that arrived and left had to pay import and export duties to the king. The king's own royal fleet was large, and most of the princes owned their own boats. As long as war could be avoided, the prospects for the new city were roseate.

Up till now Siam had been almost completely cut off from Europe. At the end of the seventeenth century, when King Narai had come under the influence of a Greek adventurer, the French had made a serious attempt to take control, but the court mandarins had suspected the plot. They had trapped the Greek adventurer, tortured and beheaded him, then wiped out the French garrison at Dhonburi. Ever since the Thais had been on their guard against European infiltration. But in the fifth year of Rama I's reign, a sloop arrived, bearing with it a letter from the king of Portugal. The envoy was courteously received, but no trade appears to have resulted from this mission.

We have no portrait of Rama I painted during his lifetime. We do not know a great deal about him. We know more about his brother — the Uparaja. In early days they had been very close. They were the two brothers in whom Taksin trusted. They had fought together in Cambodia, they had fought together against the Burmese. The Uparaja had really done as much as the king to save and restore the country. But when the fighting ended, and the bond of the battlefield no longer held them, their sense of kinship was exposed to strain. The younger brother became jealous. He resented the fact that the palace in

The Chakri Memorial Bridge, opened on April 6, 1932

which he lived, which he had embellished with his own treasures, was not really his, and would be eventually taken over by the king, to be given to his nephews not his sons. He sought occasions to humiliate the king, of which the best known example was provided by a boat race in which the two brothers were to put crews against each other. During all the practices, the king's crew made a better showing, but the Uparaja was only putting a second-grade team against his brother. He kept behind the scenes and trained secretly a stronger crew which when the day came, outdistanced the king's easily. The king was not amused.

Then the Uparaja started to complain about the meager salary he received from the civil list. The king retorted that if he needed more money, he must earn it. He must fit out junks and trade with China. The Uparaja was reminded that the royal family could only draw from the national income what was left over after the needs of the country had been met. Relations between the brothers became so bad that extra guards were mounted to protect their respective charges. Eventually their sisters restored cordial relations. But the sisters died in 1799, and a few months later the Uparaja's health started to deteriorate. He grew increasingly ill-humored. His mind began to fail. He brooded over his fancied grievances. He attempted to commit suicide, but was prevented by his courtiers. In a state of semi-delirium, he exhorted them to plot a rebellion on his behalf and see that his rights were accorded him. Unfortunately one or two of them took him at his word.

He was by now very near his death. The king was distracted with grief and nursed him personally for five days. When he died, he ordered national mourning and gave a golden urn for his brother's body.

All was harmonious until the great man's death released secret gossip about the plot that he had sponsored. Rama I or-

dered an inquiry, and his two elder nephews and a number of
officials were found guilty of high treason. For a while the king
refused to go to his brother's funeral but in the end he relented
and presided at the cremation. He charitably presumed that his
brother was no longer sane and should not be held responsible
for the traitors who had taken his mumblings as a command.
The whole story is in the classic tradition of fraternal strife. The
Uparaja is very real to us.

From Rama I himself there has come to us one anecdote that
reveals the man and shows him to have had a sense of humor.
The anecdote was repeated by his grandson, King Chulalongkorn, to Prince Chula's father, Prince Chakrabongse and reported in Prince Chula's book, *Lords of Life*. It was the custom
for the bodies of Thai royalty, instead of being laid out in
coffins, to be stood upright in urns to await the burial which
takes place a considerable length of time after death. There was
usually an inner urn of bronze and silver, and an outer golden
one. In 1808, only a little while before his death, Rama I ordered an exceptionally ornate gold urn that could be taken
apart in eight pieces and reassembled around the silver urn
when it contained the body. The king was so delighted with its
workmanship that he had the two urns placed in his bedroom.
One of his wives was distraught, and insisted that it was a bad
omen. The king laughed. "If I don't see them from the outside
while I am still alive, how can I ever see them?" In his closing
days he delivered himself of a prophecy: "This dynasty will last
for a hundred and fifty years."

3

Bangkok Grows in Beauty

PRINCE Chula Chakrabongse's *Lords of Life: A History of the Kings of Thailand* contains unquestionably the best account of that century and a half which the first of the Chakri set as the scope of his family's overlordship. Prince Chula was not only a good writer and a scholar, but he had met all the personages included in the later sections, and had had firsthand knowledge through his father of the events that had taken place during the reign of his grandfather, King Chulalongkorn. He could study material in the original Thai. A proper respect for family privacy may have counseled him to be discreet on certain issues, but we can be assured that he knew what was happening and had happened. He may not always have put down all he knew, but he does not deliberately mislead the reader, and he lets you read between the lines.

Prince Chula gave a descriptive title to each of the seven Lords of Life. Rama I he called "The Founder." Rama II was "The Artist." His accession, at the age of forty-one, was the first peaceful one in Siam for seventy-six years. As Prince Isarasuntorn, he had been made Uparaja two years before, and his father had recommended him to the accession council. There was no other serious claimant to the throne, yet within three days of

[27]

the council's choice of him, rumors of a plot came to one of the court officials. The plot had been instigated by the son of King Taksin, who had married one of Rama I's daughters, and been recognized as a celestial prince. He confessed his guilt and his execution was performed, as his father's had been, with a club of scented sandalwood. With his death, the name of Taksin vanishes from Thai history. Yet a statue to Taksin stands in contemporary Bangkok. His portrait painted from memory is shown to visitors in the Wat Arun.

Prince Chula described Rama II as "The Artist" because he was not only himself an excellent poet, but encouraged the arts and did much to restore the classical Thai ballet. Yet to many it will seem that his main achievement was the consolidation of his father's work, in the embellishment of the city of Bangkok. He did much to restore the pomp and ceremony of the city. The funeral of his father was a particularly impressive performance. It was held two years after his death; by that time grief had subsided and anyhow to a Buddhist a funeral is not a sad occasion. The populace was able to revel fully in the pageantry. Great care was taken that the various rites involved should resemble as closely as possible those that had been observed at Ayudhya. The cremation took place in the southwest corner of the lawn outside the grand palace. The palanquin on which the urn was placed was carried shoulder-high from the palace by sixty men. The huge golden funeral coach was forty feet high and weighed over ten tons. It was pulled by a hundred and sixty men; another hundred and thirty-five were in attendance to act as brakes. The urn was transferred from the palanquin to the coach in an open lift operated by a pulley and invented expressly for the occasion. Almsgiving on a considerable scale preceded the ceremonies. Offerings were made to the monks. Coins were buried in fruit and thrown to the crowd. Clothes were distributed to the poor. There were boxing matches, fireworks and ten open air theaters. It was all just as the Thais most liked it. The ashes were scattered on the river and the solid remains were conveyed to the mausoleum near the Amarinda Hall.

Rama II continued the embellishment of the city that his father had begun. But a new note enters the style of architecture. Rama I had been at pains to produce exact replicas of the old Ayudhya, but his son was an innovator. He followed Chinese and European models, so that the Grand Palace today is a mixture of two styles. He also introduced the device of decorating a building with fragments of porcelain cups and saucers, arranged to look like flowers; it is a style that is regarded as essentially Thai today. It is remarkably picturesque and is in keeping with the elegant and frivolous nature of the people. His greatest building is the Wat Arun which stands on the west bank of the river; a building that was not completed during his lifetime.

A parallel may be found between himself and the English King George IV, who in the days when he was prince regent built the Pavilion at Brighton as a playground. Rama II in the same spirit set out a garden, the Garden of the Night in the royal compound. A large lake contained a number of small islands that were linked together by exquisitely eccentric bridges. They were decorated with Chinese pagodas and European pavilions. Here the king would take his meals and listen to music. Little brightly lighted canoes would drift among the islands; the courtiers would wear fancy dress. Poets and musicians would compete against each other. On one of the islands was a tiny theater where ballet performances were given. The lake was used, too, as a bird sanctuary. The public had access to it for special festivals and when the king did not need it. It is sad that the lake has vanished. Perhaps Prince Chula was justified in labeling him "The Artist"; never has a reign been more dedicated to the arts, to a leisured enjoyment of the arts.

[29]

Rama II was fortunate in that he was given the opportunity to enjoy the pleasures by which he set such store. As a young man he had traveled at his father's side in the early Cambodian campaigns, and he had fought against each of the Burmese invasions. When he came to the throne, he was prepared to meet another attack from his country's agelong enemies, but he was spared that burden. Succor was coming to him on his western flank in the shape of the British menace. In the last year of his life the first Anglo-Burmese war broke out, and for some while before, the Burmese had been too conscious of that threat to dissipate their energies in an attack upon their neighbors. On the east flank however, French imperialism was making its first impact upon Cambodia and Indo-China. In a sense Rama II's reign was a watershed between two sets of problems. The Burmese menace was subsiding and the threat from Europe was not yet defined. It was during Rama II's reign that Britain began to take an interest in Siamese affairs. Portugal was still the country that counted first with the Siamese. And the king conferred the minor rank of Luang on the Portuguese representative who had been sent across by the governor of Macao, and gave him the house on the river where the Portuguese legation is in residence today. Profitable business was transacted, Rama II acquiring a number of modern weapons as a safeguard against a Burmese invasion.

The British mission was less successful and the reasons for its failure are not unamusing. Its main objects were to reduce the import duties and to change the system of the royal monopoly. It was also a fact-finding mission. Very little was known about Siam and it was suspected that it would soon come within the British sphere of influence. John Crawfurd was sent by the governor-general of India and the book that he eventually wrote is an important contribution to our knowledge of the early days of the Chakri dynasty. He had been a physician in the Bengal

Medical Service, had been with Stamford Raffles in Singapore, and had been Resident in Singapore. He was both capable and astute. Unfortunately his experience of Asian peoples had been derived from those who had been subjected to British rule; having acquired the arrogance that distinguished the behavior of a good many Britons in the Far East, he was not prepared for the independence of the Thais, nor for the assumption of superiority that was shown in Rama II's court. He was worried by the genuflections and prostrations. He was disconcerted by Rama's assumptions of divinity.

The king's first question set the tone for the subsequent discussions. "Have you," he asked, "been sent with the knowledge of the king of England?" Crawfurd unwisely told the truth. He explained that the king of England was too far away to deal with problems of colonial administration, and delegated his authority to governors-general. Crawfurd produced an explanatory letter from the governor-general. "The influence and authority of the British nation," it ran, "extends from Ceylon to the mountains which border upon China and from the confines of Ava, with over ninety millions of subjects and we desire not to increase it . . ." Rama II was not impressed. He preferred to deal direct with monarchs. In fact he declined to write to anyone lower than another sovereign. He would instruct his lord high treasurer to send an appropriate reply. Crawfurd protested fiercely. A governor-general might not be a king, but he represented a king. He could only be addressed by a head of state. Finally a compromise was reached. The deputy of the lord high treasurer wrote to the secretary of the government of India. The whole thing was a comedy of misunderstandings. The Siamese could not think why a man who had come in a menial capacity as a tradesman should give himself such airs. They were accustomed to the obsequiousness of Chinese merchants who were always ready to be humble if that was the way to increase their profits. Crawfurd was also worried by the Thai custom of dressing comfortably. He had not expected the lord treasurer to sit down to their deliberations naked to the waist, and he commented on the contrast between this excessive informality and the impossibility of obtaining "either by entreaty or promise of reward the services of the lowest of the people for menial purposes." He constantly complained of the vanity of the Thais. "The lowest peasant considers himself superior to the proudest and most elevated subject of any other country."

There were disagreements, too, about interpreters. And here again class distinctions contributed to the misunderstandings. There were no Thais who could speak English, and the only persons on Crawfurd's staff who could make themselves understood in Thai were of such humble origins that the court officials were reluctant to admit them to the royal presence.

Crawfurd was deeply shocked by the servility of the lower orders. He found it "quite disgusting and altogether degrading to humanity. During the whole of the visit, they lay prostrate on the earth before him [one of the ministers] and at a distance. When addressed they did not dare to cast their eyes towards him, but raising the head a little and touching the forehead with both hands united in the manner by which they would express the most earnest supplication, their looks still directed to the ground, they whispered in answer in the most humiliating tone. The manner in which he was approached by the servants of his household was even still more revolting to nature. When refreshments were ordered they crawled forward on all fours, supported on the elbows and toes, the body being dragged on the ground.

"In this manner they pushed the dishes before them from time to time, in the best manner that their constrained and beastlike attitude would admit until they had put them in their place; when they retreated themselves in the same groveling manner, but without turning round. How abominable, how revolting . . . yet this haughty chief was himself but a minister of the fifth order in importance, doomed to take his turn of beastlike groveling . . . Every man is here doomed to crawl on the earth before his superior."

Though Crawfurd's mission was not too successful, the book which he published in 1830 under the title *Journal of an Embassy* contains a number of significant snapshots of Bangkok life, in particular the description of his arrival.

"Numerous temples of Buddha with tall spires attached to them, frequently glittering with gilding, were conspicuous among the mean huts and hovels of the natives, throughout which were interspersed a profusion of palms, ordinary fruit trees and the sacred fig. On each side of the river there was a row of floating habitations, resting on rafts of bamboo, moored to the shore. These appeared the neatest and best description of dwellings. They were occupied by good Chinese shops. Close to these aquatic habitations were anchored the largest description of native vessels, among which were many junks of great size, just arrived from China. The face of the river presented a busy scene, from the number of boats and canoes of every size and description that were passing to and fro. The number of these struck us as very great at the time, for we were not aware that there are no or few roads in Bangkok and that the river and canals form the common highways, not only for goods but for passengers of every description. Many of the boats were shops containing earthenware, and *blachang,* a fetid condiment in very general use composed of bruised shrimps and small fish. Vendors of these several commodities were hawking and crying them as in a European town."

There is too a lively description of Rama II.

"The throne," he writes, "was gilded all over and about fif-

The **SEATO** Building in Bangkok

teen feet high. A pair of curtains, of gold tissue upon a yellow ground concealed the whole of the upper part of the room except the throne, and they were intended to be drawn over this also except when used. In front of the throne and rising from the floor was to be seen a number of gilded umbrellas of various sizes. These consisted of a series of canopies, decreasing in size upwards and sometimes amounting to as many as seventeen tiers. The king, as he appeared seated on his throne, had more the appearance of a statue in a niche than of a living human being. He wore a loose gown of gold tissue with very wide sleeves. His head was bare for he wore neither crown nor any other ornament on it. Close to him was a gold scepter . . .

"He seemed a man between fifty and sixty years of age, rather short in person and disposed to corpulency. His features were very ordinary and appeared to bespeak the known indolence and imbecility of his character."

The word "imbecility" is unfortunate and untrue. But no doubt Crawfurd was exasperated by the difficulty of getting anything done. This exasperation gave him a quick eye for certain Siamese characteristics. He noted for instance that the Siamese paid more attention to an actual letter than to the envoy who delivered it: that is not surprising. The envoy was a servant. The letter had been touched by a royal hand and was therefore sacrosanct.

"One of the most singular and whimsical prejudices of the Siamese," he wrote, "is their extreme horror of permitting anything to pass over the head or of having the head touched. Or in short bringing themselves into a situation of physical inferiority to that of others — such as going under a bridge or entering the lower apartment of a house when the upper one is inhabited. For this sufficient reason, their houses are all of one story."

Indeed the Siamese still are very touchy on the question of the head. Children hate being patted.

It was a harassing time for Crawfurd, and the negotiations were wearisomely protracted by the ritual of court mourning. Someone always seemed to be dying, which is not surprising in view of the large families concerned. But in the end, something was achieved. A few concessions were obtained, and by the end of the negotiations the Thais had come to realize that the stiff and formal English had certain special qualities of their own, while Crawfurd himself had come to recognize his hosts "as one of the most considerable and civilized of the groups of nations inhabiting the tropical regions lying between Hindustan and China." On the whole over the years, the relations between Siam and Britain have been cordial and sympathetic. It may well be that the atmosphere created at those first confused meetings contributed to this happy outcome.

Rama II with the cooperation of thirty-eight ladies begat seventy-three children, of whom thirty-eight were boys; seven of them, six boys and a girl, were celestial. His first cousin Boonrod was the only Thai royal mother. Boonrod was the mother of Mongkut, the crown prince or Chao Fa son, who was very much later to become universally known through the musical and film *The King and I.* There are those who will argue that Mongkut had the right to the throne because he was the son of highest rank, but in Siam at that time a son was not considered lower in the line of succession because he was the son of a minor wife. In addition to Mongkut there was Prince Chesda, the eldest surviving son, by the king's third minor wife, the daughter of a nobleman, whom Rama II when he became king recognized as a Chao Chom (Royal Lady Companion) first class.

Prince Chesda was a young man of considerable ability. When his father succeeded to the throne, he was only twenty-one years old, yet he was put in charge of the investigations of the plot in which King Taksin's son was involved. His conduct of the case impressed his father, and he was given a number of important posts. He was an astute businessman, owning a number of trading ships. He was nicknamed "The Merchant" by his father. He was punctilious in the fulfillment of his duties, regularly attending his father's audiences. He was rich and he was generous. He entertained on a large scale. He assisted his uncle, the deputy, in the law courts, and after the death of the Uparaja, he was put in charge of the royal police.

He supervised the treasury and the port authorities. Crawfurd was highly impressed by him. He asked Crawfurd if it was true that the English could cure the smallpox, and whether if this were so, the governor-general of India could arrange for the Siamese to be taught how to use this medicine. He was prominent, powerful and popular; yet at the same time his father had always indicated that he recognized a distinction in importance between celestial sons and the children of minor wives and had shown particular affection for Mongkut, taking every opportunity of showing him special honor, and reviving on his behalf the ancient Brahmanic ritual of a ceremonial bath on a sumptuous raft that was moored near the royal palace, the prince being borne to the raft in a golden litter, attended by a large procession.

The king showed him the same preferential treatment when the time came for him to be tonsured — the topknot of his hair being cut off to prove that he had reached the age of puberty — and later was to make his taking of the saffron robe as a novice priest a spectactular occasion. Prince Chesda never omitted to pay him the highest respect, and many must have imagined that the king intended to name Mongkut as his successor. Probably he thought so himself. But fortunately in the long run for Siam that did not happen. In his last months the king was struck with melancholia. His only full sister died; and very soon after two

[37]

of his white elephants died too. His grief was so great that when Prince Mongkut became a full-fledged monk, no special ceremony was arranged for him. The king was not in the mood for display. And when his final illness struck him he was in no condition to pronounce a deathbed choice.

The decision was left with the accession council, and they could hardly have done otherwise than elect Prince Chesda. Mongkut was only twenty years old. He had no experience of government. The country needed a strong man, and such a man was at hand in the presence of Chesda, who for a dozen years had been actively employed in matters of state. It has been said that he usurped the throne, but his election was constitutional, and the council's choice a wise one.

Chesda was to rule for twenty-seven years, and during those years Bangkok was to know unbroken prosperity and peace. There was no war, and while Burma on the west was to lose her independence and France's encroachment on Cambodia was to grow more insistent, Siam as a buffer state between those jealous rivals was to maintain her freedom. She maintained it in large part through the skillful diplomacy of her king. Yet even so it is not fanciful to argue that the greatest importance of his reign lay in the effect it had upon his successor.

When Rama II died, Mongkut had just entered the monastery. He had intended to stay there for the customary three months, but he had the prescience to realize that there would be very little for him to do if he came out. His half-brother would be unlikely to offer him an interesting post, when his own friends had to be considered. So Mongkut decided to remain in the priesthood and make it his career. It was a surprising decision for a young man, particularly one who was married and had children, and it has been suggested that he went there in self-defense, for fear that his half-brother might have him murdered as a precaution against his becoming the center of plots against the throne. The history of Ayudhya suggests that that is likely, but the characters of the men involved make it almost impossible. Chesda had the greatest regard for his brother; moreover many have held that he considered himself to be holding the throne in trust for his half-brother. It has been said that at his coronation he never put the crown upon his head, that he handed it to an official, saying, "I am only keeping it for him."

Prince Chula confirms this legend, adding his belief that Rama III never once wore the crown. It should also be noted that Rama III never raised any rival to his half-brother. Though thirty-five wives supplied him with fifty-one children, not one of these wives was of royal birth, so that he never had a queen. Nor did he raise any of his sons to celestial rank, as he could have done. He chose as his Uparaja not a man younger than himself, but an uncle who died within eight years. No successor was appointed, so that there was no heir apparent during the last nineteen years of his life. His only major appointment was the raising of his mother to royal rank, and the conferring of a queendom on her. It is hard to believe that this care for his half-brother's inheritance was not intentional.

Moreover Mongkut himself was a very serious and devout young man who would welcome the opportunity to devote his life to scholarship. He accepted his fate as a vocation. He could see himself living more fully in a monastery than as a courtier without responsibilities. As a result, those twenty-seven years of seclusion from the world fitted him in the end to be one of the greatest kings in the history of mankind, who led his country from a medieval backwater into the nineteenth century. Had he ascended the throne as a young man of twenty, he would not have had the knowledge, the training, the character for such a task. Inevitably his country would have been absorbed by the imperial ambitions of France and Britain, as Burma was to the west and Indo-China to the east. But for Mongkut, Bangkok would not be the city that it is today.

4

Envious Europe

Prince Chula chose for Rama III the cognomen of "The Ruler," and during his long reign the prestige and power of the city of Bangkok waxed prodigiously, while for the people themselves life continued in the same way that it had in the days of Ayudhya. They lived on the canals in houses built on stilts. They traded with one another. They were never hungry. Rice was plentiful. They tended the spirit houses on their verandahs, confident that the spirit they served would stay with and protect the house.

Rice was the cornerstone of the economy. The year was measured for the peasant in terms of the cycle of planting, growth and harvesting. In April the peasants burned the straw stumps in the fields, so as to soften the ground and make it fit for plowing. After the first rains the wet soil was plowed and harrowed. The seedbeds were then laid out. Before the planting began the headman would placate the rice spirit, and a period of intensely hard work would follow. Except for a long break at noon they worked all day long. Water had to be used skillfully — good rice needs eighteen inches of it a month. Water is controlled by banks raised between the small fields. The farmer regulates the flow of water along the channels by a windmill. About five weeks after the planting, the seedlings are transported from the beds to the paddy fields. Each seedling has to be pressed separately into the mud. Skill and care are required. Planting is carried out in the afternoon when the sun is cooler. The less experienced workers gather the fuller plants into bundles and lay them in the shade. They are taken by boat in baskets, along the klongs to the farther fields. The planting is usually a cooperative village effort, although the individual farmer owns his own land.

The harvesting starts in December. The water supply is cut off three weeks before. The harvesters use a short sickle or comblike knife. They bend to cut the stalks near the ground. The stalks are allowed to dry for four days. Then they are gathered into sheaves and carried to the threshing floor — an open space where mud and buffalo dung have been trampled into a hard surface.

The threshing time is gay like a wine harvest. A post hung with offerings to the rice goddess is created in the middle of the threshing floor. Several water buffaloes, tethered to the post side by side, tread the sheaves and dislodge the grain. As it had been in the days of King Narai of Ayudhya, so was it in the Bangkok of Rama III. So is it today in the Bangkok of the great-grandson of Rama III's half-brother.

The peasant had little to worry over. Buddhism gave him confidence in the future. Each in his own way was working out his dharma. No one bothered him. His only grievance was the *corvée*, the conscript labor either on the royal building schemes or in the army, and during Rama III's reign this burden was diminished. The periods of *corvée* were timed so as not to interfere with the people's livelihood. It was found that better work could be obtained from paid Chinese labor.

This labor was not difficult to obtain; more and more Chinese were settling in Bangkok, towards the end of the reign at the

A crowded street scene during the celebration of Chinese New Year

rate of 15,000 a year. Much of the trade of the country was in their hands, and on the whole this was to the advantage of the country. They were much more efficient as tradesmen than the pleasure-loving Thais. And the king, who had carried the nickname of "The Merchant" in his father's time, found it good policy to hand over to them a large section of his private interests. He decided that the farming out of taxes was more profitable than the former royal monopoly of trade. Most of the tax farmers were Chinese. They had to guarantee the government a fixed amount. This ending of the royal monopoly by introducing competitive practices undoubtedly increased the volume of trade that was attracted to Bangkok. Bangkok had become, indeed, a thriving port, and to improve its facilities for the seagoing junk trade, it was necessary to assist inland shipping. More canals had to be dug, rivers had to be dredged and widened; one of the new canals was thirty-three miles long.

Much of the city's rising prosperity was due to the Chinese. But they brought their own special problem — their taste for opium, which was responsible for a great deal of the crime that took place in the country. The trade was in Chinese hands; they bought from British merchants opium that was grown in India. The trade was operated by secret societies that carried on gang warfare with one another. Rama III was resolved to stamp this out. In one of the raids that he organized in the provinces he captured and had put to death as many as three thousand gangsters. Though so many Chinese traders and workmen kept coming into Bangkok, they did not bring their women with them. Instead they married Thais; the Chinese strain among the Thais was thus increased; complexions grew lighter.

In spite of the growing population and the increased prosperity of the city, its appearance did not greatly change, although Rama III was as active architecturally as his father and grandfather had been. It was, in essence, just more of the same thing;

more klongs, more temples. Nine new temples were built and over sixty were repaired. There were two main types of tower, the bell-shaped *chedi* with the spiral top and those like the Wat Arun following the Cambodian style. Much of his handiwork remains, in particular the immense reclining Buddha at Wat Po; it is ninety feet long and its mortar and brick has been covered with gold. He also set before the Emerald Buddha, two large gilt images of the Buddha, dressed as though they were Siamese kings. The country's finances were sound and he could afford these additions. He did, though, undoubtedly leave a heavy legacy to his successors. It is impossible today to maintain these temples at the standard they deserve. He also built several almshouses.

His daily routine shows how seriously he took his responsibilities. He was, as has already been told, a heavy sleeper; and he started the day later than his father had, often as late as 8 A.M. His first duty was to present food to the monks, of whom he daily invited a certain number. He had to wait for his own breakfast until they had had theirs. After breakfast he attended to his own devotions, in his private chapel with members of his family. He then fed his favorite pet, a tortoise.

His first official appearance was made in the Amarindra Hall, where a leader of a chapter of monks delivered the *pancha sila*, the five precepts by which laymen were to govern their lives. There was a chanting of hymns. Then lunch was served to the monks; he himself sat next to the senior monk, attending to his needs. Other royal princes attended to the other royal monks. This custom is still maintained. When the monks had left, he smoked a pipe and discussed matters of state with some of the dignitaries of the court. When he was ready to go into the audience hall, he ordered a cup of tea. That was the signal.

The audience lasted for over an hour, or until the king felt hungry. That was usually about half-past twelve. Luncheon was taken "inside" and was for him a heavy meal. But he had duties to perform immediately afterwards. First he would receive reports from the lady officials, then artists would show him their works or he might go to the landing stage or to the workshops for a tour of inspection. From 2:30 P.M. he relaxed in the nurseries. He was very fond of his children. He played for over an hour with them. At 4 P.M. he took his siesta. It lasted till seven o'clock or later when he would take a bath before his supper.

The evening audience began at 9 P.M. It was preceded by a sermon. It closed at midnight, unless there was extremely important business to be discussed, when it would continue until one or two o'clock. He was a devout Buddhist, and he insisted that the daily sermons should be an intelligent interpretation of the Buddhist faith. He was particularly concerned over the philosophy of Buddhism, and insisted that the monks conduct themselves with industry and decorum. As many as five hundred monks were expelled from the order because they did not satisfy his exacting standards.

Prince Chula has described him as a puritan. He did not approve of the ballet and refused to see it. He dispersed two royal companies, would not listen to music, and split the pavilions of "The Garden of the Night" with its pleasant pavilions on the lake, among the various temples. The only literature that he cared for was religious. Perhaps that is why there was in his reign a development in the standard of prose. Up to now Thai writing had been confined to poetry. He appreciated painting and embellished several of the temples with elaborate murals, in particular Wat Po, whose walls were covered with narrative pictures, telling of history, geography, biography. Indeed the library of Wat Po is a pictorial encyclopedia. Its paintings are today one of the first sights that are shown to tourists. He had the main building of the temple at Wat Yam Nava shaped like a

Chinese junk. He suspected that one day the Chinese junk would become obsolete, and he wanted to remind the people of the machinery by which their city had become rich.

If a man who had spent his adult years in Bangkok during Rama III's reign had been asked what was the most remarkable public event of the period, it is certain that he would recall the week in January 1829 when an old man of distinguished appearance was placed in a large iron cage and vociferously abused by the populace as long as daylight lasted. This was Prince Anu of Vientiane who after the British war with Burma came to the mistaken conclusion that Britain had marked Siam as her next victim, and that here was an opportunity to rid himself of the irksome obligations that were imposed by his titular subjection to Bangkok, it having been always held that Cambodia and Laos were vassals of Siam. After the defeat of Burma, the British sent a mission to Bangkok. Prince Anu felt that this was the first step; he would be wise to strike first, when Rama III was occupied with his western frontier.

He decided therefore to march on Bangkok. For a while he appeared to be successful. The Thais were unprepared and Anu, announcing that he was coming to help the Thais against the British, captured the city of Korat by surprise, and his forward troops reached Saraburi when only three days' march from Bangkok. But the Thais when they had once been warned acted swiftly. *Corvée* conscripts were summoned to the ranks, and in a very short while the Laotians were in retreat. They destroyed Korat first however, and took with them a large body of prisoners, male and female. They kept the men in close captivity on the march, but the women were instructed to act as menials, serving them at meals, and generally attending to their needs at night. This was their undoing. One of the women was the wife of the governor of Korat, who had been murdered. She took her revenge. She arranged with her fellow captives to inveigle the Laotians into a drunken revel. When festivities were at their height, she contrived to release the men prisoners who made short work of their incapacitated captors. Two thousand of them were slain. It was Judith and Holofernes in modern dress. The statue of the governor's wife now stands in the town of Korat.

The rout of Korat was followed by a six-day battle in which the invading forces were at last overcome, and Anu deserted his men and fled with such jewelry as he could collect. Rama III was ruthless in his revenge. He ordered the destruction of the walls and forts in Vientiane, and he took back to Bangkok all its arms, horses and elephants. He was resolved to remove the possibility of Vientiane being used as a military base again, and to warn his Laotian neighbors of the fate that would befall them if they followed Anu's example. For Anu himself he had reserved a special punishment. He had befriended Anu in the past; he had supported Anu's son to the post of a local governorship; he had given Anu a free hand in the running of his country. He and Anu had appeared to be on the best of terms when Anu had come to Bangkok for Rama II's cremation. But during this visit Anu's vanity had been hurt. He had asked for a troupe of ballet girls, but Rama III, disapproving of the ballet, had refused his request. The female factor in fact was responsible both for the beginning and the failure of the revolt. When at last Anu fell into Rama III's hands, he was subjected to a punishment that would have been painful for a mere politician — but for a royal personage whose subjects had to abase themselves before him it was intolerable. His wives were allowed to attend to him and at night he was housed in reasonable comfort, but all day long huge crowds assembled to revile him; the widows and children of those who had been killed in the war bewailed their loss and cursed him. How long Rama III had intended to keep him there, we cannot tell. On the seventh day he died, a disease contracted some while before being accentuated by his suffer-ings.

The war with Anu was the last with a neighboring state in which Siam was to be involved; and this good fortune was largely due to the skill with which Rama III, his half-brother Mongkut, and after him his half-nephew Chulalongkorn con-ducted their international relations. Europe was on the march. From a distance of a century and a half it is hard to see how Britain and France could justify their aggression. But they never doubted the purity of their intentions. They wanted to trade with the Far East and they wanted to trade on their own terms. If a Far Eastern monarch was difficult, he had to be co-erced. If he refused to be coerced, one looked for a prince with rival ambitions, endorsed his claim to the throne, and called his country a protectorate. That was the colonizing pattern. And the dictum of "taking up the white man's burden" justified their appropriations. "After all," they would say, "these people were always fighting among themselves. Trade was being inter-rupted by tribal raids. They had no modern medicine; no hy-giene; brigands flourished; roads were not safe at night. The police were corrupt. The people have been much better off since we came." And for all of that there was a great deal to be said. There was little excuse for Britain's Burmese war; there was no excuse for the Opium War with China, but at the time no one considered they were wrong, any more than two hun-dred years earlier Europe had considered the slave trade wrong. One has to judge public actions in the light of what was considered moral at the time, and Rama III had to move warily to preserve his country's independence.

There were several successors to John Crawfurd and Rama III dealt with them more tactfully than his father had. The first to come was an English official from Penang, trying to solicit Siam's help in the war against Burma, not with troops but with facilities for transport. He promised that in return for Siam's help, Britain would restore to Siam the port of Mergui which had been of such value in the days of Ayudhya and which the Burmese had captured during their victorious campaign of 1767. Mergui was of less value to Siam now than it had been in those early days. Moreover Rama III had an instinctive unwillingness to commit himself to either side. And later, in 1826, when Captain Henry Burney — a nephew it may be noted of Fanny Burney — suggested that the Thais, provided they did not attack the south, would be free to attack the north which the British had so far spared, he again refused to abandon his neutrality. But he did recognize that he would have to discuss problems of trade in the Malaysian archipelago. He had no doubt profited from the meetings he had had with Crawfurd. The English were arrogant but patience and tact could prove effective. So when Burney presented the first draft of a treaty on March 29, the king told his ministers to settle matters quickly. They did and by June 20th the first treaty between Siam and a Western nation was concluded — which is not long for the unhurrying East.

The treaty, which contained fourteen articles, began with the pious resolution that "the Siamese must not meditate or commit evil, so as to molest the English in any manner. The English must not meditate or commit evil so as to molest the Siamese in any manner." By and large the spirit of that treaty has been kept in spite of the Thai involvement with the Japanese during World War II. In the actual trade stipulations there was reciprocity upon both sides. The English agreed not to import opium into Siam. They also agreed that English subjects must conform to the established laws of Siam. The problems of taxation were satisfactorily solved with a fixed rate of duty on each fathom of a ship's beam. Both sides were pleased with the agreement, and Burney was honored with a final audience.

The wording of the treaty was, however, so obscure that when the Thais failed to honor it there was not a great deal to be done.

Six years later a no less warm welcome was accorded to an American envoy — Edmund Roberts. The king was anxious to have cordial relations with a nation that could act as a counterbalance to Great Britain, and an elaborate reception was given for President Andrew Jackson's representative. Roberts hoped that he would be able to get better terms than the British had. He was anxious to establish a consulate, but the king was not prepared to go that far; there was to be no question of preferential treatment. Moreover luck was not on Roberts's side. His presents were not valued as highly as he had hoped. Through ignorance he neglected the minor princes, and the gifts from the United States had been sent in a separate vessel which did not arrive on time. The Siamese were not impressed with the gifts that he had bought on his way in China.

Both Britons and Americans had at this time the belief that if they did not get what they wanted immediately from an Eastern potentate they were entitled to use force. An Englishman called Hunter, whose demand for payment for a steamer that he had brought into Siam was not met, threatened to have warships sent up the river by the government of India. But the authorities in India had the good sense to turn down the plea. A little later the balance was adjusted by an American called Balestier, the United States consul in Singapore, who wanted to present his letters of introduction to the king immediately. He was brusque and domineering, as tiresome in his American way as Hunter had been in his English way. When the Siamese official who received him inquired after the health of the American President, Balestier snapped back, "Let's get on with business." And when the minister explained to him that he could not present his letters to the king in person, Balestier lost his temper and left the room. A second meeting with the minister was equally unproductive; and eventually the ministers had to inform the captain of the United States warship that had brought Balestier to Siam that they could not admit so uncontrolled a man into the sacred presence of the king.

We have another account from a more responsible source of a visit to Rama III's court. This comes from Spencer St. John, who accompanied, in a secretarial capacity, Sir James Brooke, the first of the family that played so prominent a part in the history and development of Sarawak. Brooke, who came in the summer of 1850, had been accredited not by the governor-general, but by Queen Victoria herself. He arrived in considerable state and Spencer St. John was himself a man of distinction. The book that he was later to write of his experiences as a chargé d'affaires in Haiti is constantly referred to by those who are interested in that beautiful, dramatic and unlucky island. Brooke's purpose was to enlarge and improve the treaty that Burney had made a quarter of a century before. He wanted to establish a consulate in Bangkok. He wanted extraterritorial rights for British subjects. He also requested rights of residence. He was anxious to export rice from Siam. As history shows, Brooke was a great proconsul and a skillful administrator, but his experience with the Dyaks of Borneo had not equipped him for the independence of the Thais. It appears that he was heavy-handed. Burney and Edmonds had been successful through their amiability. The Thais were impressed but not intimidated by Brooke's eloquence. He conducted himself, they complained, "like a professor giving instructions — instruction that pours forth like waters flooding forests and fields"; he was only concerned "with advantages for merchantmen not with the interests of the population as a whole."

His mission was a failure. The Thais could not grant rights of residence, because they could not run the risk of having men like Hunter in their country. They could see no advantage in having a consul. The presence of a Portuguese consul had not led to a considerable increase of trade. The Thais did not have consuls abroad. When Thais traveled abroad they subjected themselves to the laws of the countries that they visited. They expected the same behavior from foreigners in Siam. They could not make rice free for export because rice was the staple food of the country. But though his mission failed, Brooke did not make a bad impression; and the final exchange of letters stressed the warm feelings that existed between the countries. Brooke had the graciousness not to accept the offer of the stipend that it was customary to make to a diplomat. Rama III gratefully used the money to decorate one of his many temples.

Although his ministers successfully evaded the pressure that Brooke tried to impose on them, the king was very conscious of the threat that was made to Thai independence by the growth of British power in Southeast Asia. He took a very necessary precaution. He ordered the construction of a very strong iron chain that he could stretch across the river to prevent the advance of hostile ships.

As his long reign drew to its end, the king was increasingly worried about the future. He was afraid that the various princes and noblemen would split up into various factions, plotting against each other. He remembered how it had been in Ayudhya. As a young man he had conducted the court of inquiry into the treachery of the men who had plotted against his father. Only a few months back, he had become aware that one of his uncles, Prince Raksanaret — the senior prince of the family — was plotting to inherit the throne. This charge the prince denied. He had done no more than assert that if he survived Rama III he would not serve under another king, but at his trial

Elephants provide the labor to move teakwood at an inland lumber camp

he conducted himself with arrogance. The court found him guilty, and he was executed with the traditional blow on the back of the neck from a club of scented sandalwood — the last royal prince to meet this fate.

On his deathbed Rama III gathered round him the royal princes and the chief notables of the realm. He adjured them to respect the prosperity of the country and the peace of its people and not to imperil them with civil strife. He did not intend to appoint his successor. Let the accession council make the choice. He did not consider that any of his sons by minor wives were qualified to occupy the throne. He did not himself consider that there was any alternative to his half-brother Mongkut. But he did not intend to influence them. Let them make their choice, and having made it let them remain loyal and subservient to the man they chose. The Chakri dynasty had lasted now for nine and sixty years. May the peace that it had brought to the country continue.

When he died, and the accession council met, their choice fell upon Mongkut.

5

The Original of *The King and I*

MONGKUT — King Rama IV — was to reign for seventeen years. He is one of the most unusual men in history. The bare facts of his life in outline are the proof of that. He went into the order of priesthood when he was twenty years old. He was already married to a minor wife by whom he had two children. On entering the monastery he undertook vows of chastity which he rigorously observed. On that point there is no doubt. He emerged from the monastery at the age of forty-seven to take thirty-five wives and produce eighty-two children, the largest number among Chakri kings. Many of these children were to become prominent and effective in public life. Psychologically and physically this is an astonishing performance. His studies in the monastery convinced him that Siam must be able to meet the Western world on equal terms, equipped with modern machinery and techniques. Ironically his death at the age of sixty-four, when he was in sound health, was caused by his own modernity. An accomplished astronomer, he foretold that there would be a total eclipse of the sun in Siam. He calculated the day and hour when it would be visible from a small village near what is now Hua-Hin. He not only ordered his court to move there for the occasion, but he invited the governor of Singapore to be his guest. The French sent a body of scientists. His calculations were proved correct; it was a great personal triumph for him. Unfortunately, the line of totality passed through a low, malarial swamp. It was on this swamp that he set his own pavilion. The attack of malaria that ensued proved fatal. Had he not insisted on placing himself on the exact line, had he moved to higher ground, all would have been well. But his end was in keeping with his career.

The use to which he put the twenty-seven years in the monastery is fantastic. Until his half-brother's accession to the throne, his life had followed the conventional pattern of a young Thai prince. His earlier years were spent among women, in "the inside" of the palace. It was not until he was reaching the age of puberty that he was handed over to the charge of men. He learned to read and write, to ride and shoot and fence. He learned no English; there was nobody to teach it. We may assume that there was nothing apparently remarkable about him when he decided to remain a priest, but he had to find some outlet for his great natural energy and there was no outlet other than learning. He became deeply interested in the philosophy of Buddhism. He had studied Pali, and had been disturbed to note how few of the monks bothered to study the Buddhist scripture. His learning went deep. He had nothing to distract him from his studies. He had an acute analytic mind. Rama III watched his progress as a theologian with the closest interest and appointed him as an abbot in one of the monasteries. It is not untrue to suggest that Mongkut's studies brought Siamese Buddhism up-to-date. He was the first prince-priest to stand for public examination. He passed it with such brilliance that he brought under his influence a number of young monks who came to share his view that there were many discrepancies between the Buddhism that had originally been propounded and the form of it that was practiced now in Siam. He sent to Ceylon for books, and at the king's request a number of young Siamese priests were sent to Ceylon to compare points of doctrine.

There had always been freedom of religious opinion in Siam. Mongkut's comment on the Christian religion was: "What you tell them to do is excellent. What you tell them to believe is foolish." And a certain number of Christian missionaries had starting coming to the country in Rama III's reign. They were not successful in obtaining converts. Buddhism was too deeply ingrained in the people. But the American missionaries had a considerable effect upon the lives of the people. They brought modern scientific knowledge. They also brought a printing press and set up books and papers in the Thai alphabet.

This was precisely what Mongkut needed. He extended the frontiers of his knowledge. He became friends with the Roman Catholic bishop, who taught him Latin while he taught the bishop Pali. The American missionaries taught him English. He soon learned to speak it fluently "with a literary tinge." He also learned to write English, in what one can best describe as an idiosyncratic style. His meaning was quite clear, and the prose had punch and liveliness. It was highly personal. Examples of it will be given later. Through English, he was able to read books on modern science, geography, history, mathematics. Astronomy was his favorite study. When one reflects on the amount of work that he got through as a king, in his middle fifties, with all the involvements of a strenuous domestic routine, it is not surprising that he should have accomplished so much as a young man, as a celibate with no outlet for his energy but work.

Prince Chula calls Mongkut "The Enlightened." He was the first king to be able to speak English. He made a number of English friends with whom he corresponded. He was convinced that it was only by meeting the West on equal terms that he could prevent the West from taking over his country. The country must be modernized. To this end he imported European advisers; he had an Englishman to train his army; he had a French architect who was responsible for cutting two canals through the city running from east to west so that the klongs should be sluiced each day by the high and low tides. He also had tutors for his children. One of these was an English widow, Mrs. Anna Leonowens, who spent five years at the court. She arrived in 1861, when Mongkut had been on the throne eleven years and his eldest celestial prince, Chulalongkorn, was nine years old. From the musical and the film *The King and I* the world has come to believe that the democratic changes which took place in Siam were entirely the result of Anna's influence, but actually the majority of these changes had been carried out before Anna reached the court. She spoke very little Thai, an extremely difficult language; it is most unlikely that she had more than a casual colloquial familiarity with it. She cannot really have known what was going on around her. There is no reason to believe that she had any influence on the king. He kept copious diaries which contain but one reference to her. If he asked her advice, it can only have been when he wanted to know the precise meaning of an English word; he carried on an immense correspondence, and he was most anxious to be correct.

In fact he never was. No one has written such extraordinary English. The following letter addressed to Queen Victoria is a typical example.

"We on this occasion have liberty to let our native photographers take the likeness of ourselves when we adorned with the watch decked with diamonds and the double-edged sword which were honorary royal gracious gifts from your majesty, received by us a few years ago and seated ourselves by the tables containing the gift silver inkstand and desk together with the revolving pistol and rifle wholly being royal gracious gift from your majesty."

Sometimes his exact intentions required careful unraveling as

COURTESY OF PRINCE CHULA CHAKRABONGSE AND REDMAN BOOKS LTD

King Mongkut in state robes and wearing his crown.

when he explained to Sir John Bowring, who headed a royal mission in 1855, that he wished his first meeting with him to be private. "My dear friend — I wish yourself alone be entered to my presence before two accompanied stranger a few minutes. It would appeared best than all three individuals come up the same moment as yourself along has been my acquainted by longly correspondence. The other two will have the honour to be with me on such time for yourself sake. When your excellency has received my cordial welcoming firstly; after a few minutes your excellency shall request me to let them follow your excellency's way."

He never mastered the grammar and syntax of the English language. But he was indefatigable in his search for the right word. He would ransack Webster's dictionary for words that only existed in his own fertile brain. A missionary was once dragged four miles to decide whether murky was preferable to obscure and "gloomily dark" to "not clearly apparent." The British consul was roused at night to adjudicate between deuce and devil.

He once insisted that an anecdote and an unmarried woman were the same thing. "An anecdote is something that is not yet told. An unmarried woman is something that has not yet given forth."

He was furious when he found himself described in a missionary news sheet as a spare man. "How can I be a spare man? A king cannot be spared from his kingdom. Who can take my place? I ask you that, who can fill my place?" He was only partially placated when it was explained that the word spare has two meanings, one of them being thin and this was what the missionary had meant. He was not satisfied. A language should not be imprecise when it dealt with royalty. In Siamese you used a different language when addressing a king. At a subsequent banquet the British consul displayed high tact in his proposal of the royal toast. "To his gracious majesty the king of Siam," he said. "It would be a sad day for the country if the king ever became a spare man."

It has to be remembered that Mongkut had a much more democratic upbringing than his half-brother and his father. They, except during military campaigns, spent most of their lives within their palaces. He, as a monk, traveled up and down the country. In his saffron robe he met the people on equal terms. In the days of Ayudhya the populace had not been allowed to gaze upon the monarch. The man who did was likely to have darts thrown at him by the guards. This order he rescinded. He did not need to be told by Anna that men were equal under God. Like his predecessors he was concerned with the beautifying of the city. Before his reign, transportation had been entirely by water, but he ordered the construction of a number of roads. He built, for instance, New Road which runs along the east side of the river, fifty or so yards from the bank. It was formerly an elephant track. He used to drive round the town in a two horse buggy, inspecting the alterations that were being carried out. The labor for most of this work was paid for; like his half-brother he was conscious of the disadvantages of the *corvée* system. Better work was got out of paid Chinese. He tried to keep in touch with his people. In distant days it had been the custom for any subject who had a complaint to beat against a drum outside the palace, and the king would hear the nature of the complaint. The system had fallen into disuse; no one dared to present himself this way. Mongkut restored this system and once a week he appeared in public to hear petitions. He traveled about the country; and he had a paddle steamer in which he sailed in the Gulf of Siam visiting many east coast villages. He restored the island palace of Bang Pa-In which is included in the tourist's all-day trip to Ayudhya, and he had a summer palace built on the sea near Petchaburi. He conducted his rule through a series of edicts — there were in all some five hundred of them — which opened with the phrase "By royal command, reverberating like the roar of a lion." He told his entourage that it must wear jackets in the royal presence. He was disgusted by the sight of sweating sore-scarred flesh. He considered inelegant the practice of throwing dead animals in the waterways.

His attempts to assert his authority inside his harem did not meet with equal success. It had long been the custom to "roast" the mother of a newborn baby. A brazier of lighted charcoal was placed close to her stomach. It was claimed that it dried the womb and was known as "staying with the fire." Often it raised large blisters. When she could stand no more, the attendant women turned her around and blistered her back. The treatment lasted for two or three weeks. Mongkut called it "a senseless and monstrous crime" but his wives retorted that it was *tham-niem* (the custom) and they were having the babies not he. They were convinced that if they changed the custom, they would be assailed by evil spirits. His wife, Queen Saowapa, however, eventually came to agree with Mongkut and abandoned the custom for the birth of her later children. The wives of other courtiers soon followed her example. The authority of a Lord of Life was limited where his own womenfolk were concerned.

The most important event in his reign occurred in 1855 when the people were warned that they were not to be alarmed by the discharging of gunfire from a foreign ship. This was not a hostile act but an act of deference paid by the British to the authority and dignity of the king and of his country. It was a twenty-one gun salute to the Thai flag which would be returned by Thai artillery. These salutes announced the arrival of a mission from Queen Victoria herself, headed by Sir John

Bowring. It was on Sir John's insistence that the salute was fired. King Mongkut had been afraid that his people would be alarmed, and the fact that he acceded to the *farang's* request is an indication that he was ready to be more accommodating than his half-brother had been with Sir James Brooke. After Brooke's sudden departure with nothing achieved, the ministers had been afraid that warships would arrive from Hong Kong to demand compliance. And probably they would have if Rama III had lived a little longer. But the British decided that they would wait and see how things developed under the new monarch. There was much talk about Mongkut in Singapore. It was learned that he spoke English and that he had not only read a novel by Sir Walter Scott but named one of his ships after him. It was worth giving him a trial.

The salute was fired at Paknam — at the mouth of the Menam — and a state barge was sent thither to convey Bowring to the palace. The man o' war was to come up the river on the following day. Bowring was very punctilious about protocol. He was terrified lest he should not be received in a style worthy of Her Britannic Majesty. Would his officers be allowed to wear their swords? But Mongkut was equally punctilious where the dignity of the Thais was at stake. He had set his historians to replace the records that had been destroyed at Ayudhya, and was able to reconstruct the scene that had been enacted when King Narai had received a deputation from Louis XIV. It was clear that the French envoys had been allowed to wear their swords. Bowring was ready to agree that what was good enough for the Sun King was good enough for him.

Bowring had no reason to complain of the circumstance with which he was received. A letter from the king was brought to him in a vase of ornamented gold by three high-ranking officers, one of whom spoke English. Elaborate silver salvers were weighted with fruit and sweetmeats that were protected against the sun by banana leaves. Another boat, the gift of the Uparaja, contained fowls, ducks and pigs for the crew. Later the son of the chief minister called on him. Though he was bare-legged and bare-footed, he was sumptuously clothed in silk, with a gold ornamented jacket and a belt of pure gold with a hasp of diamonds.

The barge that conveyed Bowring to the palace had a gilded and emblazoned image of an idol in its prow with flags ornamented like vanes. Near the stern was a raised and carpeted divan with scarlet and gold curtains. The rowers were in scarlet faced with green; their helmets were a kind of cape, with two tails hanging over their shoulders. They chanted a song: "Row, row, I smell the rice" — which meant that a meal awaited them at the end of their journey.

Bowring accepted this pomp as the treatment due to a representative of Her Britannic Majesty. And when on a later visit he was sent an uncurtained barge, he declined to expose himself to the sun and sent the barge back. The courtier who was responsible for the mistake was accorded thirty strokes of the bamboo.

The king received Bowring warily. He knew that truculence on his part would be followed by the same discipline that had been meted out to Burma and to China. Yet at the same time weakness on his part would make the British overbearing. Bowring tells in his *The Kingdom and People of Siam* how the king received him on an exquisite moonlit night, on a highly ornamented throne, wearing a crimson dress, a gold girdle and a headdress glittering with diamonds and precious stones. The king offered him a cigar. Tea and sweetmeats were brought in. He then showed Bowring his private apartments which were "filled with various instruments, philosophical and mathematical, a great variety of Parisian clocks and pendules, thermometers, barometers, in a word all the instruments and appliances which might be found in the study or library of any opulent philosopher in Europe." There was no doubt that he was up-to-date. Nor was there any doubt that he was very rich. Bowring was later shown the crown jewels and the sword of state, with its gold scabbard and its proliferation of diamonds. "How," he wrote, "can I describe the barbaric grandeur, the parade, the show, the glitter, the real magnificence, the profuse decorations of today's royal audience."

The king was very tactful in his appreciation of the envoy's insistence upon protocol. "He accepted my explanations of my conduct, assuring me that he should attribute my proceedings not to any want of respect for himself but to my sense of the duties I owed to my sovereign and to my country." Did the envoy realize that he was being put in his place? Probably not. He was a self-important person. At any rate the negotiations proceeded pleasantly and swiftly. Bowring got nearly everything he wanted, but on terms that were satisfactory to the king. A British consul would be nominated, but one who would have to be *persona grata* with the king. The British consul would hold jurisdiction over all British subjects — even if they were Asians who were residents in Siam. The British were allowed to import opium from India. The *ad valorem* duty on British goods was limited to three per cent. Britons were allowed to purchase land within four miles of the city walls. The concessions that Mongkut had made were considerable, but they were an acceptance of the inevitable, and the king had preserved the independence of his people. The Thais splashing in the water by their houses were unaware that the wind of change had blown along the klongs.

In fact, a whole new era had begun. The treaty with Britain held the door open for the United States and the other European nations to open negotiations with King Mongkut. Within a year both France and the United States were to sign treaties based on the British pattern. Portugal, Holland, Prussia, the

Scandinavians soon had their representatives in Bangkok. The only considerable change that the Thais felt themselves was a beneficial one. Rice could now be exported from Siam. There was no better rice than that which was grown in the delta of the Menam. The demand for it was universal. This meant that more rice had to be grown, and Mongkut ordered the digging of innumerable new canals so that the whole of the Menam delta could be irrigated. Singapore benefited enormously through this increase in production. It was a free port and most of the rice was shipped from it.

These treaties had a considerable effect on the life of the individual Thai. Up till then the country had supplied itself with everything it needed. And the princely and wealthy families had maintained their own teams of craftsmen — gold- and silversmiths, painters, woodcarvers, workers in mother-of-pearl and lacquer. Each town had its own local artificers, but now that the markets were flooded with European merchandise, the local craftsman began to disappear.

One of the first industries to wither was that of the weaving of silk embroideries. But in the opinion of Dr. Malcolm Smith, an Englishman who spent twenty years in Siam as a physician at the start of the century, its decline was not the introduction of cheaper or superior articles from Europe and the United States but the change in fashion, particularly where men were concerned. In his wish to bring Siam up to date Chulalongkorn, Mongkut's successor, decreed that at court functions uniforms should be worn instead of the sumptuous robes of office that had adorned his father's court. There was now no market for such opulent vestments. It was not till after the Second World War that an American ex-officer recognized the potential market for this exquisite material.

The economy of the country as a whole was greatly improved by the implementation of these treaties. But the changes in

Bangkok itself were even greater. It became an international city. Previously it had consisted of the palace, a conglomeration of temples, a bustling Chinese quarter, and groups of villagers living on the klongs. Now it was the home of several consulates. Business firms had to have bases there. Banks followed trade. At Christmas 1968 the Oriental Hotel sent out as a Christmas card to its clients the reproduction of a picture of itself painted in 1888 — a charmingly imposing building with its two statues standing with high-held torches in front of the verandah. Within thirty years of the signing of that first treaty with Great Britain in 1855, there had arisen the need of a first-class hotel. That is symptomatic. The presence of *farangs* meant that changes had to take place in the structure of the city. Mongkut ordered the construction of a number of buildings along New Road which could be let to commercial firms. He also had to undertake the construction of a number of new roads, because some of the consuls complained that they and their staff liked to drive in the evening to enjoy the cool, clean air; but the dirt of the narrow lanes prevented their doing this, and their health was suffering. The king accepted their strictures. He himself was ashamed of the condition of the streets. Bangkok was becoming a city that was being developed to meet the needs not only of the Thais and of the Chinese, but of the Europeans who were making it their temporary homes.

Bowring's book *The Kingdom and People of Siam* is the first authentic Western account that we have of life in Bangkok. It is a valuable book not so much for what Bowring has to tell us — he was only there for four and a half weeks and most of that time was occupied with affairs of state — as for the quotations that he makes from a book written by a French bishop: Monseigneur Pallegoix's *Description du Royaume Thai* published in 1854. There is so much information in this book that it is pertinent to make a series of disconnected quotations from it — a series of snapshots of Bangkok as it was at the beginning of King Mongkut's reign.

Bishop Pallegoix has this to say about the Siamese eating habits. He describes a favorite sauce, *nam phrik*. To make it, a quantity of red pepper is bruised in a mortar, shrimp paste is added, and black pepper, garlic and onions. Brine and lemon juice are added along with ginger, tamarinds and gourd seeds, fish in an early stage of putridity, chillies and mango sprouts. (Thais on the whole do not like very hot dishes: their curries are flavored with coconut milk. Nam phrik sounds as though it had a powerful bite.)

The Thais sit on a mat or carpet to eat. The food is served in a large brazen bowl, with covers and with a red cloth placed over it. The meat is cut into small pieces: the rice is kept apart in a large porringer. On the other side is a basin of water. Mother-of-pearl spoons are used, shaped in imitation of the half coconut shells on bamboo-stick holders that are widely used in the villages. There is no talk during meals. The Siamese concentrate upon their food. Tea is the usual beverage. (Coffee had recently been introduced.) Arak acquired from the Chinese was consumed furtively.

Rice, he said, is washed four times. It is placed in a pot filled with water. It is boiled for three minutes. The water is then poured off. The pot is put on a slow fire. The rice is steamed without being burned. The separate grains do not adhere to one another or stick to the fingers.

In those days a Siamese nobleman always had carried around with him a jeweled box. It contained his areca and betel. The betel is a creeping plant, producing a long and fleshy heart-shaped leaf with a strong flavor. The areca is a palm tree, sixty feet high with leaves only at the top. It has three or four enormous bunches, each with two or three hundred nuts. They are green at first, then they turn red. Lime is added. The leaves are wrapped like a cigar. A servant carried, in addition to this jeweled box, a spittoon.

Members of the missions were given stuffed triangular cushions with gold embroidery at the corners. The proletariat was not allowed to own such cushions. The donors said, "When you rest your head on it, think of me."

The bishop described the shaving of the head tuft — the topknot. An altar, he said, is erected of planks or bamboos. It has seven steps of ascent which are carpeted with fresh bamboo leaves. Each step is ornamented with grotesque figures of angels and animals in clay paper or carved out of calabashes. Vessels of metal or porcelain are filled with meat and fruit. On the upper stages are garlands of flowers and leaves of tinsel, gold and silver. In the middle of it all is a fresh coconut.

At the foot of the altar are nine chandeliers, whose wax candles are kindled when a musket is discharged three times. One of the candles is seized by the person in whose honor the ceremonial has been prepared. He carries it around the altar. His friends one by one seize one of the wax lights and blow it over the head of the ordained so that the smoke may envelop his forehead. Then the fresh coconut is given to the neophyte. He eats a hard-boiled egg as he drinks its milk. He is presented with a cup containing a few pennies. The band begins to play and the ceremony ends.

When a Thai is dying, priests sprinkle lustral water and recite sacred passages. When he dies they cry, "Why did you leave us?" The body is washed, enveloped in white cloth, placed in a coffin, which is then covered with gilded paper and decorated with tinsel flowers; a dais ornamented with flowers is lit with candles. The coffin is taken to a barge; wailing relatives accompany it in small boats. The corpse has in its mouth a small coin to defray the expenses of cremation. The burner washes the face with coconut milk. Sometimes the body is cut

King Mongkut in prayer

up and delivered to vultures. Then the remains are placed upon a pyre and a fire is lighted. The garb of mourning is white and heads are shaven. Opulent funerals last three days. There are sermons, fireworks, theatrical games and gambling.

"It is," he wrote, "a country of perpetual symbol. Mermaids and sirens in the waters, ogres and giants on the land, nymphs in the forests, ghosts and spirits everywhere, dragons and fire-spitting serpents, birds which feed on living men which have women's breasts and elephants' trunks. A country of unceasing pageantry." It is not surprising that the Thais should have been content with their life the way it was.

Bribery and corruption were universal. Forgery — it was called coining then — was so common that a tenth of the silver was spurious. Penalties were severe. The man who blew the bellows had the fingers of his right hand chopped off; the man who formed the coin lost his right hand. The most serious offence — it was *lèse majesté* after all — was the impressing of the king's mark upon the coin. For this the man had his whole arm cut off.

On the death of a minister, the king inherited a quarter of his estate, on the assumption that public functions are never honestly performed.

King Mongkut is the first Thai king of whom we have photographs. There is one of him in his state robes, wearing his crown. He looks like some mummified divinity. There is another of him, in prayer, in a simple white dress. His eyes are closed. His hands are raised, the palms pressed together. He is thin and bald and wrinkled. He has the air of an old and very holy man. His two roles are thus presented, side by side. He enjoyed the ceremonial of the court, and he felt that his people loved it. After his coronation he had a magnificent procession around the city; all of the gorgeous longboats were launched for it. His own was propelled by gold-painted paddles. A hundred men in scarlet coats were at the oars. He later had built for himself an exceptionally lovely barge, decorated with the seven-headed naga. One part of his nature hankered for display; but the other side of him was very holy, very simple, dedicated to the five-path road to ultimate redemption. Like all members of the Chakri family he was irascible; and he was no doubt terrifying when he was in one of his rages, but he was never ridiculous as he is made out to be in *The King and I.*

The Eastern or African potentate who is enamored of Western culture and tries to initiate Western conditions into an undeveloped country, is one of the stock comic characters of the novel and the stage. The best example in recent years is my brother Evelyn's Emperor Seth in his Abyssinian novel *Black Mischief.* And there are resemblances between Mongkut and Seth; his passion, for example, for clocks and gadgets — Queen Victoria was to present him with a model railway which can now be seen in the National Museum. There is his idiosyncratic use of the English language; and there were comic incidents in his life, such as his offering of elephants to Abraham Lincoln to help him in the Civil War; but he was not a comic character. He was an impressive Lord of Life.

Mrs. Leonowens' *The English Governess at the Siamese Court* was published in 1870. It created no stir of interest, nor did her *Romance of a Harem,* which followed three years later. Then in 1944 Margaret Landon published her *Anna and the King of Siam* which was based on the two books. It was a best seller. Mrs. Landon said that her novel was seventy-five per cent fact and twenty-five per cent fiction — which is a reasonable proportion for a historical novel. But Prince Chula raises the point: Does Mrs. Landon regard Mrs. Leonowens' book as fact? If she does, then her book is very far from being seventy-five per cent fact, for Mrs. Leonowens' book is a highly romanticized and at times very nearly imaginary portrait of court life. Then Hollywood got to work on Mrs. Landon's novel, and the picture was distorted in the best tradition of the industry. As Prince Chula says, the result was as accurate a portrait of court life as Gilbert and Sullivan's *The Mikado* is of mid-nineteenth century Tokyo. The film has been banned in Thailand.

The tonsure ceremony that the worthy monseigneur described, colorful though it was, pales before the ceremony which graced the shaving of the king's heir apparent, Chulalongkorn. First in procession came the bearers of gold umbrellas, fans and wide golden sunshades. They were followed by four hundred Amazons, green and gold and armored. Then came twelve girls in cloth of gold, with fantastic, jeweled headdresses. Court Brahmins scattered roasted rice, symbols of plenty, from golden bowls. Brahmins with tabors preceded two young nobles, carrying golden cages. The king's infantry followed the king's Japanese bodyguard.

A strip of palmyra was put into the prince's hand. It contained on one side the sacred words "Even I was, even from the first and not any other thing; that which existed unperceived, supreme. Afterwards I am that which is and he that was and he who must remain am I. I know that except me, who am the first cause, nothing that appears or does not appear in the mind can be trusted. It is the mind's *maya* or delusion. As light is to darkness."

On the reverse side was a prayer that he would obey the instructions of Nirvana.

In the final ceremony he sat on a golden throne surmounted by a three-tiered umbrella. His insignia were laid out on side tables. Then came the rites of *vien-thien,* the rotation of the candles. Selected nobles circled round the throne, keeping their right shoulders toward the prince. As they moved they passed seven golden lighted candlesticks from the one to the other; with the free hand they wafted the smoke toward him.

It is in essence the same ceremony today.

Many valuable gifts were made to the young prince. The king kept careful note of money presented by officers in the government, so that the money might be refunded by an increase of salary.

King Mongkut was, as his half-brother had been, perplexed about the succession. He married two sisters, the granddaughters of Rama III; the senior wife he raised to the rank of queendom, and she produced three celestial princes, the eldest of whom, the future King Chulalongkorn, was born in 1853, two years after Mongkut's accession. The two sons who had been born before he entered the priesthood were not celestial princes, but their seniority might have made them rivals, and Mongkut himself had always been insistent on the elective nature of the monarchy; to his relief, probably, they died before they could present a challenge. There was no Uparaja. On his accession he had appointed his full brother, Prince Chutamani, not to the position of deputy king, but of second king, restoring a custom that had been adopted in Ayudhya two hundred years before. As second king, Chutamani had a status only a little lower than the king's, and was accorded a sumptuous coronation. There is a legend that Mongkut wanted his brother to share the throne with him, the accepted reason for this being that Chutamani's horoscope had shown that he would be king one day, so Mongkut was afraid that he would not himself live very long if his brother were waiting in the wings. Prince Chula does not think that this is likely, because he does not believe that so devout a Buddhist would have been influenced by a superstition. He considers that Mongkut deeply loved his brother, was conscious of his brother's jealousy and was anxious to placate it. Even so, relations between the brothers were soon to deteriorate. The younger brother was always suspecting that some affront would be put upon him. In consequence he avoided family reunions. His domestic life was not happy. He believed that one of his wives was poisoning him with love potions. He was certainly in extremely bad health. It was fortunate for Siam that he should have died two years before Mongkut did.

The death of Chutamani left no one who could challenge the claims of Mongkut's eldest celestial son, yet Mongkut realized, on his deathbed, that a boy of fifteen was not fit to rule a kingdom. He did not name an heir; he instructed the accession council to choose the prince who was best fitted to serve the state. He used the word serve deliberately. He had from the beginning seen his kingship as a continuation of his priesthood. He had proved that at his coronation. It had always been the custom at the coronation for the princes and high officials to drink the water of fealty to their sovereign. Prince Chula tells us that Mongkut surprised the gathering by raising a glass to his own lips; thus (in Prince Dhani's words) "offering voluntarily to pledge himself to the people as their sovereign by partaking in drinking of the water of truth, thus making it for the first time a bipartite instead of the former one-sided oath of allegiance."

Nothing could have been more different from his last hours on earth than the emotion-charged scene of the musical with Anna, who was not anyhow in Bangkok at that time, promising to help Chulalongkorn rule Siam in terms of the enlightenment which she had brought to the barbarians. The king's last hours were very quiet. He would not have his children brought to see him because he did not want to disturb the mood of peace in which he was ready now to leave the world. He knew that he was dying; and he was glad to be dying on his birthday as the Buddha had. He took his leave of the senior princes and of his ministers. He asked their forgiveness for his shortcomings. He was sad that he would no longer be able to serve the state with them. The Lord Buddha had died on his right side. He asked to be turned on his right side too. "This is the correct way to die," he said. It was the last thing he said.

6

Anna's Protégé in Bondage

Mongkut died at nine in the evening. The accession council
met at midnight. It was summoned by the chief minister, Suriyawongse. The choice of membership lay in his hands. There
was no equivalent for the British Privy Council. But there
never seems to have been any dispute as to who should be
invited. The premier called upon the patriarch, twenty-four
prelates and sixteen princes. There were seven half-brothers of
the dead king, six of Rama III's sons and three sons of former
Uparajas. None of Mongkut's own sons were considered old
enough to attend, but seven who were in the junior priesthood
were allowed to watch the proceedings. When the selected
members had sat down, Suriyawongse knelt and joined his
hands in prayer. He explained that the king had not named an
heir; that he had invited the council to make their choice.
Unanimously the council agreed that the crown should be
offered to his eldest son.

The chief minister then said that King Mongkut had been
afraid that his son was too young to rule effectively. It was
therefore proposed that the chief minister should act as regent
until the king reached the age of twenty. This proposal also was
accepted. The chief figure in the council was Mongkut's eldest

half-brother, Prince Deves. The question then arose of choosing an Uparaja, and Prince Deves suggested that they should choose the eldest son of the former Uparaja. On this point however there was not unanimity. Another of Prince Mongkut's half-brothers objected. He argued that it was the king's duty to choose his own deputy and that they should wait until the king was old enough to make his choice. At that point Suriyawongse lost his temper. "Why do you object?" he said. "Is it because you want the post yourself?" He forced the election through. It is believed that his insistence was based on his own fear that the king might turn against him when he came of age; he might need therefore an ally in high office when that day came. The new Uparaja was fifteen years older than the king. He was an amiable nonentity. It was most unlikely that he and the king would combine against the regent.

The regent assessed the situation prudently. The king did not relish the regent's authoritarianism, but there was nothing that he could do about it.

The regent was a dominant personality. He was a member of the Bunnag family, which dated back to a Persian who had settled in Ayudhya in the seventeenth century. History has shown it as the most important Thai family next to the Chakris. Phya Suriyawongse was the most distinguished of them all. He had been the contemporary of Rama III, his close friend and one of his first ministers. He was equally trusted by King Mongkut, and it was he who arranged the treaty with Great Britain. He made a great impression on Sir John Bowring, who wrote of him: "He is a most sagacious man, towering above every person whom we have met, of graceful, gentlemanly manners and appropriate language . . . in a word his language is of the most high-minded patriotism." Prince Chula called him "a statesman of great integrity." Yet he was apparently tyrannical, despotic, cruel and revengeful. One must take with caution any estimate of character made by Anna Leonowens, but the portrait that appears in her book has an air of authenticity, while a very grim picture is painted of him in R. J. Minney's *Fanny and the Regent of Siam*. The king was unquestionably apprehensive of him. He could not help remembering that in Ayudhya five kings had been murdered during their minority, one of them by a regent who had been called Suriyawongse, and carried the title Chao Phya Kalahom — but much of the success of Chulalongkorn's reign must be attributed to the regent's guardianship.

Technically the regency ended in 1873, but Sri Suriyawongse continued to be chief minister until his death in 1882, so that Chulalongkorn's reign did not really start until he was twenty-nine years old. He lived however until 1910. For twenty-eight years he was an absolute monarch, during which time he imprinted his personality upon the country and the city in which he held his court.

Forty-two years is a long time, and the Bangkok he handed over to his eldest celestial son was very different in appearance from the one that he had inherited from Mongkut.

When Sir John Bowring visited the city, though there were tracks of a sort on land, roads existed only in the center and near the markets. They were paved with bricks. At the end of the rainy season the whole town was under water. There was not a single carriage anywhere in Bangkok. A few years later a road was built running around the city just inside the walls. New Road was not completed till 1864. To the south was the great market where fruit, vegetables, eggs, pork, fish were sold. The fish were sold alive. They were kept in ponds. The Marquis de Beauvoir visiting Bangkok in 1867 was surprised to find pythons floating around with soles, eels, sunfish and small sharks. This method of storing fish continued until the railway between Bangkok and Paknam, opened in 1893, brought it into desuetude.

King Chulalongkorn with the Emperor Nicholas II of Russia

There was no sanitation and no proper supply of drinking water. Dysentery was rife. Seventy per cent of the children failed to reach their fifth year of life. In spite of the fine work of the American missionaries, it was not till the start of the century when vaccination was enforced that smallpox was really controlled. When Malcolm Smith, whose *A Physician at the Court of Siam* is full of interesting matter, went to Bangkok in 1902, he found that nearly one in ten of the people he met in the streets were scarred by the disease. When he left twenty years later, he saw very few.

During the rainy season water could be collected and stored. But there was practically no rain between October and April. By April the water had grown brackish. Cholera had been imported from India in 1819, and casualties in Bangkok were very heavy in the following year. The temples could not dispose of the corpses. They lay in the grounds stacked like timber. Citizens fled in panic. The monks left their monasteries.

There was another epidemic in 1849. Mongkut, then head of the Buddhist faith in Siam, instructed the three principal temples in Bangkok that were used as burning grounds to keep a record of the number of corpses brought to them each day. Between June 17 and July 25 they disposed of 5,457. The work of the city was paralyzed. In 1873 6,600 died in Bangkok. It was some time before it was realized that the water was responsible for the pestilence. When it was, a regular supply was obtained from Petchaburi, fifty miles away, where the water ran straight from the hills over gravel beds. It was brought to Bangkok in large jars. Today you will see large water jugs on the verandah of every house along the klongs. But it was not till 1914, when the Bangkok waterworks were constructed, that the disease really came under control. Mongkut and Chulalongkorn had to consider a great deal else besides the beautifying of their capital.

Every Chakri monarch had tried to leave the city more beautiful than he found it. Each monarch in his turn thought of himself as king of Bangkok first and king of Siam second. And Chulalongkorn's additions to the city may best be assessed in terms of the roads and tree-lined avenues he laid out and the bridges, some of them in marble, that he constructed across the klongs. In his early years he loved driving in the cool of the evening in a horse carriage, later in a yellow electric car. He connected Dusit Palace which he built outside the walls, with the center of the city by means of the impressive Rajadamnoen Avenue, copied from London's Pall Mall and Paris's Champs-Elysées — an avenue that was to play a quarter of a century later an important part in one of the most dramatic episodes in the city's history.

It was in the main by means of roads that he changed the appearance of the city. He moved its traffic from the rivers to the streets, yet at the same time the houses that lined the streets were the direct outcome of the policies that he promulgated. He created a need for commodious office buildings and for comfortable houses for the men who directed them. Prince Chula has called him "The Revolutionary," but hastens to explain that it was a revolution delivered from above, as opposed to the usual form of revolution that is an uprising from below. On his coronation, he decreed an end to the centuries-old custom of ceremonial prostration before the throne. He ordered the assembled company to stand up. He also ended slavery, announcing at his coronation that everyone born during his reign would eventually be free, and because of the publicity that they received through *The King and I*, he is in the Western world primarily associated with these two acts. But slavery had in fact never weighed heavily upon the Thais. Theirs was a paternalistic system in terms of their own reverence for the monarchy. And in the end it was only by ingenious litigation and a certain amount of personal philanthropy that the reform was carried through. Children automatically ceased to be slaves at the age of twenty-one and no one over twenty-one could be sold into slavery. But that was not enough. He needed to protect those who might suffer destitution when they were no longer housed and fed by their masters. He needed to fit the liberated slaves for subsequent employment, so he instituted schools where they were given what would now be described as instructional training; to ensure that these schools were well attended, he himself freed slaves by buying them from their owners on the stipulation that they attend the schools. It was a slow business and it was not until 1905 that abolition could be regarded as being finally achieved.

Chulalongkorn himself would have regarded abolition as one of his minor achievements. He prided himself on the methods with which he Westernized his country without subjecting it to foreign usurpation. He had taken note of what had happened in Burma and in Indo-China. He was resolved to make himself a modern monarch. He was a short, chubby man, with a zest both for living and for work. He was well educated. He spoke excellent English, and he decided to make himself known to British and Russian royalty. He met them as an equal, which is possibly one of the reasons why his relations with France were not at the start as cordial as those with Russia and Great Britain. He was not quite able to meet the president of a republic on equal terms.

In 1897 he made the first European tour ever made by an Eastern potentate. Nicholas II of Russia had visited Siam when he was heir apparent, and very cordial relations had been founded with King Chulalongkorn. These relations were strengthened and confirmed now that Nicholas was the Czar. Chulalongkorn had a warm reception in Germany from William II. In London he stayed at Buckingham Palace, and though Queen Victoria was resting at Windsor in view of the exhausting duties that would attend her Diamond Jubilee, he was received by the future Edward VII. In Austria he was entertained by Francis Joseph. In Paris he was met by the French president at the railway station in his carriage, and in view of the difficulties that he had experienced with French imperialism in Cambodia, he was surprised by the warmth of the reception that he received from the populace during his drive along the boulevards. But probably his happiest hours were spent in Denmark. The links between Denmark and Siam have always been close. The Thais have been called "The Danes of Asia," as has already been noted, and there are resemblances between Bangkok and Copenhagen — each is a city built on waterways — but there is a kinship, a character deeper than that resemblance; both are happy, lively, laughter-loving, independent, with an engagingly basic frivolity. There is an automatic response between the two peoples. The East Asiatic Company, whose offices are situated on the river next door to the Oriental Hotel, was one of the first European firms to trade extensively with Siam. The Danes with their teak concessions in the north have always occupied a special and privileged position. Even today Denmark is always careful to choose as its minister a man of family and culture and the writer of this narrative recalls gratefully the hospitality he received in 1958 at the Danish Embassy. The minister was a highly distinguished Dane, who did not seem overworked, but who quietly and richly acted as a social lubricant. Denmark is a democratic country and in early days one of its royal princes, the brother of Queen Alexandra of England, frequently visited Bangkok for business reasons. He became a close friend of Chulalongkorn and carried back to Europe warm accounts of the charm of the Siamese court.

King Chulalongkorn's first visit to Europe had been prepared by the series of close links that he had initiated with European courts. He had sent most of his sons to Europe for their education. He had seventy-seven children, thirty-two of whom were sons. Prince Chula considers that he had ninety-two wives, but a large number of these were ladies of nominal qualification. Since they saw him only at the audiences in the yellow room they were known as "the Chao Choms of the yellow room."

With the exception of the crown prince, all of his chief sons were educated abroad. Vajiravudh, who became Rama VI through the early death of the crown prince, had his entire education in England. After studying history at Oxford, at Christ Church, he went to Sandhurst, the Royal Military College, and was commissioned in the Durham Light Infantry. He was an ardent Anglophile; possibly too ardent a one for there seems little doubt that in England he developed homosexual tendencies. He took little interest in the female sex, and though he eventually married, he produced only one child, in the last weeks of his life.

Another of Chulalongkorn's sons went to Germany to have a distinguished period of service in the German army. Prince Chula's father, Prince Chakrabongse, went to Russia where he deeply offended the king, whose favorite son he appears to have been, by marrying a Russian lady without asking for the royal consent. His explanation was that he knew the permission would not be granted and he did not want to put himself in the position of flouting the royal command.

The story as told by Prince Chula is not unamusing. On his return from Russia Prince Chakrabongse prudently established his bride in Singapore, took up residence in Bangkok in the main building of Paruskavan Palace next door to his brother the crown prince, and assumed his army post as commandant of the military academy. Not surprisingly the prince paid frequent visits to Singapore. The king was curious; and as a result of his inquiries learned that there was a certain Madame de Bisnulok, one of the many names to which the prince was entitled. As a joke at a public audience, the king asked his son if it was true that he was married to a Russian lady. "Yes, Sire, I am." *Consternation générale.* At length there was a reconciliation, but the succession to the throne may well have been affected by this romance.

It is impossible to enter imaginatively into the mind of an Eastern Lord of Life whose chief wives were his own half-sisters and whose own mother was the granddaughter of his father's uncle; a man moreover who eighty years ago saw nothing unusual in such involved relationships. It is impossible to assess his feelings towards his thirty-two sons and his innumerable cousins. Chulalongkorn was by all accounts a devoted family man; he wished the best for them, and he wished the best for the city that they were to inherit. Much of his concern for his country was conditioned by his concern for them. He saw the country and his family's dependents as working for each other's good. He was anxious that they should see themselves as "members one of another." His two chief wives — his queens — were sisters, and they accepted the Thai philosophy of polygamy. The mother of the future Rama VI wrote to her son while his half-brother, the heir apparent, was still alive: "You know what Vajiravudh is going to be. Apply yourself to love him and be loyal to him. You are both far away from home, so if you can be intimate and affectionate to him now, it will smooth the way for both of you in the future. As for the rest of your half-brothers in Europe, remember that they are all your father's sons; be correct, affectionate and united with them all."

It is not easy for a Western father with four or five children to give each one of them the best chance possible. Though Chulalongkorn must have had favorites, he appears to have been devoted to all his sons. He was anxious to give each one the opportunity of playing an important role in the country's fu-

King Chulalongkorn leading Queen Alexandra and followed by King
Edward VII at a garden party at Windsor

ture. He gave them the best education that he could devise and
he trained them for administrative office. He knew that the
Chakri family had saved, defended and built up the country,
and he believed that members of the Chakri family were the
best qualified to run the new late-nineteenth-century country
that he was creating. Perhaps it is that resolve that was the
basic cause of the political confusion that has distracted the
country for the last quarter of a century. A number of his sons
were men of remarkable powers — indeed one of the most
striking features of Siamese history is the qualities of industry,
power and intelligence that have been a part of the Chakri
royal princes' hereditary endowment — but it is not possible to
rule a modern country through a single clan, and it was Chulalongkorn's plan that each of the new ministries that he founded,
and he founded a great many, should be directed by a royal
prince.

He gave his sons strict instructions as to how they should
conduct themselves overseas. They must not, he said, style
themselves as princes, even though he acknowledged them as
his sons. His reasons for this were sensible. In Europe, he explained, there were very few princes and those few maintained
an elaborate entourage. In Siam there were so many princes
that they could not maintain an equivalent state abroad, and in
consequence if they conformed to modest standards they would
lessen the dignity of the Siamese royalty. Let them, therefore,
be regarded as Siamese boys of good birth. This would not in
any way diminish their self-respect, since foreign princes had
no privileges in Europe. Entrance into good society was easy
for a royal prince, but any other person of good birth could do
this if he wanted. He stressed the purpose of their mission to
Europe. Prince Bidya, in Prince Chula's *Lords of Life,* quotes
Chulalongkorn's advice: "If after acquiring proficiency in foreign languages, you cannot turn them into Siamese, little ad-

vantage will have been gained, for we can employ as many foreigners as we need. What will be required of you is an ability to
turn a European language into Siamese and Siamese into a European language. You would be useful then."

He regarded the training of his sons as his own obligation.
The discipline of the daughters he left to his queens and minor
wives, who for punishment would bend back their arms and
fingers at the joints giving them the double-jointedness that the
Thai male found attractive. The king was a most diligent correspondent when his sons were abroad. He never let them forget their destiny — it was through them that he was to create
modern Bangkok. He was well aware that the country was not
yet ready to run itself, so he introduced foreign advisers. The
British dealt with finance; the French later in his reign controlled the law; he regarded Americans as the best fitted to advise him on foreign affairs, presumably because they were neutral. Danes, Germans, Belgians all had their roles to play, and
under the guidance of these advisers he entirely reorganized
the country. He enlarged and modernized the army. He formed
a ministry of justice, and established criminal and civil courts.
Though the French were ultimately the chief advisers on legal
matters the procedure was very much the same as that of the
English courts, and a majority of the Thai lawyers had been
called to the English bar.

There was a ministry of agriculture. A police force was created under British officers. The health facilities of the country
were improved, though the king met with difficulties through
the reluctance of Thai doctors to divulge their secrets and
through the faith that the people as a whole had in the medicine on which their ancestors had relied — which indeed
achieved highly effective results with concoctions brewed out
of herbs and the bark of trees. Later it was as hard to find pa-

tients for the hospitals as it had been to find doctors. A British physician whose advice was sought, suggested that a number of the beggars who were suffering from sores should be rounded up and cured so that the Thais could see how excellent Western medicines were, but the beggars refused. Their blains and blisters were the proof that they needed help. They would starve if their skins were whole. Finally the committee insisted on their own servants attending hospitals. The results were so obvious that the public was convinced. The public was also beguiled by the device of not labeling the origin of the bottles or pills, but by simply stating the purpose each was to serve. The labels read "For Fever," "For Bronchitis," "For Headaches." One of the advantages of Western medicine was apparently its less copious need of liquid content. When the people had once begun to appreciate the effectiveness of Western medicine they were ready to accept surgery.

Education was, naturally, one of Chulalongkorn's first concerns and the university that now bears his name is a testimony to the extent of his achievements in this field. In earlier days the monasteries were responsible for all education. The temples were in fact colleges, and when the need for modern equipment was recognized, many of the old temples and their grounds were adjusted to meet changed conditions.

A teacher's college was instituted. It was the king's wish in his own words "that all my own children to the poorest should have an equal chance of education." He, in fact, instituted secondary education.

One of the ways in which Chulalongkorn modernized Bangkok was in the opening of the first railway station. He was aware that British engineers were examining the feasibility of running a railroad between Burma and China, and he was resolved that any railroads that existed in Siam should be under

Siamese control. He did not want to have the British and the French extending their systems across his territory. So he gave a British-Danish company permission to construct a railroad connecting Bangkok with Paknam, a town at the mouth of the river. He bought shares in it himself, and formed a Royal State Railway Department. The first project was a line to Korat. For this, in search of neutrality, he employed German engineers. The king cut the first sod in 1882. By 1887 a line ran to Ayudhya; three years later the line to Korat was ready; by the end of his reign there were 520 miles of railroad in the country. The king interwove his railroad plans with those of his road development. He did not build roads in areas that were served by railways, and his roads led to railheads. The first railroads were built out of ordinary revenue. It was not till 1903 that the first foreign loan was floated.

The economy of the country, in spite of the lavish expenditure at court, was extremely flourishing. When he came to the throne, Chulalongkorn had owned all the land. The peasants were in fact peasant proprietors, but the king was their landlord and instead of their paying him rent, he was entitled to demand *corvée* service of them. But Chulalongkorn surrendered these rights. He instituted the process of titled deeds by which private owners could bequeath property to their heirs. This was to prove of immense value to his grandchildren. He set up a Privy Purse which was kept separate from the national treasury: and from this purse he sent his children to be educated in Europe. Under the efficient guardianship of his British technical advisers, he was able to conduct the nation's finances in a manner that would fill a modern Chancellor of the Exchequer with envy and despair. There was no public debt. The annual budget showed a profit. Nobody was hungry, nobody knew want. Exports exceeded imports. The Chinese were so well contented that they began to bring their wives with them.

This meant that Chinese profits remained within the country; a painless and profitable switch had been made from the medieval Bangkok of Rama I to a modern sovereign state. European royalty was met on equal terms.

7
Europe Outwitted

BANGKOK had become a modern city, with streets and pavements and electric light. Yet the river remained the center of its
life. Much of its pageantry was displayed, much of its drama
was enacted between its banks. High matters of state reached
their climax there. One such climax occurred in 1879, at the
start of the wet season on a morning of heavy gales, when the
populace was astonished to see a British gunboat fighting its
way upstream. Its commander was unfamiliar with Bangkok.
He recognized the British consulate since the Union Jack was
flying from its flagpole, but the river was too congested with
wharves, barges and houseboats for him to anchor there. He
looked for a suitable anchorage, and saw an empty space in
front of a series of gold pagodas which seemed appropriate to
the dignity of his vessel. It happened to be within the sacred
precincts of the royal palace. Confusion convulsed the palace
guards. Nothing as unexpected had happened in the city's history.

The explanation of how this came about has been entertain-
ingly told by R. J. Minney in his *Fanny and the Regent of Siam.*
Mr. Minney has told the story in the form of a novel, but it is
based on solid research, on the examination of state papers. Mr.

Minney has earned the respect of historians with his *Clive of India,* and his book can be accepted both as a statement and an imaginative interpretation of the facts, hard though it is to believe that events such as those that he relates were taking place less than a hundred years ago. It was the love affair of the daughter of a British consul general that brought H.M.S. *Foxhound* from Singapore on a mission of high urgency.

In April 1875 Fanny Knox, then a girl of nineteen, was met on her arrival in Bangkok by two men. One was the grandson of the chief minister of the country, Sri Suriawongse, who had been regent to the young King Chulalongkorn. The other was Louis Leonowens, the son of the Anna of *The King and I.* They had come to meet her in the British consulate's launch. On the landing stage of the consulate were her mother and her sister, Caroline, her junior by two years. Her mother was a Thai, the daughter of a nobleman, who had been a lady-in-waiting in the court of King Mongkut's Uparaja. Knox, after serving in the Indian Army during the China Wars, had been persuaded by the deputy king to help in the training of the Siamese. It was thus that he had met Fanny's mother. When a British consulate was established, Knox joined it as an interpreter. He had in England relatives in high places, Lord John Beresford and Lord Ranfurly. He was soon made vice consul; and when a vacancy occurred he took over its administration. He had been consul for eleven years when Minney's narrative begins. Most of his service had been spent in the Far East. He had had no diplomatic training, but he was clearly admirably fitted for the post. His connection with the Thai royal family ensured that he would appreciate the Thai point of view and that he could explain the British attitude to them. But things did not turn out the way it had been hoped.

Fanny was a headstrong lady. She was anything but a Victorian miss. In early years she had seen a great deal of Louis

Leonowens; they had been childhood sweethearts and Louis had imagined that on her return from Europe they would become engaged. But Fanny was not interested in marriage for the sake of marriage. She was resolved that her marriage should be a real romance. She had also noticed that Caroline during her absence had fallen in love with Louis. It was not difficult for Fanny to convince Louis that he would be happier with her sister, and in that she was very probably right. Fanny was not the kind of woman to make happy a man whom she did not adore. Caroline, though she died sadly young at the age of thirty-five, made a contented marriage and was the mother of two children. Fanny in the meantime was waiting for the real thing.

She was soon to find it in the person of a nobleman called Preecha, a dashing warrior, fourteen years older than herself, who had recently become a widower. He was not perhaps the husband that an Englishman, even though he was himself married to a Thai, would have chosen for his daughter, but Preecha was rich, he was powerful, and he had found a gold mine on his province which he had presented to the State. No doubt Knox would have come to welcome him in the end as many fathers have done in the past and will do in the future. Unfortunately fate intervened. The chief minister decided that Fanny would make a suitable bride for his grandson Nai Dee, the young man who had met Fanny at the consulate. The chief minister saw her, presumably, as a pawn in the devious power game that he was playing with the king. Suriawongse was as much a king as ever Mongkut had been. His authority was unquestioned; only one man could question it, the king himself. Sri Suriawongse was anxious to avoid a showdown. He fancied that it would be useful to have a family link with the representative of Her Britannic Majesty. He, therefore, approached Knox in the matter. Knox was not unimpressed. He liked Nai Dee. He considered that it was his first duty to maintain the best possible relations with the chief minister. That was what he was here for, after all. It would be disastrous if, through Fanny's irresponsibility, the queen's representative in Siam was unable to fulfill the duties for which she had, through her ministers, appointed him. He forbade Fanny to see Preecha. He urged her to prevaricate with the chief minister. The chief minister, he reminded her, was no longer young. He would not live forever; at the same time he urged patience on the chief minister. English girls were not like Thai girls, he explained. They did not regard their parents' wishes as commands. The prime minister exercised as much patience as was possible for one who considered himself a Lord of Life. He was assiduous in his attentions to Fanny. At a performance of *The School for Scandal* he presented her with a large brooch of yellow diamonds and emeralds.

But guile and diplomacy were alike ineffective. This was "the real thing." On the tenth of March Preecha and Fanny were married in Preecha's house in Bangkok. Neither her father nor her mother attended the ceremony, Knox insisting that it would not be politic. The next morning the happy couple left for his residence in the country. They made a tour of his estate. They were received everywhere with jubilation. Elaborate festivities were arranged. But their happiness was brief. The chief minister struck with speed and with ferocity. Preecha was summoned to the capital. On March 28 they were back in Bangkok. Preecha did not seem to be suspicious. He asked his father to take Fanny to the ballet, while he paid his respects to the chief minister and the king. He would join them as soon as his audience was over. But he never did. On his arrival at the palace he was put under arrest.

During the next weeks Suriawongse showed how he interpreted the powers of a Lord of Life. Authority for ultimate decisions had to be given by the king, but the king was under the chief minister's orders. He could not act on his own. It was easy in those days to trump up charges. Preecha had insulted the king by marrying without his permission. There were accusations of mismanagement on his estate, of cruelty to the workers in the gold mines. It was also stated that Preecha had taken Fanny on his yacht for a whole night, before they were married, without her father's consent. For this there was a factual basis. Fanny had spent a night on Preecha's yacht; but not alone: there had been female chaperones. It was pointed out that Fanny's father had not attended the wedding. He had only agreed to the wedding because his daughter had been compromised. The dignity of Her Majesty Queen Victoria's representative had been affronted. The representative of Her Britannic Majesty ranked with the high nobility of Siam. Preecha was tried by the council of state, and was found guilty. The sentence ran "For such irregular, contemptuous and outrageous conduct let Phra Perim Worathep take Phra Preecha and cause him to receive thirty strokes so that other officials may not follow his example."

In the meantime there remained the charge of mismanaging the gold mines. Judges were appointed to audit his accounts. That was how it started.

Knox indignantly denied the allegations. Facts had been misinterpreted and thrown out of focus. He demanded an apology and the immediate release of his son-in-law. "I shall, of course," he said, "inform Lord Salisbury [the Secretary of State for Foreign Affairs] that the Prime Minister wanted my daughter to marry his favorite grandson and was furious at her choice of another suitor."

Fanny and the Regent of Siam reproduces a facsimile of this letter which begins: "My Lord, I very much regret to have to lay before your Lordship a report of an occurrence in which I am to some extent personally concerned through another closely connected with me" . . . and the letter concluded, "I

King Chulalongkorn with one of his favorite sons, Prince Chakrabongse

am sending for one of H.M.'s gunboats and on her arrival here, I will make a final demand for an apology and for the release of Phra Preecha. If I find that there is a *prima facie* case against him on the new charges, I shall place no difficulties in the way of a fair trial. On the other hand, if he has committed no offence and I find that the king wishes it, I shall have him sent out of the country. I am convinced that on the arrival of the gunboat, I shall at once obtain compliance with my demands."

That was how diplomacy was conducted in the 1870s. Knox telegraphed to Singapore, and soon H.M.S. *Foxhound* was on her way. The sight of her plunging through the troubled waters of the Menam on a gale-shaken summer morning may well have been taken by King Chulalongkorn as a salutary warning. He must be on his guard against the repetition of such incidents. When he ordered in 1892 a private yacht, the *Maha Chakri*, in which he was to make his trip to Europe, although he had it charmingly equipped for social and state occasions, with a round smoking room in the stern, and a circular banquette under the portholes, he also had it fitted as a gunboat. She was of three thousand tons and was armed with four 4.7 inch guns, and ten six-pounders. Her deck was plated with steel armor. Such a boat might have a useful part to play in the maintenance of Siamese independence. But at the moment there was nothing that he could do. The British gunboat was anchored in the river, and its presence ensured that Knox's complaints were thoroughly investigated.

The events that followed would belong to comedy had not a man's life been at stake, for in the end Preecha was executed, the victim of trumped-up charges inspired by an old man's hate and sense of injured vanity.

The arrival of the *Foxhound* was the most exciting thing that had happened in Bangkok for very many years. The people once they had recovered from their first alarm, were excited by this unusual visitant. It was the first time that the majority of them had seen a gunboat. They clustered around it in their boats and barges. They stood on their roofs to get a better view of it. But some of the more serious citizens — the Chinese in particular — were apprehensive. They sent petitions to Knox. They were afraid of war. They organized demonstrations in front of the consulate. Boys threw firecrackers from their boats. Men paraded New Road with placards bearing the Siamese equivalent of "Knox Go Home." The officer in charge of the gunboat did not know how to comport himself. He had no clear instructions. He did not call on either the king or the foreign minister. The chief minister invited the officers of the *Foxhound* to a garden party. The captain did not attend himself but dispatched three junior officers. The next day he issued instructions that there must be no intercourse between his officers and Siamese nationals.

But behind the scenes a great deal was going on. Fanny's brother-in-law Louis Leonowens had been a childhood friend of King Chulalongkorn. She begged him to intercede on her behalf. Knox interviewed the king; he was assured that the trial would be conducted in terms of the due and proper processes of law. The king had to walk warily. He did not want to quarrel with the chief minister. He had to bide his time. The chief minister was concerned only with revenge. Let the other princes take note of what happened to any of their number who challenged his supreme authority. It took ten weeks to get an answer to a letter dispatched from Bangkok to London. Lord Salisbury had a great deal upon his hands. He did not intend to let Britain become involved in war because of a consul's daughter's love affair. He did not reply at once to Knox's first dispatch announcing the arrest of Preecha. Let the matter solve itself. But when Singapore informed him that a gunboat had been sent to Bangkok, he knew that he had to move and quickly. He telegraphed: "The information in your dispatch does not justify your official interference in regard to Phra Preecha. You must not use force or threaten to use force."

The next day the Siamese consul general in London informed him that a special envoy was on his way from Singapore. The Siamese consul general was instructed to inform the Foreign Office that a gunboat was at Bangkok at Knox's request and to plead that no hostile acts take place before the arrival of the envoy. Salisbury's habitual placidity was disturbed. Knox must not think that as the man on the spot, his hands were free. Salisbury's cable ran: "Siamese consul general in London intimates you are contemplating warlike operations in Siam. Is it true? If so, why? Reply by wire." Knox answered that the report was utterly untrue; it was a ruse to get the gunboat recalled, the chief minister having boasted that he, Knox, would get no support from home, and that he had taken steps to have the boat recalled.

Lord Salisbury shrugged. It was an occasion for the exercise of that patience for which he was renowned and to which he was temperamentally so attuned. Let the gunboat stay, he said.

Its stay did little good. The chief minister was acting with un-Oriental speed. Trials usually take a long time in the East, but the evidence against Preecha was quickly put together. He was accused not only of a couple of minor murders, but of having employed a sorceress to make a wax image of the king, and by prayers and incantations to the image induce in the king a love for Preecha that led to his promotion. The sorceress had also made wax images of the chief minister and foreign minister on which she had laid spells; she had written their names on a sheet of paper and placed it together with the wax images in a coffin. She had prayed for their speedy death. She was caught just as she was preparing to lower the coffin into the ground.

Had she not been discovered, the two ministers would most certainly have died.

The chief minister took elaborate steps to assure that his own position should be cleared. Every Englishman in the Siamese Service was instructed to write to the London Foreign Office, condemning Knox's action. He wrote to the lieutenant governor of the Straits Settlements in Singapore. He expressed a wish through the envoy in London, to confer the Order of the White Elephant on Queen Victoria. Would she be so gracious as to accept it. A slight note of comedy was struck when Knox received from London the order of St. Michael and St. George which had been, at his request, awarded to the chief minister. He did not make the gift. He put the box in a drawer and locked it.

The chief minister won his battle. Power corrupts; absolute power corrupts completely. By the end of the year, Preecha had been beheaded; under the eyes of his enemy, his lands and property had been confiscated. The gunboat had left the river. The consul general had been recalled to England, with the consolation that Britain invariably gives to the man on the spot who has backed the wrong horse. He was awarded the honor of Knight Commander of the Order of St. Michael and St. George and a pension that was estimated at being two-thirds of his final salary — roughly £1,000 which was in those days not a negligible sum. And the widow, his daughter Fanny, the mother now of Preecha's son, was back with him in England.

Her escape to England was not undramatic. For the chief minister was resolved that she and her child and her stepchildren — the children of Preecha's dead wife — should be fully punished for Preecha's insolence. She went first to Singapore and while she was there, the Siamese consul telegraphed London that the question of Fanny's nationality must be taken up. She had married a Siamese official — she was therefore a

Siamese subject, under Siamese jurisdiction, and her child and stepchildren must be handed over to the Siamese.

The case eventually reached Lord Salisbury. He deliberated with his secretary, who reminded him that the act governing the marriage of female British subjects to aliens states that the wife automatically assumes her husband's nationality. The secretary was of the opinion that Fanny would have to be handed over to the Siamese. His lordship asked to be shown the act. He studied it carefully. He had mastered the arts of compromise and evasion. He was confident that if there was a loophole he would find it. His confidence was justified. "I do not see it stated anywhere in this document that the provision which relates to English women marrying aliens is applicable to heathen countries. You can inform the Siamese government that His Majesty's government deems that the lady is entitled to be counted a British subject and consequently will enjoy our protection."

There it would seem the story had reached its melancholy curtain, but there is a sequel and one that fills a special corner in a biography of Bangkok. Fanny did not, as might have been expected, remain in England, in retirement with her father in Bath or Cheltenham nor — after a decent lapse of time — did she allow herself to be consoled by some pukka sahib from the colonies, for whom she would produce, almost in the Siamese tradition, a quota of half-sisters and half-brothers for Preecha's son. On the contrary, Fanny returned to Bangkok, two and a half years later, with the fantastic idea of helping the French in Cambodia — the French who had only recently been routed at Sedan — take over Siam and install a constitution that would destroy forever the tyrannical power of men such as Sri Suria-wongse.

The story of this absurd adventure is admirably told by R. J. Minney. There can be little doubt that Fanny was off her head — as was not surprising in view of what she had endured. Her life was only spared through the fact that in the course of her insane escapade, death in its turn came to Sri Suriawongse, and Chulalongkorn became king not only in name but in fact. Fanny now felt that she could abandon her conflict with authority. But she still felt that she had a duty to perform to her husband's memory. He had loved the people of Siam. Ought she not carry on his work? She decided to dedicate the remainder of her life to their service. She could very easily have made herself a home in Europe. She was still young; she was attractive. She would probably have found a husband. At least one very eligible Englishman, a diplomat, had courted her for many years. But her duty, as she saw it, recalled her to the service of her husband's people.

She took a small house in one of the alleys running off New Road near the Hong Kong and Shanghai Bank. The king, in recompense for the injustice that had been done her husband, paid her an annuity that sufficed for her simple needs. She worked for the people and among the people until her death as an old woman in 1925. She helped them when they were sick; she fought their battles in the courts when she felt that they were the victims of injustice. It was one of those curious, dedicated lives that were quite often led by Victorian ladies, widows and spinsters, who worked as missionaries in Africa and Asia or lived in English slums.

She had returned to Bangkok in a spirit of revenge; and though that spirit had not survived the death of her enemy, she retained a relentless animosity against the system that had made possible the emergence of a villain such as Sri Suriawongse. What had happened once might well happen again. And in her quiet, unobtrusive way, she tried to convince the young men whom she met that the system, by which the kings were Lords of Life, was opposed to the standards of contemporary thought. It was a system, she argued, that undermined the dignity of Bangkok, that prevented its development, that tied it to the servitude of a barbarian epoch.

Did she accomplish anything in this direction? It is hard to say. Newspapers with immense circulations are unable to swing the fortunes of an election. A small journal selling a few thousand copies weekly whose readers include the men and women who influence decisions may be more powerful. Lenin issuing cyclostyled arguments from Zurich started the Russian Revolution. Fanny may well have been contributory to the climate of opinion that was to turn Siam into a democratic monarchy. One episode in her last years has certainly an ironic twist, like that of a magazine short story. She was active among the students, in particular those who were planning to leave for Europe for their final training. For one of these called Prosit, she had a special regard. He was eighteen years old. But his parents were poor. He had little chance of getting himself to Europe. She resolved to help him. Among her jewels was the large brooch of emeralds and yellow diamonds that Sri Suriawongse had given her after the performance of *The School for Scandal*. She sold this brooch and on its proceeds Prosit went to Paris. While he was there, he joined the group of young men who were to carry through in 1932 the coup d'etat which was to rob the Chakri dynasty of its power. Prosit was only one of several, but he was not a negligible participant. It is ironic that Sri Suriawongse, by his gift to the girl whom he hoped to install as his grandson's bride, helped to overthrow the dynasty he represented.

Chulalongkorn was not unmindful of the anchoring of H.M.S. *Foxhound* outside his palace when in 1892 he ordered the *Maha Chakri* to be built as a gunboat as well as a royal yacht. In the following year he was to have another and more serious example of gunboat diplomacy. The incident is recounted in H. Warrington Smythe's *Five Years in Siam,* published in London in 1898. It was the result of the spread of French influence in Southeast Asia. After her defeat in the Franco-Prussian war France had come to feel that her prestige could be recovered more easily in Asia than on the battlefields of Europe. In Asia she had only the British as a rival, and her ministers felt, with foresight as it was to prove, that France and Britain should find no difficulty in driving a thieves' bargain and sharing the swag. Britain had taken over Burma; why should not France have control of what was to become Indo-China? In 1863 Cambodia had become a French protectorate. Within the next twenty years the whole of Vietnam passed into French control. In 1883, France assumed the protection of Annam. It was at this point that trouble started. The boundaries between Annam and Siam were vague; and the French with their practical love of precision were insistent that the Mekong was the natural frontier. They also ignored — or perhaps it would be truer to say made no effort to understand — the shadowy and complex interrelationships between the various countries of the Indo-Chinese peninsula; how fealty was acknowledged here and tribute exacted there, although the countries retained independence. The French were prepared to admit that the king of what is now Laos was the vassal of the king of Siam, yet they argued that he was also a vassal of Annam because he had sent tributes to Hué in 1831 and 1832. During the late 1860s some warlike Chinese refugees, known to the Thais as Haws, had invaded Tonkin and the Laotian states. In 1872 they threatened Luang Prabang, the capital of Laos. Its king appealed to Bangkok for help — which was duly sent — and the Haws were defeated. But since they remained a menace, Thai forces remained to protect Luang Prabang, and the French when they took over Annam complained that Thai troops were constantly raiding Annamite territory. A treaty was

Prince Chakrabongse of Bisnulok in the full dress uniform of the 1st
Infantry Guards

eventually signed agreeing that France was to be in control of land west of the Mekong, with Siam retaining its rights over Luang Prabang. However since the Haws remained a menace, both the French and the Thai forces went into action against them.

There were constant frontier clashes, and on occasions the two sides found themselves fighting one another. The situation became acute when the ex-marine officer, Auguste Pavie, who had been in charge of the French forces, was posted to Bangkok as the first minister plenipotentiary, the French consulate having achieved the status of a legation. The pace quickened with his arrival. He was hoping to weave Siam into France's colonial empire. He followed the traditional technique. French nationals were in danger; they had to be protected. It was the technique which Hitler was to follow in Czechoslovakia in 1938, in Poland in 1939. By April 1893 the tension had grown so acute that the British, who were apprehensive of French aggrandizement, sent a gunboat, the *Swift*, to Bangkok. There was a serious frontier incident. A French captain was captured by Siamese troops. A French officer was killed. The Siamese were anxious to go to arbitration. But that would not have suited the French plan.

In June a French gunboat anchored outside the French legation. Pavie informed the Thai foreign ministry that two more gunboats would arrive to protect the three Frenchmen who lived outside the embassy: he asked for the loan of pilots. He was informed that no boats were allowed to travel to Bangkok without permission. Pavie promised that the boats would stay outside the bar at Paknam. The captains of the ships ignored his instructions. They sailed straight ahead. A battle had been joined for which no one was prepared. The German harbormaster at Paknam ordered the French ships to stop. The officer in charge of the first fort fired a couple of blank shots, then a round or two across the bows of the invading gunboats. The battle had begun.

It lasted for twenty minutes. Two of the Thai ships were hit and narrowly escaped collision. Three French sailors were killed and two wounded. Fifteen Thais were dead or lost and twenty wounded. The Paknam forts suffered no casualties, but chaos supervened. They were manned by Danish volunteers from the survey department: only one of them spoke Thai. It was all in the best tradition of comic opera and the Thai foreign minister tactfully complimented the French commander on the skill with which he had forced an entry.

In the city itself there was not a great deal of excitement, although troops were called out. The crowds gathered to look at the gunboats. They expected a fight: when one of the French ships fitted a machine gun platform on each of her three masts, the people wanted a good view of it. A city that loved spectacle and parade imagined that a fine performance was about to be staged for its benefit without any danger to itself. It was disappointed. The real drama was to take place in the council chambers of Europe. Two British ships were on the spot, but the British foreign secretary had urged the Thais to move cautiously. He told the French that the British had warned the Thais. And the French had promised the British that London would be kept informed of their intentions. The Russian emperor because of his friendship with King Chulalongkorn urged the French to be amenable. Pavie issued an ultimatum. France as the protector of Annam and Cambodia must have all the territory on the eastern bank of the Mekong even though some of it might be occupied by Laotians who the Thais considered to be Thai subjects. The Thai officers responsible for frontier incidents were to be punished. Siam was to pay France an indemnity of three million gold francs — at that time the exchange rate was twenty-five francs to the pound. When the Thai government's reply did not come promptly, Pavie withdrew with his warships to the mouth of the river leaving the gunboats anchored by the French legation, and informed Bangkok that it could consider itself blockaded.

A minority of the Thai ministers felt that these demands should be resisted. The king himself was so distraught that he took to his bed, refused medicine, and delivered himself of a lugubrious poem which he dispatched to a number of his brothers. The response to this poem was so warm and loyal that he rose from his bed and persuaded his advisers to be prudent and accept the French demands. He felt that the British should have given him more support, but he recognized that the French and British had a great many irons in a great many fires and that his country was only one of them. The Siamese capitulation was complete. They agreed to demilitarize the territory close to the west bank of the Mekong and the French were to maintain a garrison in the southeast near the coast to guarantee that the treaty was carried out.

They were hard terms but it was to Siam's advantage that France should get all she wanted at a single bite instead of nibbling away little by little. France would have been prepared, no doubt to take over Bangkok had she been forced, but the occupation of a city of 350,000 would have been extremely costly and a drain on her resources. Moreover there was Britain to the south in Malaysia and to the west in Burma. There were problems enough between the two countries waiting to be settled in North Africa. The crisis of Agadir was not so many years away. It was wise surely to compromise here in the Far East and keep Siam as a buffer state, a Far Eastern Switzerland.

Siam suffered a diplomatic humiliation. An examination of the map will show that in loss of territory she had suffered as severely as France had twenty years earlier in her war with Prussia, and no doubt Paris had that treaty in mind when she imposed her *dictat* on Siam. But there is no real comparison between the loss of Alsace-Lorraine and a few thousand square miles of paddy field and jungle. Siam's lordship over Laos had been a shadowy basis for self-defense, a guarding of the frontiers. It is doubtful if those subject tribes brought in very much revenue to the exchequer. The city of Bangkok did not suffer; probably it profited because the French presence in Indo-China added to its own trade. And the Chakri dynasty had thought of itself as kings of Bangkok first and kings of Siam second. But the incident was decisive in directing Siam's future foreign policy. Chulalongkorn recognized that Siam could not resist a foreign invasion from one of the major powers. Her army and navy could do more than make a powerful neighbor wonder whether it was worthwhile invading her, whether it would not be wiser to be conciliatory, to reach agreement over the council table. So that the big nations should pause before they acted, it was necessary to have an efficient if small army, and a navy. He must be on his guard against casual gunboat diplomacy. He ordered therefore several yachts which could act as gunboats if required.

Probably as an outcome of King Chulalongkorn's first trip to Europe, and his warm reception in Paris, relations between France and Siam improved, and a few years later Siam's three remaining Cambodian provinces were peacefully handed over to France. This involved the loss of the fabulous Angkor Wat, which from the world's point of view was undoubtedly an advantage, since the French possessed the skill, scholarship and money to restore the ruins. In return France relinquished her extraterritorial rights over her Asian subjects. This made things very much easier for the Siamese police who had not been able to distinguish between Thai subjects and French Asian subjects. They looked alike and they talked alike and the Thai police kept arresting men who lay outside their jurisdiction. Soon after the signing of this treaty, an arrangement was made by which a number of French lawyers were brought into the country to act as technical advisers and revise the Thai laws. This was to have a very big effect on the life of Bangkok. It meant that a number of its young men went to Paris to study. There were already close links with Germany and England. Now the Thais became truly polyglot, speaking French as easily as they had German and English. They were also meeting other students; sitting in Left Bank cafés they acquired modern democratic ideas. Those ideas were to play an important part in the drama that awaited Siam's capital.

In 1907 Chulalongkorn made a second and more ambitious tour of Europe. He had been on the throne for nearly forty years. He was internationally well-known, and now that Queen Victoria had been succeeded by the lively, pleasure-loving Edward VII, London had much more to offer him than it had when the widow was resting at Windsor before subjecting herself to the strain of her diamond jubilee. He spent an enjoyable weekend at Windsor Castle, but though he appreciated the hospitality that he received, he was not in the same robust good health that he had been ten years earlier. He had lived at a fast pace, working hard and playing hard, and indulging the pleasures of the table — he was himself an admirable cook and composed a book of recipes of European food that contained among other succulent dishes forty-six different kinds of soup. He loved to do the cooking on a picnic, but he had a serious kidney complaint which his enjoyment of rich foods did not improve, and his second trip to Europe was largely in search of medical advice. It was a quieter trip than his first. He came not in a yacht, but in a German liner of which he took over the entire first class for himself and for his staff. He also wanted to see his sons, and discuss their problems with their instructors. He was aware that radical changes were taking place in Europe. He was wondering how his sons would adjust themselves to a Bangkok that was still, in large part, medieval. His visit to his sons in Europe confirmed him in his belief that change was not only inevitable but imminent.

He returned to Bangkok a sick man. He returned also with the idea of abdicating from the throne. He knew that the days of absolute monarchy were ended, but he suspected that it would be better if the takeover took place during his son's reign rather than in his. It would be difficult, it would be impossible for him who had been an absolute monarch to become a constitutional monarch such as Edward VII. Prince Chula quotes from a letter that he wrote after his stay at Windsor Castle: "It must be pleasant to be a British king, as long as one does not want to have too much of one's own way. One must let others do the work. They usually come and tell you about it before, and if you have any ideas of your own you can always state them. But if they persist in having their own way you must let it go, otherwise it might lead to a disastrous quarrel."

The system worked well in England. How would it work in Siam? Or rather how would it work for him in Siam? He did not believe it would. His son, who had been educated in England and was addicted to the English way of life, would be far better fitted for the new role. He had bought for his Queen Saowabha, slightly north of Bangkok, a small farm with a collection of large wooden buildings, which he converted into a palace called Phya Thai. He proposed to spend his declining years here. "I will not for all my life remain king; instead I want to be the king's father." He fixed in his own mind his sixtieth year as the final one. Whether he would have had strength of will to step aside when the time came, we cannot know. He died when he was only fifty-two.

He was not alone in his belief that the management of the

Prince Chakrabongse of Bisnulok with his son Prince Chula, a military
cadet

country must be changed. As early as 1886, four years after he had assumed full powers on the death of Sri Suriawongse, a group of eleven people, four of them royal persons, all of whom had visited or studied in Europe, pointed out in a petition that it was dangerous for all the power to be concentrated in one person; if the king was lazy, if he was unwise in the choice of his ministers, the stability of the country would be threatened. Colonizing powers would be given an excuse for intervening. Would not the country be safer if collective responsibility was vested in a cabinet headed by a prime minister?

The king received this petition with sympathy. He could have regarded it as an impertinence, as an act of *lèse-majesté;* but he was conciliatory. He reminded them that he had greatly suffered when he was a powerless figurehead during the regency. He was now, in contrast with those days, overburdened with authority and would welcome the compromise of constitutional government such as European monarchs had been forced to accept. Yet he did not believe that the country contained men of sufficient caliber to run the country on their own. He did not feel that he could abandon his responsibility to his present ministers. "Until," he said, "we can get the right kind of people to be our future legislators, we are better off without them." As Prince Chula has pointed out, he wrote this answer eleven years before he made his first trip to England and to Europe. His point of view was the one that is invariably adopted by the conservative politician, namely that a certain section of the community is not yet ready for a voice in the government. The conservatives are not always wrong. Perhaps Chulalongkorn's ministers were not at that time fitted for rule by cabinet, but it would seem that he was mistaken in arranging that at the head of each ministry there should be a royal prince; particularly in a country where there were so many royal princes that royalty stood above the law. He believed with some justice that his sons, his nephews and his cousins were the most gifted of his subjects, but it was dangerous to have so much of his own supreme power delegated to a narrow and family oligarchy. This was to become apparent during the next reign.

8

A King without a Harem

CHULALONGKORN'S successor — Rama VI — to whom reference has been already made, was in his thirtieth year. He was short and rather plump; but he was good looking and he spoke well in public. He had spent a large part of his life in England. He was a good shot and an enthusiastic soldier. He had not in his earliest years expected to be king, as he had an elder brother who died young, and he would have probably preferred to remain in England. The post of deputy king had been recognized as obsolete and he had been officially proclaimed heir apparent fifteen years before. The choice of him by the election council was automatic. He was a bachelor, and content to stay one.

One of his first acts was to recognize his brother's marriage to the Russian lady which had caused such irritation to King Chulalongkorn, and give her the title Mom. There is no doubt that he looked on his brother as the heir presumptive and it was in that light that Prince Chakrabongse was regarded not only by the royal family but the ministers. Later a law was passed that prohibited the accession to the throne of a royal prince who had married a foreign lady, but by that time Chakrabongse was dead. Had he lived longer, it is improbable that the law would have been passed — or perhaps it would be truer to say had he remained on good terms with his brother.

There is certainly no doubt that in the early part of Rama VI's reign, Chakrabongse was treated as the heir. In 1911 he was sent to London to represent the king at the Coronation of George VI. He was made a Knight Grand Cross of the Royal Victorian Order, and as the king's representative at foreign functions he received fifteen other Grand Crosses. At that time no one doubted that the two brothers had many years of life ahead of them.

The city to which Rama VI succeeded was very different from that which his father and grandfather had known. It had become a modern city and it had to accommodate the many *farangs* whom its prosperity brought to it. Not only the East Asiatic Company had teak concessions in the north; two other British companies, the Borneo and Bombay-Burma were active there. They had large administrative offices in Bangkok, and there grew up around them all the appurtenances of colonial Britain, the clubs, the tennis courts, cricket and golf, the general gymkhana atmosphere. Yet Bangkok retained its distinctive features, the festivals and ritual celebrations whose observance was so dear to the Thais.

Some of these have been abandoned now. There was for instance Songkram, the water throwing festival. This comes in April, with the start of the New Year, when the first rains fall. In Rama VI's time, people carried silver bowls of scented water from which they sprinkled a few drops on their friends in blessing. Later it became a spree, with young people throwing great bowls of water indiscriminately. It was rather like London's Hampstead Heath on August Bank Holiday before 1914. Banners were waved, tin cans were beaten; boys drove around with water pistols; girls were elegantly dressed, but the boys wore only shirts and shorts. It was a form of courtship. Songkram has been banned now in Bangkok, because it disorganizes the city's work, but it still continues in the countryside.

Another festival that has now been abandoned is that of the Giant Swing — Sao Chingcha — though the swing itself remains. Two scarlet poles, a hundred feet high, lean towards each other, joined by a carved crossbar, surmounted by an elaborate carved headpiece. It has a Japanese look. It is set near the only temple in the middle of the city, the Wat Sutat, built by Rama I, with doors carved by Rama II. The swing stood once in an open space; now it is a traffic circuit. By comparing contemporary photographs of it with those taken a hundred years ago, you can see how the avenues of the city have become cluttered up. Tall though the swing is, you do not notice it until you are beside it. It was not till my fifth visit that I myself saw it. I had not known about it, and I had never glimpsed it on my trips through the city.

The ritual that was enacted here was of Brahminic origin, and Brahmin priests officiated. Siva visits the world for ten days and likes to be amused. Vishnu follows him for five days. The whole thing is a kind of Lord Mayor's Show. The best account of it that I have read occurs in Norman Bartlett's *Land of the Lotus Eater.* In early days the king himself presided at the ceremony, but possibly because of their innate Buddhism the kings did not care to deputize for a Hindu god, and a deputy took his place. The subject who was honored by the king's choice was hung with gorgeous robes, and was carried on a palanquin with the sacred seven-tiered umbrella held above his head. Dancers and drummers accompanied the procession. Acrobats kept the crowd amused. The king for two days impersonated Siva and was installed in a bamboo hall, hung with white cloth, erected for the occasion. He had to sit motionless, with his left foot over his right knee, his right foot on the floor. If he allowed both feet to touch the ground, his godhead vanished. Three sets of swingers, with four acrobats to each set, performed for his benefit highly dangerous exhibitions on the swing. Each swinger wore a cobra headdress; a purse of gold tied to the top of a bamboo pole was set at an awkward distance from the swing; the leader of each set had to catch the bag of gold between his teeth. When each set had performed this exercise, the king retired.

The performance was repeated on the following day. On this second occasion it was concluded with an elaborate piece of Brahmin ceremony. It was always held that the Brahmins were the kingmakers since they held the source of divine power which they transmitted to the king. When the king became a constitutional monarch, he was no longer the recipient of this divine power, so that the ceremony became invalid. Many thousands used to watch these ceremonies, but the number of fatal accidents that occurred at the swing turned public feeling against it. At one time it was used to test the loyalty of courtiers. If the accused did not fall off, he was judged innocent.

The most popular festival — and one that has survived unchanged — is Loy Krathong, which comes at the start of the dry season, with the new moon in November. "Loy" means "to float" and "Krathong" is a cup. Lighted candles and flowers and joss sticks are floated down the river and the klongs. It is claimed that you thus float away your sins. The city also atones for its sin of boating over the footsteps of the Buddha and the images of the Buddha that are embedded in the sand of the river. The krathong is a small tray or dish made of banana leaves or matting. They are often very elaborate, shaped like a dragon, a houseboat, an airplane, a battleship. It is one of the gayest evenings in the Bangkok calendar.

Then there is the day in September when the king leaves the

palace in his royal barge to present the monks with their robes. There are also the three changes of clothes for the Emerald Buddha. They are golden and studded with jewels. In the rainy season the Buddha is dressed in a prince's robe. In the summer the robe leaves the right hand and shoulder bare. In winter a woven saffron robe covers the entire body.

In early days the populace was frequently offered the spectacle of a public execution. In 1926, when I went there first you could buy photographs of an execution. The condemned man was seated on the ground, with his legs extended. He was tied to a stake. The execution was preceded by prayers and genuflections, just as there would be before a Thai boxing match. There were two headsmen. They danced round the victim so that he would not know who struck the blow. If he knew who was going to strike, he could put a curse on his executioner. I saw a photograph taken a few seconds after the head had been struck off. Two columns of blood rose from the neck to the height of about a foot.

Jacob T. Child, who was American minister in Bangkok in 1892, witnessed the execution of three dacoits who had been operating openly in the city. His description is slightly different from that which was presented by the photograph that I saw — but only very slightly. According to Child a bamboo yoke a yard in length was placed round the prisoner's neck and fastened to a round piece of wood that enclosed his wrists. A small bamboo cross was stuck in the ground. The yoke and chains were taken off; the prisoner squats in front of the cross to which his arms are fastened. He bends forward with his face to the ground. Flowers and a few lighted joss sticks are placed in front of him. Prayers are said before the execution. An attendant then takes some mud, blocks his ears, and makes a mark on the back of the neck. In this case, as there were to be three simultaneous executions, there were three executioners. They were dressed in scarlet with gold fringe trimmings on their coats. They entered as soon as the mud marks had been made on the prisoners' necks. Each carried a heavy shining sword. They advanced dancing and saluting. They whirled their swords. The moment they were behind the prisoners, they struck. The three bodies rose upright, then fell forward, but the head was still connected with the torso by a small piece of skin. This piece of skin was now severed by a man with a large knife. He stuck the heads on small bamboo poles six feet high. The eyelids flickered and the jaws opened and closed as the blood ran out. The heels of the dead men were then cut off, for reasons of economy so that the chains might be slipped off and taken back to the prison. The torsos were left on the ground; friends carried them away.

The chief differences between these executions and the one presented in the photograph I saw were that there was only one executioner to each prisoner, and that the prisoner bent forward: in 1926 the prisoner sat upright so that his neck was cut right through. In 1926 the executioners did not wear uniform.

Child says that there were very few executions in Bangkok because better use could be made of prisoners. A life prisoner became the slave of a noble. He wore a chain fastened to a steel ring that was riveted round his neck, and to another ring round his ankle. He worked in the nobleman's garden.

Few kings can have entered upon their inheritance with more promise of success than did Rama VI. The throne was secure. The country was prosperous; its prestige stood high among other nations. The world itself seemed a stable place. The coronation took place in 1911, in November, and there was a considerable gathering of foreign potentates. The Prince of Wales, the future Edward VIII, was then only seventeen and it was considered that he was too young to attend, but George V sent his brother-in-law, the future Earl of Athlone. Russia sent

the Grand Duke Boris. The King of Sweden sent his younger
son, Prince William. The King of Denmark was represented by
his brother, Prince Waldeman. Prince Fushimi of Japan was
there.

The coronation was carried out in the traditional sumptuous
style. No one who attended it could have foreseen that the disaster
of the European war, three and a half years distant, which
was to overthrow the thrones of Russia, Germany and Austria-
Hungary, was to have as part of its backlash the shaking of the
power of the kings of Bangkok. Nevertheless that future might
have been apparent in the character of the king himself. Great-
ness is not hereditary. The Chakri dynasty had produced five
great men, of whom the last — Chulalongkorn — was the
greatest. But the creative power was spent. Rama VI was not
fitted for the role of Lord of Life. He was not popular with his
people. He did not present himself sufficiently in public. The
fact of his being a bachelor did not improve what is now called
his "image." Tradition decreed that the king, who in Brahmin
philosophy is Indra on earth, should be served by a large
harem. Polygamy was an instrument of statecraft. How else
could the loyalty of princes and nobles be assured? Rama VI
was a recluse to the extent that he did not lead the traditional
social life. As his reign progressed he attended fewer and fewer
cabinet meetings. He dealt with the individual minister concerned. Probably as a result of his long stay in England, he was
happiest in the company of the younger army officers. He organized a special elite force called the Wild Tiger Corps, which
he made responsible for the maintenance of internal security. It
was an equivalent of Hitler's S.S. — an army within an army.
He was on his guard against foreign interference. He did not
think that the climate of public opinion would tolerate the ag-
gressive colonialism of the nineteenth century, but he still believed that any domestic explosion, any collapse of order would

The Golden Buddha

be leaped on by the European powers as an excuse for "police action" to protect their nationals. The Wild Tiger Corps was to be an insurance policy against this danger. It was not an unsound policy. Rama VI regarded the army as the bulwark of the state. He wanted to increase the power of the armed forces. But he might have recalled the warning of the Duke of Wellington, who did not approve the promotion of the professional soldier. He preferred to have armies commanded by peers and landowners. Inefficient generals like Lord Raglan and Lord Cardigan might lead to the confusion of the Crimean War, but the social order remained intact. Men like Cardigan had a stake in the status quo. Rama VI raised his Wild Tiger brigade of guards from his own courtiers. The Bangkok command had a comfortable clubhouse that was open to all ranks, and here the king spent most of his evenings from five to seven. He lectured the members and he was an inspiring lecturer. He met the members on equal terms. Civil servants and businessmen who would not normally have had access to court circles, were eager to join so as to improve their social status. But members of the regular armed forces were excluded: and so it happened that senior military and naval officers appeared on fashionable occasions dressed as private soldiers. This caused a great deal of jealousy among the regular officers who with justice considered themselves underprivileged. It is not surprising that a group of conspirators were soon plotting to kidnap and depose the king. Prince Chakrabongse had the foresight to guess that this would happen. He watched the army closely, and soon one of the suspects was induced to confess. Before the conspirators knew they were suspected, they had been arrested. Several of them were condemned to death. But the king was lenient and commuted their sentences to life imprisonment.

In another and surprising way the Wild Tigers diminished the king's popularity. England had taught him to appreciate football. He decided that soccer was more suitable than rugby to the climate, and he organized leagues and clubs with school-masters and resident Englishmen acting as coaches. The games drew large and enthusiastic crowds; unfortunately the king was desperately anxious that the Wild Tigers should always win. The best players of other clubs were given minor posts at court, so that they could join his teams. The public did not en-joy seeing all the cups going to the Wild Tigers, yet even so Bangkok has cause to be grateful to him for having added im-mensely to its enjoyment of life by his introduction of the game. There is a superb stadium there now. Rugby football has also proved popular.

Another of his well-meant but unfortunate experiments was in the theater. He was a reasonably skillful poet and while he was a student he translated and adapted some hundred plays from French and English. He organized a company of amateurs in Bangkok and gave the proceeds of their performances to charity. He acted in some of them himself. But the Thais did not like the plays and they were shocked at the spectacle of their revered monarch on the stage.

Not all of his innovations were unsuccessful. He ordered that all families should have surnames. This has made social relations with foreigners a great deal simpler. He was also to alter the appearance of the city by persuading the women to wear their hair long. This habit of short hair had been acquired during one of the sieges of Ayudhya, when the women cropped their heads so that the Burmese seeing them on the battlements should mis-take them for men and believe that the city was more strongly defended than in fact it was. He also persuaded them to aban-don the *panung* — a garment for the legs not unlike plus fours — and wear skirts instead. Thai women are considered to be among the most elegant and beautiful in the world. They owe a great deal to Rama VI. He was also extremely generous; many charities and objects of charity were supported from his Privy Purse. In 1912 there was an outbreak of smallpox. He did not force the people to be vaccinated, but he launched a publicity campaign which persuaded them to go to a modern doctor. He also instituted a snake farm where serums could be obtained against poisonous snakebites; and he was active in the program to prevent rabies. A very large sum of money had been contributed to purchase an equestrian statue to his father — far more than was needed — and with the surplus he founded Chulalongkorn University. To this, too, he made a large contribution from the Privy Purse.

All these activities were exceedingly expensive. He inherited a balanced budget. In the first year of his reign a revenue of sixty-three and a half million bahts stood against an expenditure of fifty-nine million bahts. But he was soon in the red. There was little direct taxation, and it was estimated that in 1914 the Chinese traders, who had no voice in their politics, sent one hundred and twenty-six million bahts back to China — thirteen bahts were at that time worth four dollars.

Much of the government's revenue came from the duties paid by Chinese gambling houses and from the sale of opium that the government had imported. Rama VI was convinced that both gambling and opium were evils for the Thais, and though both the Thai minister of finance and the British adviser assured him that he could not afford to close the gambling houses, he got his way.

One of the great difficulties for the Thai financiers was that King Mongkut had limited the import duties on goods from Europe at a three per cent *ad valorem;* and in those days there was no unilateral canceling of treaties. But the state railway system was a source of substantial revenue; and the founding of the Treasury Savings Bank for which the King was responsible greatly added to the prosperity of the individual subject. Exports still exceeded imports.

The finances were not improved by the outbreak of the war. Usually neutrals do well out of wars and for the first three years Siam remained on the touchline. But in 1917 Rama VI brought his country into the war on the side of the Allies. It was believed in diplomatic circles that this was achieved by a member of the British Embassy whose amatory tastes were similar to the king's and who promised that in return for a declaration of war, he would persuade his own catamite, in whom the king was interested, to accept the royal favors.

For the country as apart from the king, there was some immediate profit, for forty or so German and Austrian merchant ships were taken over by the government and became a valuable part of the Siamese merchant navy. News traveled slowly in those days, and *farangs* working on the teak plantations knew little about the progress of the war, still less that Siam had joined the Allies, until groups of international "teak wallahs" sitting around their table, outside their tent at the end of the day's work, would be interrupted by the arrival of Siamese soldiers to march the Germans and Austrians away to prison.

Their treatment as internees was humane; they were content with their condition, but the British insisted on their being moved to India. The British, so Prince Chula thought, did not like white men being subject to Asians.

Rama VI had been from the start violently pro-Ally. He wrote anonymously a number of pro-British articles for the press, but the people on the whole were anti-French; they resented the loss of Cambodia and they suspected that their humiliation was partly due to the British who had, if not actually supported, failed to resist the French demands. The Germans on the other hand had never trespassed upon their rights, and

[129]

had supplied them with the kinds of merchandise they wanted and at a price lower than the British. The word "people" in this connection must be taken to mean the equivalent of the white collar class, the Thai merchants, the lawyers, the schoolmasters, the army officers. The Chinese stood outside politics, and the peasantry were only interested in their paddy fields and garden produce.

At the outbreak of war, in 1914, a German light cruiser, the *Emden*, broke out of the British cordon and shelled Penang. Its gallant exploit won the praise even of "the ranks of Tuscany." The king felt that if Siam entered the war, a Thai cruiser could perform similar feats, and bring high honor to his country. Extra taxes would have been required to commission such a vessel. The king was reluctant to do this, so he formed a Navy League that would raise the necessary funds by public subscription. In order to please the king, the governors of provinces and the heads of the various departments coerced the public into subscribing. This did not increase the king's popularity; nor was the campaign successful: only enough money was raised to buy an old British destroyer, which was not able to fly the Siamese flag until the war was over and the opportunity of its shedding luster on the throne had passed.

Nor did Siamese participation in the war confer much glory on the nation. The Allies were not prepared to arm and train a Siamese force capable of fighting on the Western Front. It is possible that the British and French were not anxious to have Asian troops in the trenches. The Japanese had not sent any troops. The Chinese supplied only a labor corps. Indian and Sengalese troops were another matter. They had been trained by British and French officers, and were at that time British and French subjects. In the end the Allies agreed to accept a motor transport corps and a certain number of air pilots.

Wars are usually popular at the start, and when the king

called for volunteers, thousands of civilians applied and the
armed forces offered their services to a man — the king having
decreed that the expeditionary force must be composed of volunteers. Twelve hundred men were accepted. They never actually saw action — they were still being trained in the South of
France, accustoming themselves to the northern climate when
the Armistice was signed. The motor transport corps did, however, operate with the French forces and are reported to have
come under fire. At any rate they were represented in the victory marches in Brussels, London and Paris, and elaborate re-
ceptions and parades were staged in Bangkok "when the boys
came home." The king, who had been made an honorary general in the British army, delivered a number of rousing patriotic
speeches. Siam was, on the whole, through its acquisition of
enemy property, better off as a result of its participation in the
war. But the finances of the country were no longer identifiable
with those of its sovereign, and the king himself was even more
in debt, through his personal generosity.

Perhaps the most lasting result of Siam's entering the war
was the changing of the national flag. Originally a white elephant was shown on a red background. But the design was not
always skillfully carried out, and the king felt that the elephant
looked too much like a pig, which did not confer credit on the
country when it was flown at Allied functions in Europe and
the United States beside the flags of the other allies. The flag
was therefore changed to one of horizontal stripes, red, white,
double dark blue and red.

Wars usually create a sense of unity inside a country. There
is a closing of the ranks, but during 1917 King Rama's popularity sank considerably. That spring there was a severe flood in
Bangkok, and for several weeks the whole city was underwater.
The young people thoroughly enjoyed paddling their boats
down the majestic avenues, past the statue of King Chulalong-

Two ancient statues grace a temple garden

korn, but the damage to the rice crop was severe. The king could not be blamed for the flood: it was not due to inadequate precautions on his part. But people are illogical; in England general elections have been lost and won by the irritation that follows a bad summer and the good humor that follows on a good one. And in 1917 Bangkok was in a discontented mood. There were rumors of a military plot, and though no corroboratory evidence was discovered, a newspaper called the *Daily Mail* that was issued in both English and Thai strongly attacked the king, the court and the general conduct of the country.

To Prince Chakrabongse in particular this was disturbing. He felt that the king was carrying too heavy a responsibility. He was being blamed for everything. The days had passed when a monarch could prosecute a paper. A war was being fought for freedom. He suggested that a legislative council such as Chulalongkorn had used should be revived. The president and members should be chosen by the king: the council should discuss each act before it became a law; members should be allowed to question ministers; meetings should be held in public, and reported in the press. This would reduce the power and arrogance of individual ministers. The king would not be solely responsible.

It was a long way from democracy, but it was too large a step for Rama VI to take. He would have liked, he said, to announce a constitution, soon after his own coronation, but he did not believe that the Thai people were ready yet to choose their own representatives, and if as his brother suggested, he were to choose the members of the council himself, everyone would complain that he had surrounded himself with "yes men." Better leave things as they were. The matter was allowed to rest.

In spite of the excitement and pageantry of an entrance into war as an independent ally of France and Britain, 1917 was a year of calamity for at least one prominent Bangkok family. The Russian revolution was a sad blow to Prince Chakrabongse's Russian wife. She and her husband had indeed been on the point of going out to Russia to see the Czar, Nicholas II, when the revolution started. She was desperately anxious for her relatives. Then the flood destroyed her garden to which she had devoted much loving care. She was in such a state of nerves that it was decided to send her on a holiday, to a cool climate. She went to Canada. The marriage had been a very happy one. She and her prince had set a remarkable example of domestic coziness in a country where fidelity was not highly prized or practiced. But the marriage was not to survive absence. Prince Chakrabongse was a youngish man: he had a romantic temperament. He was working at extremely high pressure. He was also a dutiful son to a mother who had become in her declining years a severe problem to her "best and dearest." She spent most of her time in her bed, and in the subfusc atmosphere of the Palace had turned night into day. She breakfasted at 10:30 P.M. Visitors began to arrive half an hour later. She was vital mentally; she had a number of activities: the Red Cross, household duties, affairs of the court. She lunched at 2:30 A.M. Her last visitor left at about 5:30 A.M. It was more than the king could take: every four months he satisfied his filial obligations. But Prince Chakrabongse was extremely dutiful; quite often he would leave his mother at 5 A.M., drive out to supervise the training of his troops at 6 A.M., then after a bath and a change of clothes proceed straight to his office desk. As she grew older, the queen spent more and more of her time asleep. Sometimes the prince spent hours waiting for an audience. Her English doctor asked why he did not complain. She was, after all, his mother. The prince replied that she was more than that. She was the queen mother.

He had a great deal upon his mind. He was living under con-

siderable strain. It was not surprising that he should have relaxed as completely as possible on the few occasions when re-
laxation was a possibility. The only place where he could relax
was Hua Hin, a stretch of beach near an old fishing village
some fifty miles from the city on the west coast of the Gulf of
Siam.

For its development Chakrabongse was himself in large part
responsible. After his brother's coronation festivities, he had
taken a number of European notabilities on shooting expeditions
and sited his camp there. He found wild elephants and tigers.
The sand was white. The prince and his wife were so delighted
with their discovery that they built a house there. Today Hua
Hin has a railway, a hotel and a golf course and has become —
along with Pattaya — the chief weekend and holiday resort
for city dwellers. It was here that the prince spent every unoc-
cupied hour during his wife's absence. He organized swimming,
sailing and hunting parties for young people. Inevitably he
soon fell in love with a very young and very pretty girl, the
daughter of a royal prince. A busybody wrote to inform his
wife. She did not, as might have been expected, hurry back.
Perhaps she thought it was prudent to give the thing time to
burn itself out. When she did return, it was to find that the
romance was still in flower. She issued an ultimatum. Either the
prince must give up the girl or give her a divorce. Chakrabongse was not only distraught but off his guard. Most of us in
moments of crisis tend to think "this is the kind of thing that
happens to someone else, not me." Certainly this was not the
kind of thing that happened to a Lord of Life. It would have
been outside the comprehension of his grandfather and father,
with all their consenting wives. Chakrabongse asked for time.
It was not granted him.

It is hard not to feel great sympathy for his wife. She had met
Chakrabongse when she was only sixteen years old; both her

parents were dead; her father had been chief judge of a province, her mother had come from a family of landed gentry. She was in St. Petersburg training to become a volunteer nurse in the Russo-Japanese war. Chakrabongse fell in love with her at once; but she insisted on going to the war. She served there bravely and efficiently. She received three decorations, one of them the Order of St. George. Two years later the prince returned to St. Petersburg. He met Catherine again, he found himself still in love with her, and he proposed. She was only eighteen. We know nothing of what she felt. But it cannot have been difficult for her to fall in love with this handsome, dashing prince, who had about him that "something different" for which a romantic young girl pines. The emperor of Russia was his guardian. His skin was no darker than that of the Georgian students whom she had seen at college. She was a Christian and a dutiful daughter of a family — she asked her brother's permission. He was then a student at the university; later he was to join the diplomatic service. He gave her his permission.

She can have known practically nothing about Thailand; its curious history and its curious *mores*. It may not have surprised her that Chakrabongse did not tell his parents or his guardian, Nicholas II, or that on their arrival in the Far East she was not brought straight to Bangkok to be presented to the court, but kept in Singapore as Madame de Bisnulok. It may well have seemed to her that everything was in keeping with the whole Cinderella quality of her romance, the rich and charming prince falling in love with a commoner and transporting her to a far country and a palace; perhaps, who knows, a throne; for she must have realized that, in view of her brother-in-law's irregular aptitudes, there was every likelihood of her one day being queen of Siam.

In her nursery she had been told that the course of true love never did run smooth. But she was soon to find that it sometimes did. Early in 1908, she gave birth to a son — Prince Chula — with whom the queen was delighted. Rama VI, on his accession, conferred on her the Chula Chom Klao Order, and raised her to the rank of Mom, the equivalent of being a princess without being a royal highness. Her son was recognized as a Mom Chao, a serene highness. When they returned to Russia in 1911, the emperor made her husband an honorary colonel in the Hussar Guards and conferred on him the Order of St. Andrew, the equivalent of the English Garter. Every girlhood dream was being fulfilled for her. And then within the space of a few months every dream was shattered. Her native country was thrown into anarchy and defeat. Her emperor was imprisoned. Her garden on which she had lavished so much love, in whose carefully tended borders she had cherished the memories of her girlhood, had been submerged in mud. And then while she was trying to recover her faith and strength in a cool climate, her husband had fallen in love with a woman fifteen years younger than herself. It may well have been that the ruin of her garden symbolized for her the foreignness of this country, with its oppressive climate, its rains, its heat, and its mosquitoes, where strange gods were worshipped, where spirit houses placated the powers of darkness, and men married their half-sisters and the daughters of those half-sisters. She may well have felt lonely for the clean cold snows that she had known in childhood, for the ikons and altars of her cupola-domed churches, where men kept their marriage vows, maintaining where necessary their deviations in a back street. She was tired of it all. She would give her husband his one chance, his alternative, then if he failed, go. He hesitated, he prevaricated, and she took her leave. She left her son behind. What could she do, in exile, for a Thai prince, who one day might be king? She accepted only a small allowance from her husband. Her brother was in China and she went to join him. She hoped to work as a nurse for the White Russian forces, but the Bolsheviks were victorious before she could get to them. So she went to Shanghai, to help the Russian refugees. In 1921, after Prince Chakrabongse's death, she married an American citizen who was working then in China. It was not till 1960 that she died, in Paris. One day perhaps, her story will be written, taking its place in a collection of biographies of lovely and unlucky ladies who in spite of misfortune maintained their dignity; a companion volume to Leslie Blanch's *Wilder Shores of Love*.

Catherine's departure had a catastrophic repercussion on the inner circles of Bangkok's society. Rama VI had strongly opposed the divorce; so had the queen. The army was disconcerted. Nobody had been happy when Chakrabongse married a European, but the world tends to approve eventually what it must accept. And the evident happiness of the marriage had endeared Catherine to the country. A divorce was unheard of. There was much ill feeling, much taking of sides. When Prince Chakrabongse asked for permission to marry the object of his affections, he was refused. The queen mother on the other hand felt that once the divorce had gone through, her son had better marry the girl. She was so furious with the king that she refused to take any medicines to restore her ailing health. When he called on her, she turned her face to the wall and would not look at him. The king sat in silence for an hour, then went away. That was the last time that mother and son saw each other.

The old queen died in 1919, and the atmosphere of the funeral ceremonies was disturbed by the knowledge that the two brothers, who had been so close, were now on bad terms. There were rumors of plots against both the king and Prince Chakrabongse. When the rites were completed, Chakrabongse was so worn out by the strain of the last months that he asked for leave of absence to take a holiday. He planned a long trip to Singa-

pore, by boat, then up the Malay peninsula by rail, finishing up
with several days of swimming and sailing in his beloved Hua
Hin. But within a few hours of leaving Bangkok, an attack of
Spanish flu had developed into double pneumonia and that was
that. There were many who believed that he had been poi-
soned. He had been engaged during the preceding months on a
scheme of army retrenchment that would have led to the retirement of a number of elderly and inefficient officers. Shortly before he left for Singapore, he was invited to a large dinner
party. Several of the senior officers who attended were subsequently struck by illness whose symptoms resembled those of
Chakrabongse. A few of them died, but no investigation was
held.

So often historians and semi-historians write: "If only so-and-
so had lived, how different it would all have been," and there is
strong reason to believe that Prince Chakrabongse's death was
a great loss to Siam. It seems as though the full vitality of the
Chakri dynasty had concentrated upon him. Though many of
King Mongkut's and King Chulalongkorn's sons by minor wives
were men of high distinction it would seem that the perpetu-
ated custom of breeding from half-sisters, and granddaughters
of one's uncle, had in the end a debilitating and etiolating
effect. None of the other royal princes had the same drive and
power as Prince Chakrabongse, while his son, Prince Chula,
was a man of great charm and great effectiveness, who made a
mark and a life for himself in a changed society. Had his father
succeeded to the throne, and he, in turn succeeded him, the
history of Bangkok might have been very different. As it was,
the sands from that moment appeared to be running out.

To Rama VI, his brother's death, in spite of their recent di-
vergence of point of view, was a catastrophic shock. He suddenly realized that the succession had become a problem.

Three of his full brothers were still alive, but none of them

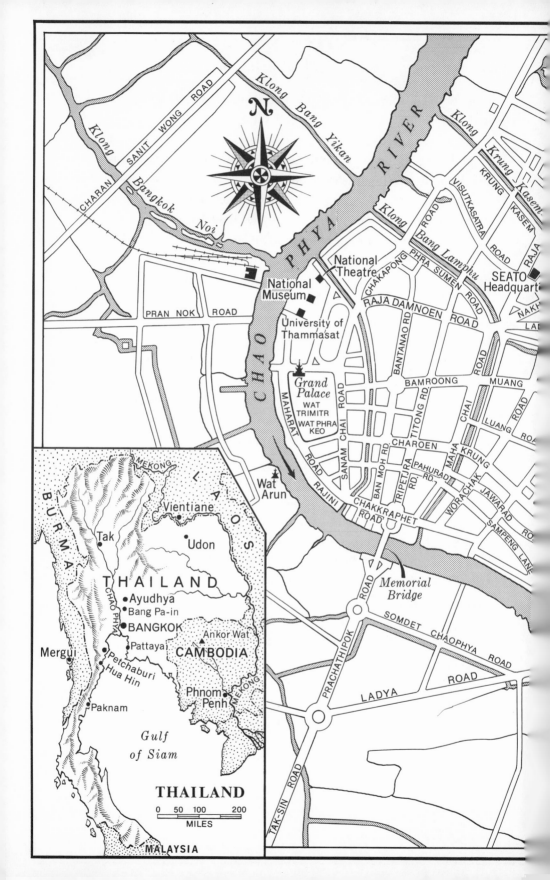

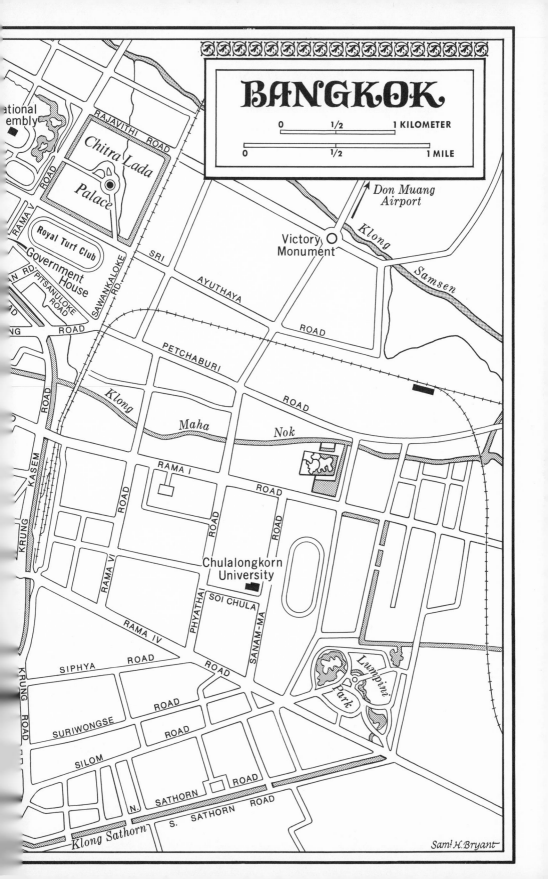

had yet produced a child. Two of them were still unmarried; and the one who was married had not chosen a royal lady as his bride. He had, however, a half-brother, Prince Mahidal, who had married into the royal family but was absorbed in his career as a doctor and was currently studying in the United States, in Boston. King Rama VI decided that it was his duty to produce an heir himself.

Politically this was no doubt a very wise decision, but as regards his personal happiness it was disastrous. He was in his fortieth year. He was not only a born bachelor but a homosexual. His plight was pitiful. Soon after the cremation of his brother, he began to ask young women to the court. Most of them were his cousins. His whole pattern of life altered. He had done little architecturally in Bangkok. But in the garden of his mother's palace at Phya Thai he had built a miniature city of the kind that you see in exhibitions. It contained a replica of the grand palace. There were shops, temples, stores, theaters; he imported dwarfed trees from Japan; a river wound its way between the buildings; a water tank hidden behind a mound of earth that was called a mountain, kept it supplied with water. It was charming in the evenings when it was lit up, and Prince Chula as a young boy spent many happy hours there. The king's courtiers entered into the spirit of the toy. They rented houses; they elected a mayor and councillors. The king attended their meetings. He claimed that he was educating them in the arts of municipal politics. It was a model for the Bangkok of the future. It was all very coy and charming and it made the king very happy. But he could not expect the young ladies with whom he was beholden to surround himself, to be entertained by it. He arranged for plays to be written for them, in which they could act along with his courtiers and himself. Within a short time he was able to announce his engagement to one of

King Mongkut's granddaughters, a lady of twenty-eight. He announced at the same time that he proposed to be a monoga-
mous king, following the example of Europe's monarchies.

The court was delighted by these announcements. The celestial princes staged party after party. Bangkok was very gay and
the princess, who made herself charming to everybody, held a
court of her own, at the Palace of Chitra Lada. He himself
moved to Phya Thai — in the hope possibly of being consoled
by his toy city. He was punctilious in his performance of the
courtesies that are considered appropriate to a fiancé. He telephoned her daily from his study. He called on her at teatime.
He escorted her to parties. But the engagement did not last
very long. In March 1921 it was announced that because of in-
compatibility of temperament, the marriage would not take
place. In September he announced his engagement to her sister,
whom he married in the following August, raising her to the
rank of Phra Nang. In the meantime he had married in the Siamese manner, in October 1921 and January 1922, two sisters of
good birth who became Chao Choms. No one could say that he
was not doing his best to adjust himself to the amatory conduct
that his unlucky fate imposed on him.

His marriage to his official wife did not prove fruitful, and
after a short time they separated. They remained, however, on
friendly terms. By this time, in his desperate search for a male
heir he had definitely lost faith in the demands of monogamy.
His union with the younger of the sisters, without proving precisely fruitful, did declare itself to have been consummated.
She had more than one miscarriage. And she was raised to the
rank of supreme queen. But his need for a male heir had to be
assuaged. In September 1925 he announced that she "lacked
efficiency to hold the rank of supreme queen" and her title was
altered to that of an ordinary queen. At the same time it was

rumored that a lady of the court was shortly to give birth to a royal child. She was created a junior queen — as Phra Nang Suradhana.

A top secret report on the nature of his predicament was forwarded to the British throne. King George V, so rumor has it, shook his head and penciled in the margin, "It is sad to remember that this man was educated at Oxford."

During these months so full of strain for him, the king was in addition saddened by the death of two of his remaining three full brothers. The death of Prince Asdang, in 1925, left Prince Prajadhipok, who was in weak health, married but childless, as the heir apparent. This increased Rama VI's need to produce a male heir. In the year before he had had enacted a law of succession, which followed a system of primogeniture. It decreed that the son of a deceased heir would succeed before his uncle, and that the line of succession of the sons of Queen Saowabha should precede those of Queen Sawang, whose sons in their turn would precede those of Queen Sukumala. Women could not occupy the throne. Princes who married foreign ladies were disqualified. But there was nothing in the law to say that the mother of an heir had to be of royal blood. At the same time the king was left with the right to nominate his successor. In a sense this left things very much as they had been before, except that in the case of sudden death as later in King Ananda's, the elective council had a clear law of guidance.

The last five years of the king's life were as unhappy as the previous forty had been happy. For he had a sunny nature. But at the end not only was he burdened by this obligation whose fulfillment was opposed to his own instincts, not only had he the private sorrow of seeing his full brothers die one by one, but he was worried by his debts. He was incorrigibly extravagant in the running of his household, and the state budget had begun to show a deficit; he had not only all that to harass him but in

Wat Arun as seen from the Bangkok side of the Chao Phya River

addition his health broke down. Appendicitis and peritonitis had been followed by complications. By the time of his final marriage he had reached the climax of despair. He knew that he would not recover. When he learned that his long-expected child was after all a girl, he does not seem to have minded. It was all too late. "It's just as well," he said.

In the meantime, while Rama VI was frantically striving to secure the succession and preserve the despotic powers that had been handed down to him, nine thousand miles away by the banks of another river, the fate of his country — or rather of his capital — was being decided. For it cannot be repeated too often that outside Bangkok, life in the teak forests and rice fields and in the tin mines to the south, continued unaffected by the turmoil in high places. And it was the conduct of affairs of state that young Thai students were eagerly discussing in Paris cafés.

Paris was at its liveliest in 1925, the Paris of Hemingway and Scott Fitzgerald, of Left Bank avant-garde magazines, of high talk and wild ambition; of youth and of rebellion. The war was six years away; no one could foresee the Depression. "Lands fit for heroes to live in" were being built and the young men from Siam drank deeply of a heady wine.

The law school in Bangkok was the center of advanced ideas, and it was from there that most of the young men in Paris had won scholarships. Chulalongkorn's treaty with France was bearing fruit. Of those bright spirits, the brightest was Pridi, well-built, sturdy — "chunky" is the adjective that Rayne Kruger applies to him in his absorbing *The Devil's Discus*, with his hair cut *en brosse*, with brown eyes and an easy laughing manner. He was born the son of a rice merchant in a small village near Ayudhya. He went to a local primary school. A senior official took interest in him and moved him to a monastery school. He enjoyed football, but he was more interested in his studies. The law school saw him on his way to Paris. His quick brain set him above but not apart from his contemporaries. They listened to him, but he was one of them. They nicknamed him "the mentor": mentor, not leader, be it noted.

One of those of whom he was the mentor was a very different type of person. He was a soldier. His name was Pibul. His family grew fruit outside Bangkok. He was born on July 14, 1898. He liked dressing himself up and the army appealed to him. He went to the royal cadet school. He attended the staff college and won a scholarship to the artillery school at Fontainebleau. It was here that he realized that he had been born on Bastille Day. As a Thai he could not fail to respond to the significance of the date; it may be doubted if he recognized the star of his own fantastic destiny, but it stirred his blood. In those days he was a junior army officer, listening to the brilliant mentor.

He remembered these law student harangues on his return to Bangkok, and when he found many of his brother officers exasperated by the overbearing way in which the princely executive dragooned the army into conformity, he explained Pridi's views to them. They listened and remembered.

9

The First Coup d'Etat

Pᴙɪɴᴄᴇ Prajadhipok — King Rama VII — succeeded his brother in November 1925. I paid my first visit to Bangkok in 1926. It is, I hope, pertinent to compare my impressions of the city at that time, as I expressed them in a travel book called *Hot Countries*, with Somerset Maugham's as he expressed them in *A Gentleman in the Parlour*. He was there in 1925.

It was my first visit to the Far East. I was on my way around the world. I had spent two months in Malaya, based in Penang, and was on my way to join the British technical adviser to the Siamese forestry department, on a month-long tour of inspection of the teak forests north of Chiengmai. I spent a day in Bangkok, before going north, and three days on my return, before going south again. That was not very long, but I obtained a first impression.

I do not know where I stayed, except that it was not in the Oriental, on the river, where Maugham stayed and where I have myself stayed on subsequent visits. I was not in funds; I asked my advisers for something cheap and clean — if those two characteristics ever went together. I was glad to find that they did. I did many of the things that are expected of the short-term tourist. I saw the klongs and I saw one or two temples. I had most of my meals in the British Club — which was comfortable enough. In the hallway was a green notice board, crisscrossed with narrow stretches of tape in which visitors inserted their calling cards, inscribed to "the President and members of the Bangkok British 'Club." The Phya Thai Palace was now a country club and in the evenings I sat out by the tennis courts, drinking a gin sling. The women were given pillowcases in which to put their legs as a protection against mosquitoes. The men were not given pillowcases. Never anywhere have I been bitten so painfully. I was kept awake at night by my tormented ankles.

In certain ways when I went back to Bangkok in 1957, I felt that I was seeing the same city, just as I did when I went to Chiengmai. The river was the same, so were the klongs, so were the temples; so was the confusion of rickshaws and carts and cars along New Road; but one of the features that struck me most in 1926, and it will astonish the modern tourist that it should have done so, was the emptiness of the avenues that had been built by Chulalongkorn. I wrote, ". . . the prevailing impression is of dust and heat and squalor. The temples and the palaces are far apart. They are divided from one another by hot, white roads and sequences of ugly buildings. The city was planned by an earlier monarch who did not realize that Siam was without enough rich people to adorn fittingly those avenues with spacious bungalows." Maugham said, in essence, the same thing. "The Chinese," he said, "live their lives apart and indifferent to the western capital that the rulers of Siam have sought to make of this strange, flat, confused city. What they have aimed at you see in the broad avenues, straight dusty roads, sometimes running by the side of a canal, with which they have surrounded this conglomeration of sordid streets. They are handsome, spacious and stately, shaded by trees, the deliberate adornment of a great city devised by a king, anxious to have an imposing seat, but they have no reality. There is something stagey about them so that you feel they are more apt for court pageants than for the use of every day. No one walks in them. They seem to await ceremonies and processions. They are like the deserted avenues in the park of a fallen monarch." And no doubt it was for purposes of parade and for his personal enjoyment as he drove in the cool of the evenings in his yellow electric car that these avenues were built. But with the eyes of vision, Chulalongkorn, who so loved his capital, must have foreseen its growth and must, knowing the haphazard nature of the Thais, and the Chinese indifference to order other than their own, have guessed how confused that growth would be unless a pattern for development were imposed. What chaos there would be today if Chulalongkorn had not eighty years ago cut those broad avenues through the paddy fields.

How often in recent years have I not paused in cities that were on the brink of violent change. Aden in 1955, Baghdad in 1955 and again in 1963 — and seen no warning signal. For Bangkok in 1926, the overthrow of the monarchy as the early Chakris had interpreted the word was only a few years distant. Did anything happen to make me suspect that under the heat and dust of summer, discontent was stirring? The only intimation of change was a growing sense of nationalism, similar to though completely different from that which I had noticed on the same trip in Egypt. The man who was my host during my trek through the teak forests was the technical adviser to the forestry department. He was to retire shortly. He was in a disgruntled mood. He had had, he said, really no work at all to do during the last eighteen months. He had sat idle in his office. The minister had resented his presence, not on personal grounds, but because he had considered there was no longer any need for a *farang* in his department. The Siamese were no longer ignorant barbarians. They were college trained: they were graduates of European universities. They could run their own show unaided. "Siam for the Siamese." "That's the way it is," my host complained. That was the only sign I received that all was not for the best in the best of all possible worlds.

But then that is how it was pretty well everywhere in the world in the summer of 1926. And in Bangkok, the auspices for Rama VII's reign were roseate. In most other countries, he would not have succeeded to the throne, since an older brother had left a son, but that son was only three years old. No one wanted a long regency and Rama VI had left behind him a letter appointing his brother Prince Prajadhipok as his heir. The law of succession that Rama VI had promulgated was only operative when a king did not appoint an heir. Had he not done so, the elective council might very well, in spite of the law of succession, have chosen Prince Paripatra, who was twelve years older than Prajadhipok and was a celestial prince, the son of Chulalongkorn's third queen, Sukumala. Perhaps it would have been better if he had. Not that Prajadhipok was not an able and conscientious ruler, but he was diffident of his capacity to serve his country as an absolute monarch. His whole training had been military and much of his youth had been spent in England. He was sent to Eton, and afterwards to the Royal Military Academy at Woolwich. He was commissioned into the Royal Horse Artillery and was very disappointed when he could not accompany his brother officers to France in World War I. He begged George V to let him go. But the king had to point out to him that he was not a British subject. It was then that he returned home to join the Thai Army and serve as a subaltern in the 1st Regiment of Artillery.

Soon after the war, however, for reasons of health, he returned to Europe. He recovered quickly and entered the French Staff College. He did not return to Siam until 1924 when he was made a major general in charge of a division in the provinces. His entire training was military and most of his life had been spent abroad. As he had no experience in the technique of government, of administration and the workings of a ministry, he decided to form a supreme council consisting of his uncles and elder half-brothers. In Prince Chula's opinion this was a good idea at the beginning. But even when the king acted under the advice of the council, he was himself ultimately responsible for the decisions that were taken. His surface reliance on the council made people suspect that he doubted his own ability to rule — and the country was accustomed to a king who knew his mind. There was also the fear that the supreme council was a permanent institution. As soon as one of the royal members died, another took his place. The council had been originally started to advise the king on his choice of ministers, but it now came about that several of the new councillors were holding ministerial appointments so that the cabinet became a cabinet within the cabinet. Vacancies were invariably filled by a senior prince. No commoner, however brilliant, however extensive his experience, was ever appointed. Even an absolute monarchy was less rigid. It is not surprising that such a system of government should give ample scope for captious criticism from talented young men like Pridi who found themselves permanently excluded from any point of influence in public life.

The fact, however, that so many of his formative years had been spent in Europe, gave the new king a detached, an unprovincial outlook on his country's problems. His brother had spent money recklessly, and had called on the treasury to meet the bill for his personal extravagance. Prajadhipok saw that that could not go on. He started on a rigorous policy of retrenchment. He cut down staffs and reduced the civil list. The time had come, in his opinion, for men to seek careers outside government service. Let them concentrate on industry and commerce. This was sound finance. But it was not a popular policy.

It might, however, have worked had not luck loaded the dice against him. In the first place the king's eyesight failed him. His health was sound. He played golf, tennis and squash. But he had cataract in both eyes and it was soon evident that an operation would have to be performed on one of them. Feeling that he could not risk having this performed in Thailand, he decided to make a tour of Japan, Canada and the United States; at its conclusion he could have the operation performed in the home of an affluent American, Mrs. Whitelaw Reid.

The tour was a considerable success. He was popular everywhere; the new Waldorf-Astoria in New York saw to it that his presence there as its first royal guest was amply publicized. He told an interviewer that he was planning to give his country a constitution in the immediate future. The operation was successful. The auguries for his return seemed admirable. But he could not have chosen a worse time to be away from his own country. A regent had to be appointed in his absence, and there was no alternative to the choice of his half-brother Prince Paripatra, the son of Queen Sukumala, who was twelve years older than himself, and whose claims to the throne at the death of Rama VI had not been inferior to his own. The elective council would have gladly accepted him had he been nominated by his half-brother. Prince Paripatra was a man of distinction and integrity, but he was not popular, and with the economic blizzard raging, he had to sponsor cuts in the armed forces that alienated the loyalty of many officers. The minister of defense, Prince Barosa Def, was only a minor royalty, and was not a member of the supreme council, but he was four years older than Paripatra, and he was a close friend of the king's. He had had an English education, at Harrow and the Royal Military

Academy at Woolwich. His resignation as a protest against these economies made him the hero of the army.

King Prajadhipok returned to find an electric atmosphere in his capital. The slump had hit Wall Street in one traumatic day in late October 1929, but its effect was not fully felt in Europe until two years later. The peak of the boom had been reached in the United States more swiftly, had risen higher and the subsequent collapse had been spectacularly precipitate. In Europe the boom had been reached more slowly, the fever of speculation had not been so hectic, the decline had been consequently gradual. The casual visitor to France and Britain during the summer of 1930 would not have been aware that anything was disastrously amiss. And the Siamese economy was linked with Europe, particularly with Britain, rather than America; but by the autumn of 1931, the situation had step by step become so serious that in September Britain had to abandon the gold standard and a national government of Labour and Conservative forces was formed to deal with the situation. Siam had always traded mainly with the sterling group, and there is little doubt now that her financial adviser was mistaken in recommending that she should stay upon the gold standard. As a result Siamese rice was too expensive for the sterling market. The king was confronted with problems that he was not trained to solve. "I'm only a soldier," he complained. "How can I understand things like the gold standard?" He was exasperated and exhausted by cabinet meetings that went on for hours. It was often as late as three o'clock that he sat down to lunch. He was advised by innumerable experts but the responsibility for the ultimate decisions was his alone, and even those members of the intelligentsia who were loyal to the throne and to the dynasty were doubtful of his ability to deal with an international disaster that was confusing the world's most astute financial mandarins.

The Temple of Dawn at Wat Arun

In November 1931 the king tried to explain the general position to a large group of army officers. He addressed them as brother officers, as a soldier speaking to his brothers-in-arms. He hoped that they would sympathize with him on a basis of shared experience and training. Prince Chula tells us that a young artillery captain left the meeting in tears: that officer was Luang Pibulsonggram who as Field Marshal Pibul was later to play so important a part in the country's history for the next quarter of a century.

Pibul was a remarkable man. His parents had given him the nickname of Plack, which means "odd," because his eyes were above the level of his ears. He knew what he wanted and what he did not want; as a newly gazetted second lieutenant he was chary of getting himself involved with any of the young girls on whom his good looks made an instantaneous impression. He was content to bide his time. Then he met a thirteen-year-old girl whose name, Lia-iat, meant delicate. He approached her without an introduction. "Little sister, stop and talk to me," he said. She shook her fist at him and ran away; but he did not forget her; he wrote love poems to her. He persisted in his courtship. Within two years she was his wife.

He knew what he wanted, and he considered himself entitled to everything he wanted. His horoscope credited him with a rare ability to see wrong as right. When he first met Pridi he was merely one of the bright man's followers. In Paris Pridi was the leader of the young students who gathered round him. Pridi was eloquent and inspiring. Pridi no doubt at that time looked on Pibul as one of several, but Pibul was soon to fill a very vital point in the organization that Pridi and his friends were building up. He was an efficient soldier. He had soon reached the rank of major. He was in touch with a number of the senior officers who resented the autocratic administration to which they were subjected by a hierarchy of royal princes. Pibul was the channel of communication between Pridi and these disaffected officers. Intellectuals alone were not powerful enough to overthrow a dynasty.

Pridi's group was known as the People's Party and it contained barely two hundred members. Within the party was a smaller and very secret group, fifty-seven strong, who were known as "The Promoters" and of whom twenty-seven were soldiers. They did not understand the economic measures with which Pridi proposed to reorganize the national economy, but they leaped on the word "democracy" as though it were a talisman to protect them against the royal masters.

Apparently the chief of the police was aware not only of the existence of the People's Party, but of an actual plot to take over control of the country. The king did not however consider that there was enough evidence to justify the arrests that would have saved the dynasty. He had been trained in England. He had a European not an Asiatic respect for legal procedure.

Nineteen thirty-two was a bad, slow-passing year. In the United States, a distracted people was waiting for the November elections that would establish a new regime in the White House. The world was waiting for that new regime. In the meantime the sands were running out. In Siam no less than in Britain, in France, in Portugal, in Spain. In Bangkok preparations were being made to celebrate on April 6 the hundred and fiftieth anniversary of the ascendancy of the Chakri dynasty. It was remembered that Rama I had prophesied that his house would rule for exactly that sum of years. Was the tocsin about to sound? Rumors were on the wind. The inefficiency of the supreme council was causing a universal resentment against the princely caste. It was whispered that the wealth of the princes had not been affected by the slump. They were as affluent as ever. It was rumored that a large part of the revenue found its way into the coffers of Prince Paripatra. The minister of commerce and communications, Prince Purachatra, though himself a minor prince, was married to a celestial princess. Bitter accusations were made against his extravagance, his trips to Europe, his cameras, his radio sets, though in fact they were far more justifiable as "deductable expenses" than the entertainment account of the average contemporary tycoon.

Slowly the heatening spring passed. Prince Chula received royal permission to return to Cambridge for two more years of historical research before taking up a post in the ministry of education. The king accompanied him from the Dusit Palace to the private royal railway station. It was a singular tribute that the king was paying to his nephew. Neither Rama VI nor King Prajadhipok had gone to the station except to honor the deceased senior members of the royal family. Courtiers had little doubt that the king, who was childless, was already regarding Prince Chula as his heir. De Quincey once wrote that we never do anything consciously for the last time without regret. How often do we not do something familiar, without recognizing that it is for the last time. Prince Chula never realized on that spring afternoon that he was seeing for the last time the royal standard, the red garuda on the saffron yellow background.

April 6 came and went, the threatening rumors were dispersed. No demonstrations interrupted the official ceremonies. The Rama I bridge across the river between Bangkok and Dhonburi was opened. The crowds dispersed, and the hot humid night began. The prophecy of the first Chakri monarch had not been fulfilled. April passed. The rainy season was about to start. On May 11 Siam abandoned the gold standard, linking its currency with sterling, at eleven bahts to the pound. But there was no change in the economic crisis. The downward slide continued.

The *New Yorker* writer, St. Clair McKelway, then in his later twenties and at the start of his career, was editing the Bangkok *Daily Mail*, a daily newspaper that appeared in the late afternoon and was directed to the resident British and American colonies in Bangkok. His mother presented the files of the issues that he edited to the Library of Congress. Those files possess for us today a poignant, dramatic irony.

The fateful third week in June started like any other week. On the preceding Saturday, the eighteenth, the patrons of the Queen's Theatre had been urged "to drown depression in the sparkling comedy of comedies, *Peach O'Reno* starring Bert Woolsey, Bert Wheeler and Zelma O'Neal." The sports columns discussed the prospect of the Sharkey-Schmeling fight, and Kaye Dori's hopes of driving Miss England III across Lake Garda at 120 miles an hour and breaking Gar Wood's record. The leading article considered the probability of the United States' abandoning Prohibition. It rained on the Sunday, and the big football match in the Royal Dusit Park grounds was canceled. The king was enjoying his summer holiday in his new palace at Hua Hin which he had called Klai Klangwol, "far from worries." The Monday issue of the *Mail* had as its chief headline "Stocks slip as gloom darkens trading markets." But Charles G. Dawes announced reassuringly that the turning point of the Depression had been reached. Walter Lippmann in an editorial reprinted from the New York *Herald Tribune* wrote with indignation of the lack of discipline in Washington. London socialites were diverted to learn that Elvira Barney, a prominent "bright young person" had been arrested for the murder of her lover in a Mayfair mews. On the Tuesday Prince Damrong celebrated his seventieth birthday and the next day's issue was filled with photographs of the celebrations at his Varadis Palace. Prince Damrong was one of the most distinguished of King Mongkut's minor sons; a man of scholarship and enterprise, he had controlled in his time the ministries of education and the interior. He was a historian and an archaeologist; his history of Rama II and his memoirs are accepted authorities. His prominence can be gauged from the fact that he received a telegram of congratulations from the king and queen of England. The paper carried photographs of him with the Princes Chumbohl and Devawongse. It seemed an agreeable curtain to a crowded and illustrious life. Two mornings later, however, he was standing in pajamas and unshaven in the marble throne room of the Dusit Palace, having been arrested by the People's Party along with Prince Paripatra and a number of other royal princes in charge of ministries.

The Bangkok *Mail* later in the day announced in banner headlines that the People's Party had seized the government, that the chief royal princes were in custody, and that a limited monarchy would be founded. In the meantime a coast guard cutter had been sent to Hua Hin to bring the king back to his capital.

No revolution in the turgid history of mankind has been carried through so swiftly, so efficiently and so pacifically. McKelway was to write in a subsequent article in the *Mail:* "Not a single measure that would ensure the prevention of bloodshed, violence or disorder was overlooked in the meticulous plan that was carried out. The soldiers and sailors were trained to a fine point of discipline so that not only did they act with marvelous precision and dispatch but they refrained from a too-exuberant enthusiasm even when they saw that their long dreamed of plan was at last a success." Their task had been made the simpler by power having been concentrated into a minutely small area. Only a very few princes held positions of executive authority, and they were arrested by tanks at dawn. Senior naval officers were on their annual leave. Their ships and shore units were taken over by junior naval officers who were in the plot.

The inner pavilion of the Grand Palace

The promoters had enlisted in their support Colonel Phya Bahol of the artillery and Colonel Phya Song, an engineer. Song was commandant of the staff college, he had influence over the weapons training school, the military cadets academy, the armored regiment. Pibul, since he was lower in rank, worked in the background; another important promoter and one of the Paris group was Kuang Abhaiwongse, who was employed in the postal services. He knew which telephone and telegraph wires needed to be cut. He was able to show the military which important post of communication, radio stations and general post offices needed to be occupied; though there were so few "promoters," every key point was covered. For some reason the Thai air force was not involved, and very few infantry officers had a role to play.

The staff work was superb. Shortly after dawn the greater part of the Bangkok garrison was marched down Rajdamnoen Avenue which Chulalongkorn had had constructed for his yellow car, to a square in front of the Dusit Palace; they were told that they were to be shown an antiaircraft exhibition, so they came unarmed. On their arrival at the square they found that a large body of tanks was drawn up facing them. Colonel Bahol then mounted upon a tank and informed them that a revolution had taken place and that the king would be invited to grant a constitution. There was nothing that unarmed troops could do but raise their hands and voices in a cheer.

Only a few yards away from the square was the Second Battalion of the First Infantry Regiment, Chulalongkorn's own bodyguard in their special barracks. They were ready to take action, but no orders came. The guards divisional commander had been arrested. The promoters did not miss a point. In the whole operation there was only a single casualty, a policeman who had misunderstood his orders. Later in the morning Prince Paripatra from his enforced seclusion issued a broadcast appeal that between Thai people there should be no bloodshed. He accepted the new government and ordered public services to continue.

In the meantime for the king in his palace named "Far from Worries," the day of June 24 began just as most other days. There was no immediate threat of rain, and the air of Hua Hin is considerably cooler than that of Bangkok. All the same he decided to start his daily round of golf while the weather held and the sun was still low in the sky, so that he was well into the second half of his round when his concentration was disturbed by the spectacle of an ill-kempt figure hurrying towards him down the fairway. At close range he recognized it as being that of Prince Purachatra who had been overlooked in the series of arrests, and had made his way to Hua Hin in a detached railway engine.

Prince Purachatra brought with him both the news of the revolution and the report that its aim was not to dethrone the king but to establish a limited monarchy on the British model. This was the kind of change that Prajadhipok had for a long time himself considered necessary and inevitable. He had said, indeed, precisely that to an interviewer in the United States, and had he been given any encouragement by his advisers, he would have probably by now taken steps for the promulgation of a constitution. One part of him was ready to welcome the People's Party's coup d'etat, but Prince Purachatra brought out with him two documents that were being circulated in Bangkok. Both appeared to have been authorized by the People's Party, though each was an unsigned manifesto. One was in the king's eyes inoffensive, in view of the turgid atmosphere that must be existing in his capital. It was an apologia; it complained that the king had conferred all the important government posts on to his relatives and favorites; who had been allowed to act "as they chose in their own aristocratic way, satisfying their greed and desires, accepting bribes in construction undertakings, profiting from the rise in sterling. The royal families were in fact robbing the people of their means of livelihood." That was the kind of thing that in England was said at election time by radicals of Tories and vice versa. The king was prepared to accept an election manifesto of that nature, but he was disconcerted by the second document that attacked the whole Chakri family, all the way along the course, accusing Rama I of having usurped Taksin's throne. This document falsified the facts of history.

The two royal heads of the army and the navy happened also to be in Hua Hin and that afternoon they held a conference as to what the king should do. He had three courses open to him. There was the traditional escape abroad. It was to be presumed that he, like every prudent monarch or dictator, had a numbered account in Switzerland. He could on the other hand return to Bangkok and accept the role of a constitutional monarch. Or again he could rally the troops stationed in the provinces and march on Bangkok, where there must be many loyal battalions waiting to see how he would act.

A march on Bangkok might well have proved successful. But he had the intrinsic built-in Buddhist reluctance to shed blood — a part of the Thai temperament that must never be forgotten. Moreover he knew that if he provoked a civil war, the senior princes in captivity would be in mortal danger. He was a soldier and the idea of running away to Switzerland was repugnant to him, yet at the same time he had not relished the manifesto attacking the Chakri family. He considered, and few historians would contradict him, that Siam owed everything to the Chakris. He was reluctant to subject himself to the whims of a group so ignorant of history, so ungrateful to his ancestors. Finally and surprisingly enough he sought the advice of his womenfolk — his mother and the queen. They both insisted that he should return to Bangkok — even if it was a return to death. His thoughts that night were those of the soldier who will have to go over the top next morning.

The most dramatic day in Bangkok's history had come and gone, yet a traveling salesman from Singapore who had checked in at the Oriental Hotel the previous night would not have realized for quite a while that anything was happening. From his bedroom balcony as he looked out over the river across his breakfast table, he would have seen the small boats ferrying their passengers and produce to the Dhonburi bank; barges would have chunked slowly to the sea. There was no commotion in the streets, the police were on duty. The priests carried their begging bowls, the traffic in New Road was neither more nor less congested than it had been the day before. When he made his business calls, he would learn something of what had happened in the Dusit Palace. If he went to the British Club for lunch, he would have been entertained with rumors. But he would at the same time have learned that the machinery of the city was revolving smoothly. Mails had been delivered. Courts were functioning. The salesman from Singapore, because he had contacts with residents, would pick up gossip. But a tourist at the Oriental would not have known that anything unusual had happened until in the late afternoon he read the headlines in the Bangkok *Mail*. There was no equivalent of the storming of the Bastille. There were no barricades in the streets. The revolution was not the spearhead of a people's movement. The people were not interested in theories of government. They had been trained to the demands of a paternal, absolute authority. That was what they understood. That was what they wanted. They worshiped the king because he was the symbol of divine authority, the incarnation of Vishnu. They lived under his orders and protection.

Next morning the warship arrived at Hua Hin. It brought

with it the People's Party's ultimatum. It informed His Majesty that a party consisting of civil and military officials had assumed the administration of the country and had taken members of the royal family as hostages. If members of the People's Party were injured, reprisals would be taken against these royal hostages. The People's Party did not intend to appropriate any of the royal family's possessions. Their aim was a constitutional monarchy. "We therefore," it concluded, "enjoin Your Majesty to return to the capital to reign as king under the constitutional monarchy as established by the People's Party. If Your Majesty refuses to accept the offer or refrains from replying within one hour after the receipt of this message, the People's Party will proclaim the constitutional monarchical government by appointing another prince whom they consider to be efficient as king." The ultimatum was signed by three Army colonels — Bahol, Song and Riddhi. It has not been divulged which prince they had in mind.

While the king was reading this ultimatum, the press was gathered in the Throne Hall, waiting for his answer. There was an atmosphere of enforced occupation. Machine guns were mounted in all the upper floor windows; the soldiers and sailors on the front lawn had their bayonets fixed. But their smiles and the badinage that they exchanged with the crowd belied the menace of the bayonets. At last the message came: the king accepted the proposal of the People's Party and would return immediately to the capital by special train. The radio was read out by a press officer. The three words "the king accepts" were shouted triumphantly in Siamese and English. The soldiers on the lawn cheered. The news swept down the avenues to the royal palace.

It was by train, not ship, that the king elected to return to Bangkok. In a ship he would have felt himself a prisoner. The letter which he addressed to the People's Party was dignified,

with the dignity of a tired man. The following English transla-
tion of it appeared in K. P. Landon's *Siam in Transition*. It was
addressed to the military in defense of Bangkok. "I have received," it said, "the letter in which you invite me to return to
Bangkok as a constitutional monarch. For the sake of peace and
in order to save useless bloodshed, to avoid confusion and loss
to the country, and more, because I have already considered
making this change myself, I am willing to cooperate in the
establishment of a constitution under which I am willing to
serve.

"Furthermore, there is a possibility that, if I decline to continue in my office as king, the foreign powers will not recognize
the new government. This might entail considerable difficulty
for the government.

"Physically I am not strong. I have no children to succeed
me. My life expectancy is not long, at least if I continue in this
office. I have no desire for position or for personal aggrandizement. My ability to advance the progress of the [Thai] race
alone constrains me. Accept this sincere expression of my feelings."

Only a Boy Scout detachment and a few civilians were awaiting the arrival of the train at the royal station. Prince Alongkut,
the vice-minister of defense, left the train at the public station
and was promptly arrested by troops of the provisional government and taken to join his fellow princes in the throne room of
the Dusit Palace. But Princes Svasti and Purachatra because
they actually accompanied the king were not arrested but allowed to proceed with him to the royal palace.

At ten o'clock on the following morning the minister of the
royal household conferred with the leading civilian and military representatives of the People's Party. A little later the nu-
cleus of that group, accompanied by two armored tanks and
two detachments of soldiers, proceeded to the king's palace to

hold a conference. Pridi was the spokesman for the group. As the representatives were admitted to his presence, the king stood up. He said, "I rise in honor of the People's Party."

St. Clair McKelway, in addition to editing the Bangkok *Mail*, was the *Herald Tribune*'s correspondent in Siam. He was the first foreigner admitted to the headquarters of the provisional government on the afternoon of the coup, and on the following day he was allowed to speak freely to members of the government. He cabled the *Herald Tribune* that it was to him as an American "a stimulating and memorable experience for the familiar phrases 'all men are created equal' and 'government of the people, by the people, for the people' figured prominently in the conversation of the young idealists who for years have been planning a peaceful overthrow of the clique of princes who have enjoyed too much power and who sometimes have prevented the carrying out even of the king's own wishes to the detriment of the country. The People's Party," he went on, "is composed of a mixture of young and brilliant government officials, educated abroad but not royally born, and middle-aged army and navy officers who firmly believe that they are acting in the best interests of their king and country."

McKelway considered highly significant "the fact that thus far no government funds have been used by the provisional regime, despite its present absolute control over the country. The leaders of the movement ride to the Throne Hall on their own motorbicycles or in their own motor cars, though each prince in custody has dozens of fine cars which might have been seized." This was a standard that clearly could not be maintained in a country that regarded the desirability of a post not in terms of the salary it brought, but the opportunity for being bribed that it presented. King Mongkut, when Anna Leonowens complained that her salary was inadequate, retorted, "But what about all these petitions that you bring to me. That should earn you a substantial sum."

McKelway was particularly impressed by Pridi. He wrote of him in the Bangkok *Mail:* "His manner is extremely modest, yet in his bright eager eyes and decisive gestures, one catches a glimpse of the force of character and the strength of conviction that have made him a leader in one of the most unique political movements in the modern world . . . He is an official of the ministry of justice, but being a man of quiet, studious mien, he is not widely known outside the immediate circle of his friends."

At the start there was universal approval of the leaders of the People's Party. In another article McKelway wrote: "Despite their absolute power during these first days, the civilian leaders have refrained from the slightest suggestion of arrogance or showiness. All of them are believed to be men of very modest means living on their small salaries and supporting families therewith — a precedent for government officials which it is indicated will be continued by the present leaders."

A leader in the same issue of the Bangkok *Mail*, entitled "The Initial Task before the New Government," referred to the new leaders as being "activated by the highest ideals of patriotism," but it had one qualification to make about the roseateness of the immediate future. Was there not the danger of a financial slump; while the political mind of the nation was being adjusted to the new order, the economic body of the nation might fail and waste. Was there not also the danger of a countermovement? But the general atmosphere was euphoric and Siamese citizens in Washington cabled their congratulations making the suggestion that only the children of a king's first queen should be princes and princesses.

There was an admirable lack of rancor in the immediately

The compound of the Temple of the Emerald Buddha

subsequent proceedings. As soon as the king had signed a provisional constitution that had been drafted by Pridi, the royal
princes were released from custody. In only one instance was
an exception made. Prince Paripatra had stood too high, had
inspired too much opposition to be allowed to remain a part of
the Bangkok scene. He could not be trusted to accept obscurity.
He had, moreover, to face a charge of corruption in his handling of public money. He was invited to leave the country and
on July 4 he took his family to Java. There was no one at the
station to see him off. His many friends had imagined that he
was leaving by a later train and did not discover their mistake
until it was too late. There was often an atmosphere of comic
opera about the most solemn events in Bangkok. Paripatra
never returned to the country of his birth. He died in 1944.

By the time he left, the city had resumed its habitual routine.
On the previous day large crowds had assembled at the Royal
Turf Club to cheer the winner of the Luk Pasom Cup. The ban-
ner headlines of the Bangkok *Mail* were concerned with the
Lausanne economic conference and the Democratic Conven-
tion in Chicago where the partisans of Al Smith and F.D.R.
were arguing over their choice for the election in November.
Walter Lippmann was deliberating the burdens of taxation.
Local news was put back into its usual secondary place. Public
announcements invariably stressed the royal presence. It was
announced for instance that it was with the sanction of His
Majesty the King that an investigation was being started into
the recent administration of the ministry of commerce and
communication. Every attempt was made to preserve the appearance of his authority. And indeed he did still possess far
more power than most constitutional monarchs.

The document that he had signed on his return from Hua
Hin was only a draft, and during the next five months the king
and his ministers deliberated the wording of the constitution in

which he would formally hand over to the Thai people the power and privilege he had inherited. It required very careful cooperation, and it was not till the middle of November that the final draft of it was published, and St. Clair McKelway was cabling the *Herald Tribune* that the king was arranging a gala celebration for December 10 when he would sign it, inscribed on palmyra. McKelway described it "as a long step away from dictatorship towards true democracy . . . the king actually took the leading part in its drafting, virtually all of his suggestions being included. All possibility of Prajadhipok's abdication has now vanished and Siam is entering a new era promising real social and economic development."

McKelway explained how the new constitution granted the king power to dissolve the newly formed legislative body, the People's Assembly. The Assembly, pending a ten year educational program, was composed half of members appointed by the king and half of members elected from the various provinces. The king would also appoint an executive committee composed of legislators, ministers and the revolution leaders. It was indeed not so much the king's power that had been limited as that all power had been taken away from the royal princes. It was against their misuse of power that the revolution had been directed, and the constitution expressly stated that members of the royal family were "above politics"; they must therefore take no part in active politics or run for elective office, although they might hold any appointive position in the government including that of minister.

McKelway hailed this constitution as "a brilliant victory for the moderate members of the coup d'etat group over the radicals who are young idealists with socialistic if not communistic theories." Copies of this new constitution were carried to remote country districts, with appropriate pomp. But it cannot be pretended that the villagers had any idea what it was all about.

With puzzled faces they inquired, "Who is this Mr. Constitution?" The word "democracy" meant nothing to them. The king was still in his royal palace, that was all that mattered.

Never had the king been more popular than he was during those final months. His public appearances were cheered vociferously. On his birthday the city was decked with flags and bunting. There was a blaze of illuminations. It was very possibly a happy time for him. He had never wanted to be king. Maybe he was glad to be rid of the authoritative autocracy of his elder relatives. But even so, he was loyal to the memory of his ancestors. He insisted that before he signed the constitution, the promoters should present themselves to him and apologize not only to him but to the royal family as a whole for the abuse that had been contained in the Rama I manifesto. The promoters agreed to this. It has never been established who was responsible for that manifesto. The other document was unexceptional. The promoters said "We take this opportunity before Your Majesty to make a solemn declaration that we shall be faithful to Your Majesty for ever." There is no doubt that that promise was made sincerely.

The king devised a special and solemn ceremony for the occasion. He wore his crown for the first time since his coronation. He sat under the sacred seven-tiered umbrella. "I had," he wrote to his nephew Chula, "thought out such a ceremony for years, knowing that it will have to come in my lifetime. Even the proclamation that was read, had been drafted in my mind for a long time." He expressed his regrets that things had turned out in exactly the way they had, but he wrote: "If I had granted a constitution myself those people who want power and now have got it would have been still left in the cold, and there might have been a severe agitation for a republic and a much worse form of rising . . . I feel that my life work is done and that I have nothing more to do except live on peacefully if possible." He was only thirty-nine years old when he wrote that. He concluded by saying: "I don't know whether you realize it or not as you are far from Siam, but the actual fact is that this movement for a constitution is not as popular in Siam as one might expect."

Never, indeed, can a revolution have been less inspired by a spontaneous outburst of public feeling. But that is in fact the Bangkok pattern. The city has known a number of coup d'etats since the day when the seventh Chakri monarch resigned his power, but not one of these has been dictated by mass hysteria, such as there has been in Paris and Baghdad. Bangkok is a Buddhist city. Prajadhipok wished that the revolution could have come in a different way. He may have wished that another king had been on the throne when the revolution came, but it may well be that it was a good thing for Siam that a man with his particular character and point of view was there. He handled the situation in terms of his own nature. Prince Chula in the succession of definitive labels that he gave to the various monarchs called Prajadhipok "the philosopher"; and it was philosophically that his uncle bowed before the storm. Had he resisted it, the traditions of monarchy that the Siamese themselves so much respect might have been disrupted, thereby outraging their deepest hereditary instincts. It is very possibly because Prajadhipok was the man he was, that the Thais have been able to remain their unique, delightful selves.

10

Uneasy Lies the Head

W<small>HEN</small> Chulalongkorn's princes begged him to reconstruct his government on the British pattern, he assured him that the Thais were not ready yet for independence; when Prajadhipok suggested to his advisers that he was anxious to give the people a constitution, he in his turn was assured that the Thais were not ready yet. The same advice has been tendered in recent years by innumerable on-the-spot experts who assured metropolitan ministers that the colony in question was not ready to elect its own representatives. "In twenty years' time, perhaps, not now." But the wind of change has blown. Independence has been granted, and the man on the spot, now in suburban retirement, sighs as he sees on his television set massacres of Sikhs and Moslems, riots in Aden, starving children in Biafra. "They wouldn't listen," he thinks. "They wouldn't listen." And no doubt during the next decade, Prince Paripatra in his exile must have often shaken his head wryly. "I warned that half-brother of mine." But the wind of change cannot be stopped blowing. If you try to check it, it becomes a hurricane. And in Thailand democracy as it is understood in what is called by "Westerners" the Free World, never stood a chance. It was not that the Thais were not ready for it. It was that they did not understand it. They had no wish for a voice in the management of affairs; certainly they did not get one under "Mr. Constitution." They liked their traditional life of the klongs and rice fields and they had no wish to alter it. Politicians might be distracted by a series of coup d'etats. That was no concern of theirs. Up till 1932 the story of Bangkok had been the vicissitudes of the seven Ramas and their divergences with their brothers, uncles and half-brothers. Now it became the vicissitudes of politicians — in particular during early years the rivalry between two of the youngest and most brilliant of the promoters, Pridi and Pibul. For fifteen years they were the protagonists, and even now the changing situation is colored by their divergent fortunes.

Within a very few weeks the main features of the drama had become distinct. The premiership had been given not to one of the promoters, but to Phya Mano, president of the supreme court of appeal, while several of the other new ministers had served in one way or another under Prajadhipok and his predecessors. This was, of course, an attempt on the part of the promoters to prove their disinterested devotion to their country's good. Pridi and Pibul were ministers without portfolio. But though Pridi had been given no official standing, he was allotted immediately the intricate and highly technical task of reorganizing the budget. Of the six main aims that the People's Party had presented, the third had been "a national economic policy must be drawn up to provide remunerative work for everyone." In Paris and at the university, Pridi as the mentor had exposed the antediluvian system by which the profits of the country's trade had been diverted into princely pockets. His hearers had applauded, but they had not appreciated all that was implied in his denunciations. It is one thing to attack an existing system; it is quite another to produce a practical alternative. And the plan that Pridi presented came as a considerable shock to those of the promoters for whom the coup d'etat had been intended as no more than a transference of power to themselves. Pridi's plan involved the nationalization of all agricultural land. It would be acquired not by cash, but with the issue of bonds, so that the farmers would become government officials with a fixed salary — a salary which was to be paid not with cash but with checks that would be honored only in government stores. This would reduce the price of consumer goods by destroying the profit system. The government would also take over the distribution of rice: the middleman would be thus eliminated. This meant, of course, the Chinese.

Pridi's plan was, not surprisingly, opposed to all the ideas that were held by the more conservative members of the cabinet, particularly by the military ones. They considered it communistic, as indeed it was. But the minority who supported it were vehement in its defense. Mano, the prime minister, showed the plan to the king. He too considered it communistic. He also said that the farmers would never accept it. They were free and independent people. Rather than be dragooned by city supervisors, they would vanish into the jungle and live on roots. The king produced a lengthy, carefully reasoned argument, which Mano had published and distributed as a pamphlet. This act showed at the start how little he understood the niceties of a constitutional monarchy, the English principle being that though the monarch may warn and advise his ministers, this is a private matter which should not be made known to the public. The sovereign should never be the cause of controversy.

The Thais are a gentle people, but feelings grew so high that loaded revolvers were brandished during the parliamentary debates, and Colonel Song had troops stationed at the door of the Chamber of Deputies, to search members for firearms. The disturbances became so violent that Pridi resigned from the cabinet and left the country unobtrusively, while Mano requested

A view of the northern half of the Temple of the Emerald Buddha; in the foreground is the roof of the back entrance with statues representing the heads of legendary birds

the king's consent to prorogue the assembly, for fear of violence. "Mr. Constitution" had reigned for less than four months. Prince Paripatra in his exile must have chuckled.

Mano now prepared to rule by royal decrees, and the diehard royalists began to wonder whether the days of absolute monarchy were not about to return. But Mano, though he appeared to have made his point about Pridi's plan, had not the support of the promoters, and the two chief colonels, Bahol and Song, resigned not only from the government but from the army too. Mano thought that he could manage without them and he appointed as army chief a retired general who had not taken part in the 1932 coup.

It did not work. On June 14, Pibul and four others met at a secret rendezvous in an open field. They went quietly to avoid notice. A number of soldiers stood on guard. A few hours later Bahol and Pibul recalled the assembly and forced Mano into exile in Penang.

It was, like nearly all Bangkok coup d'etats, bloodless, and it sent expressions of loyalty to the king who asked Bahol to form a government. Pridi was recalled to be cleared by a tribunal of the charge of communism and given a portfolio as minister of the interior. On the surface it looked as though everything was exactly as it had been two months earlier, except that the original promoters with Bahol at the head were in complete control, with Pridi and Pibul confirmed in the succession.

Their troubles were, however, far from over, one of the chief troubles being that because the new leaders lacked experience, senior officials were allowed to remain. Moreover the brief period during which Mano had ruled by royal decree had encouraged a few unwise reactionaries to believe that "happy days were here again." Pibul was aware of this and on July 16, he and Subha Jalasarja had the following letter sent to men as prominent as Prince Devawongse:

SIR:

Both times that the People's Party seized the power of government, they acted in an orderly fashion for the sake of the peace of the country and the freedom of the people. It appears from our investigations that you are planning to overthrow the peace of the country by attempting to overthrow the present government. Such a move would interfere with the orderly progress of the nation. In our position of responsibility as guardians of the peace, we advise you to desist. If you insist upon causing trouble, our group will use strong measures to assure the peace of the country. This is not a threat designed to intimidate you, but is advice hopefully given.

With high respect,

The recipients were furious and sent the letters to the press. The press too was indignant. The two officers claimed that they had acted as private citizens, but some editorials pointed out that as private citizens they were not in a position to use "strong measures" in case of disobedience.

Trouble was clearly imminent. On October 11 it became known that Prince Bavoradej, who had been minister of defense in earlier days, was indisposed and staying at Korat with Lieutenant Colonel Phya Vijaycnor and was being visited by army officers and officials. On the next day, with a body of provincial troops, he marched on the capital. The prince's presence did not improve the image of the revolt because it gave the impression that it was a royalist plot, which it was not. The rebels announced that Bahol had usurped authority, that the people had no voice, that the spirit of the revolution had been violated: their aim was to deliver the king from the People's Party. They hoped that several units stationed in Bangkok would act as fifth columnists and join them, but almost entirely as a result of Pibul's skillful handling of the defense this did not happen and the rebels were defeated in a battle near the Don Muang airport, where the leader of the retired generals lost his life. Bavarodej and a number of the other leaders escaped to French Indo-China.

When all this was happening the king was once again at Hua Hin, "Far from Worries"; Bahol in his radio talks had begged the king to return to Bangkok and place himself at the head of his legal government. He would, as events turned out, have been wise to do so; but not only did he not return to Bangkok, he deserted Hua Hin, making a dangerous trip across the gulf in a small motorboat to a village called Songkla, only a very few miles from the Malayan border. It was not an act of cowardice — for the trip he made was very dangerous — but of exhaustion. He had had enough. He could not be expected to feel any particular affection for Bahol, Pridi and Pibul. Fifteen months before they had been scarcely names to him. Nor had he much sympathy for the retired generals. He had probably been bored by most of them. A group of upstarts were in conflict with a group of "dug outs." "Let them fight it out between themselves and then tell me what they have decided." Had he gone to Bangkok and Bahol's forces been defeated, his position might have been very awkward, even though the rebels had claimed that their aim was to release him from the domination of the People's Party. His wisest course probably would have been to stay on at "Far from Worries" even though he ran the risk of being captured by the rebels. There was, in fact, no satisfactory solution to his dilemma. As it was, he was never trusted again by the People's Party. They felt that they had been deserted by him in their time of peril. They suspected that because the rebels were led by a royal prince, he had given them his support. There could never be glad, confident morning again — and all the time the king's health was worsening.

On November 1, the first general election took place. It was a curious election, because the deputies were chosen not by popular vote, but by elected village representatives. There were seventy-eight deputies in all. Historians differ as to the amount of public interest taken in the election. One authority — and a sound authority — states that "less than a tenth of the electorate voted and comparatively few candidates offered themselves for election." Prince Chula on the other hand says that so many candidates presented themselves that there was confusion at the hustings, and gives ministry of the interior figures to show that out of an electorate of 4,278,231 there were 1,773,532 voters. A percentage of 41.45.

There was heavier voting in the provinces than in Bangkok where there was relative apathy. For the country dwellers an election was a novelty. The sophisticated citizens suspected that as far as they themselves were concerned, it did not very much matter who got in. Bahol remained premier, and Pibul, now a colonel, was virtually commander in chief of the army. Pridi was still with the interior department. The race was starting to thin out, with these three old campaigners well ahead. But the king was not destined to be there to watch the finish. His eyes were growing worse. He explained to his ministers that it was essential for him to return to Europe for an operation. They were reluctant to have him go. His presence in Bangkok gave them an air of stability. They offered to bring out any surgeon that he wanted, no matter what the cost. But he stuck to his point, and at length his ministers agreed. On January 12, 1934, he sailed for France.

He was never to return. In the England where he had spent his happiest years, surrounded by so much that was both dear to him and familiar, the now changed Bangkok seemed increasingly remote and alien. It was no longer the city that his father and grandfather had built up. He had no wish to return to endless arguments with people who were strangers to him. His difficulties with his ministers were now magnified by distance. On his arrival at Victoria Station he was met by the Duke and Duchess of York (later to be George VI and Queen Elizabeth) and he was invited by George V to lunch at Windsor. This was the world in which he had been brought up. This was where he belonged. He could not be bothered to argue across nine thousand miles with a Colonel Bahol. He objected to what his government was doing under the excuse that a crisis demanded emergency controls. He claimed that he had given up his power to the Thai people, not to one particular group. It would seem that he no more understood the limits and techniques of a constitutional monarchy than his first prime minister had done. The bickering continued; a mission from the government begged him to return to Bangkok; the mission was headed by an old friend, the president of the People's Assembly, one of the men who had served under earlier regimes, but the deadlock remained unbroken.

Finally the king decided that there was no alternative to abdication. On March 2, 1935, he accepted the logic of the situation. In his announcement of this step, he wrote: "I am happy to turn over my power of rule to the people as a whole. I am not willing to give it over to any person or to any group to use in an absolute manner without heeding the voices of the people." In this insistence he was surely in the wrong. A constitutional monarch cannot choose his government. He has to accept the verdict of the majority, even when he disagrees with it. He thus avoids responsibility for the mistakes that his ministers may make. He has to accept his ministers' advice.

"I wish," he continued, "to give over all of my kingly privileges, but I desire to retain all of those privileges which were mine before becoming king. I do not care to name my successor, although it is my privilege according to law." Had he chosen a successor, it would almost certainly have been Prince Chula, of whom he was extremely fond. But he had no wish to inflict such a burden on his nephew. "Furthermore," he continued, "I do not care to have anyone rise up in rebellion in Siam against the government on my behalf. If anyone names me as their instigator in rebellion kindly understand that I have no share in it and am not pleased. I am exceedingly sorry that I am unable to serve my people and country according to my plans and hopes which I received from my royal ancestors. There remains only a sincere prayer that Siam will prosper and that the people will have peace and happiness."

Prajadhipok took a house in Surrey, in Virginia Water, where he spent the last six years of his life in restful peace of mind.

11

A Throne without a King

Under the laws of succession that had been laid down in 1924 by King Vajiravudh there was only one possible successor to the throne and that was a ten-year-old schoolboy, who was being educated at the time in Switzerland. His father, Prince Mahidol, who had died in 1929, was the son of King Chulalongkorn and Queen Sawang. He had been born in 1892 and nothing at the time had seemed more unlikely than that he or any son of his would ever ascend the throne. Six lives at least stood between them. There was first of all his brother Vajirunhis, who was named crown prince but who died in 1895. Then there were the five sons of Chulalongkorn and Queen Saowabha, two of whom did ascend the throne, but neither of whom had a son. There was Chakrabongse, who ruled himself out of the succession by marrying a Russian lady, but whose son Prince Chula could have been nominated by an uncle. Queen Saowabha's other two sons were Asdang, who died childless in 1925, and Chutadhuj who, dying in 1923, left a son but not one with a royal princess as his mother. Finally there was in the background Prince Paripatra, the son of Queen Sukumala, who had been born in 1881 and was an undoubted candidate because of his seniority in age. A great many unlikely things would have to happen before Mahidol could be in the running. And from the start he ruled this highly improbable contingency out of his calculations. He conducted his life in the light of his own tastes and character, never expecting to have the obligations and responsibilities of state imposed on him, acting, except when he was in Siam, as though he were not a royal personage, but simply as Mr. M. Songkla, the name of one of his titles, and later as Doctor Songkla because he qualified as a doctor of medicine at Harvard.

Mahidol was a remarkable man. He had the same kind of education that his father had designed for his celestial and the most promising of his minor princes. He was educated at Harrow, then transferred to Germany where he was trained as a sailor. But he had only just been commissioned into the German navy when the war broke out and he returned to Siam. His service in the Siamese navy was, however, brief. His European experience had convinced him that Siam needed more than anything experts to supervise public health services. So he went to the United States to study at the Massachusetts Institute of Technology. He was there when Siam entered the war, and he was anxious to serve in France. Devoted though he was in many ways to the German way of life, he resented the idea of Siamese peasants being sent to their death in the trenches, while the sons of the rulers remained behind in safety. Permission was not granted him, but he did his best to help his compatriots whenever the chance came to him. He tried to help every Siamese student who came to the United States. He lived modestly, and was thus able to endow scholarships for study overseas. He adopted American customs; a student who had come to Boston from England had learned there the English habit of putting his shoes outside the door at night to be cleaned. He did so when he was the prince's house guest and was disconcerted next morning to find his footwear being polished by a celestial prince.

A little later Mahidol was to show even more startling independence. He became engaged to and subsequently married a Siamese student nurse, a commoner. This caused considerable surprise and not a little scandal in Bangkok. The lady — she is now the Princess Mother — was in her own way as remarkable as her husband. Nine years younger than Mahidol, orphaned when she was very young, she was brought up, through the intervention of one of her father's relatives — he had been a minor official — in the crowd of young women who constituted Queen Sawang's court. As a young girl she must have frequently seen Prince Mahidol, though it is unlikely that he would have noticed her. She was not happy there, and when an accident sent her for treatment to the queen's surgeon general, she found the atmosphere of the doctor's home far more congenial than that of the court. A friendship sprang up between the doctor's daughter and herself, and the doctor and his wife were so delighted to find a bright and cheerful companion for their daughter that they adopted her. Both girls after a preliminary education in a state high school were sent to study nursing at a hospital. She showed such intelligence and skill that she earned a scholarship in the United States. It was thus that she met Prince Mahidol.

They married in 1920 and had nine years together, during which they had three children. They were supremely happy years. They traveled constantly in connection with his work. He took a number of courses in Europe. Their first child was born in London, their second in Heidelberg, where Mahidol was undergoing treatment for dysentery — his health was never robust — their third, the present king, in Boston where Mahidol enrolled for his degree as a doctor, feeling that his public health course was inadequate for his requirements. Boston was, indeed, as much his home as Bangkok. He was quite often in Paris, at the time when Pridi was developing his theories in the Left Bank cafés. They met and the young students were impressed by the charm, sincerity and capacities of a prince who stood for everything they admired, and had none of the arrogant self-importance of the royal mandarins of whom they saw too much. Everything might have been very different, had he lived longer. Had he succeeded his half-brother, there would have been on the throne a man whom both Pridi and Pibul could have trusted; those two men might have managed to work together in harness, under the guidance of a wiser man who stood above the battle. Who knows?

Mahidol spent a great deal of his time in traveling, but his love of his own country never lessened. In 1917, when he was in Boston, he was writing to his half-brother, Prince Chula's father — Chakrabongse. "In my early years, as a student in Europe, I never did realize what my country, what my home were to me. Not until I have learned to love my people through contact with them, have I known their valuable and lovable qualities. I am not exactly homesick, but I have learned through my work here that my place in the world is among my people, the Siamese."

He was to do a great deal for them, and the frugal manner in which he lived personally made it possible for him to endow a number of important charities. At one time he worked in Bangkok, in the department of public health, but he refused further government posts. He wanted to work in the field. He had hoped at first to work in Bangkok's Sirras hospital, and complete there the mandatory year's internship that is required of a newly qualified doctor. But this was not possible because court etiquette would not allow him to treat commoners. His hands were sacred and could not touch certain proscribed portions of

A stone giant guards the entrance to the Temple of the Emerald Buddha

his patients' anatomy. He had to work outside Bangkok. Leaving his wife and children in Bangkok, he went to the American hospital in Chiengmai. One of his first concerns was the leper colony which had been established there by the medical missionaries. On my first visit to Chiengmai in 1926, I visited the colony and was moved and impressed by the hopeful, friendly atmosphere that pervaded it. Sometimes one feels indignant at the harm that has been done to simple people, like the Polynesians, by hard, bigoted, emotionally thwarted missionaries, but in a place like Chiengmai one can recognize what the medical missionaries have done. Even in the leper colony, Mahidol was not free from family interference. Royal circles were horrified to learn that he was bathing his peasant patients.

He worked for nearly a year in Chiengmai, but his health soon proved unequal to the strain imposed on it. He was suffering from an amoebic abscess in his liver. He died in 1929. This left his four-year-old son Ananda heir presumptive to the throne.

We are now entering upon a period of Bangkok's history with which the recorder has to deal with caution and discretion. He is describing events that took place within living memory. Several of the chief figures are still alive. It is not merely a question of being exposed to the law of libel — that can usually be avoided — but of causing pain and offense to persons whom he holds in high regard. He cannot impute motives. He must content himself with the recording of events. The main authority for the drama and tragedy that was to cloud the life of Mahidol's widow and his children is Rayne Kruger's *The Devil's Discus*. It is a magnificent and exciting book, to which the reader is strongly recommended. It is banned in Bangkok.

It has been suggested that Princess Mahidol never completely recovered from the grief of her husband's death. Her personal life was over. She had now to live in and for her children and it must be remembered that she was a commoner, that she had not felt at home as a young girl in Queen Sawang's court, that she had nothing in common with the majority of the royal circle. Moreover a great deal of her married life had been spent in Europe and the United States, where she had lived simply as Mrs. Songkla. She had no taste for ceremony. It may well be that she welcomed the revolution. Now her son would not be personally responsible for any misfortunes that might befall her country. She may also have welcomed the opportunity that it gave her of taking her children away from Bangkok. She sent Ananda first of all to a Roman Catholic convent, then a year later she moved him to the Bepsiriad school for boys, which is in the heart of the city and is not unlike an English preparatory school such as Summerfields or the Dragons; that was in March 1932. Within a few months she was petitioning the king to allow her to take her children out of the country for their health's sake and for their education. The king agreed and suggested Switzerland. She sailed in May 1933. She had seen Lausanne on her honeymoon. She believed that its climate would be preferable to Geneva's. She went first of all to a small hotel, the Windsor. But the government decided that it was not adequate to Siamese prestige, so she was moved to a large luxury flat in the Avenue Tissok. It was here that twenty months later three high emissaries of the government called to inform her ten-year-old son that his uncle had abdicated, and to ask him if he would accept the crown. It is reported that the boy who was in bed with a cold, said to his mother "I want to do whatever you say is right."

She answered, "It is for you to decide. You have your duty."

He said "Then I must."

The news of his decision was welcomed in Bangkok. But

there were those who were disturbed by the fact that he did not own one white elephant. He was the first Chakri monarch to be in this predicament.

The promoters — or rather what was left of the promoters — now had it their own way. A council of regency was appointed, but the real power lay with Bahol who was still premier, with Pibul minister of defense and Pridi in charge of foreign affairs. Bahol was the eldest of the three, and the senior in experience, but it was questioned whether he possessed the staying power of his younger colleagues. Democracy did not exist in any form that would be recognizable to a European, and the government owned the power of summary arrest. There was a special kind of victim known as the political prisoner — indeed this was one of the issues on which Prajadhipok had found himself in disagreement with his ministers — and the royalist plot of 1933 had given the government an alibi for unconstitutional action. A crisis or a threat of a crisis was always the excuse required. The game of power politics was in full operation, and Pibul was playing his own hand with the cards held close against his chest. He was building up for himself a strong following inside the army by a series of judicious promotions and government appointments. Pridi was teaching in the law school. He was known as the mentor still. His influence among the young intellectuals was as high as ever, but in the political arena his followers were being pushed into the background. It is doubtful if he was actuated by hopes of political aggrandizement. He was, far more than any of his contemporaries, an idealist.

In the summer of 1937 there broke a crisis which though it might well have ruined Pibul, in the end strengthened his position because it proved him to be capable of taking ruthless and decisive action even when he was in the wrong. The crisis was known as the Land Scandal. Prajadhipok had owned a good deal of land in Bangkok, which the regency council had decided was not actually his, but belonged to the state. This land was put on sale, which was legitimate under the circumstances. It was the kind of thing that happens after a revolution. No one objected until rumors began to spread that some of the promoters had been allowed to buy portions of this land at a very low price and at easy installment terms. The land was practically given away. There was high public indignation, and the civilian members felt that their chance had come. They clamored for the resignation of the regents and the premier so vigorously that the regents and the premier actually did resign. But Pibul was equal to the situation. It was believed that he had himself been given some of this land, but if he had he quickly managed to return it so that his name would not appear upon the record. He then swore by the Emerald Buddha that he was innocent — and a grisly and grievous fate befalls him who swears falsely by the Buddha. Then he surrounded the Assembly with tanks, and informed the deputies that their behavior was out of order. The military expressed their loyalty to the premier and the council, who withdrew their resignations because "the defense forces wished the premier and the present regency council to remain in office."

It was clear from this moment that it was in Pibul's hands that the real power lay. Pridi had not been involved in the scandal in the slightest way. He was now foreign minister and was busily engaged trying to arrange treaties with the European powers that would allow Siam to abandon the import duty which as a result of King Mongkut's treaty with Sir John Bowring had been in operation ever since. Under a treaty made by Rama VI this small tariff rate had been slightly modified, but apart from tobacco at 25% and wines and beer at 12%, most of the imported commodities only paid a duty of 5%. Pridi was brilliantly successful in his negotiations — the rates of duty were raised and the gain to the country's fortunes was considerable. But Pridi, though he was doing a great deal for his country, was not doing a great deal for himself. Pibul was in the saddle.

That is how it was in 1937 with the military in control and that is how it has been ever since with the people themselves taking the minimum of interest in what was being transacted in high places on their behalf. Pibul knew that he had powerful enemies. He was the intended victim of a continuous series of assaults. He was shot at once as he was getting out of his car at a football match. At another time when he was preparing to leave for an evening party, his valet drew a gun on him. As so often in Siam, there was an air of comic opera about this assault — with his half-Wellington boots on, he had not buttoned up his trousers — but even at this disadvantage he was agile enough to dodge the bullets and to collar his man. Later an attempt was made to poison both him and his wife. They had strong constitutions and survived, but for a long time afterwards they declined to eat any food or take anything to drink outside their own home. Although the Thais were and are an extremely gentle race, loath to shed blood or to cause pain, they regard assassination as an inevitable factor in the conducting of practical politics.

In November 1938 the king paid a visit to his capital. He stayed two months and made himself extremely popular. He was dignified and courteous, with a shy, slightly puzzled air that reminded his courtiers that he was only a schoolboy after all. He arrived by ship and the premier and the regency council went out to welcome him. The flagship of his navy, the *Ayudhya*, honored him with a twenty-one gun salute. As the battleship sailed up the river, a hundred airplanes flew overhead: small boats festooned with silk and flowers thronged the water. The procession was one of the most superb in a country that

The Marble Temple

has made a specialty of sumptuous display. Members of the royal family were waiting with cabinet ministers and ambassadors in full court dress on the royal jetty by the Grand Palace. When the king appeared on deck, there was a triumphant outburst of harmony from drums, fifes, trumpets and conch shells. The princes, their excellencies and the ministers rose to their feet. The king in his royal robes carried the symbol of power, the golden sword. The nine-tiered umbrella, the particular perquisite of kingship, was held above him. Monks chanted as he stepped ashore.

The populace of the country listened reverently while addresses of loyalty were delivered. He worshiped the Emerald Buddha. He paid appropriate homage to "the august predecessors of the Royal House of Chakri." His grandmother, Chulalongkorn's seventy-six-year-old third wife Queen Sawang, prostrated herself before him. Two months of lavish gaiety had begun. The weather was growing cool, the rains had ceased; crowds lined the avenues whenever the king drove by in his open carriage, in a plumed helmet, the gold braid on his white tunic glittering in the sun. The people had again what they really needed, a king in a royal palace. When he left the country in mid-January, the riverbanks were lined by a crowd of three thousand; the auguries could not have been more propitious. But nearly seven years were to pass before he again sailed down the broad brown waters of the Menam.

They were to be crowded, fateful years, tragic but lit by comedy as everything in Bangkok is. During the months that separated the departure of the king from the outbreak of war in Europe, on September 3, Pibul took drastic measures to assure his position. Bahol had resigned his premiership, and Pibul took his place, with Pridi as minister of finance. Studying with admiration the careers of Hitler and Mussolini, Pibul started to model himself on them. He established an equivalent for the

Hitler youth movement. He noted with approval how his heroes had dealt with their rivals, Mussolini with Matteotti, Hitler with Roehm and Streicher. Pibul was well aware that he was the object of fierce hatred; the three attempts against his life proved that. There were rumors of plotted coup d'etats. He decided to strike first. He announced that a repetition of the 1933 Royalist coup was being prepared, in secret, and certainly there was. But he did not, as Prajadhipok had in 1932, wait until the evidence was ready. He arrested everyone who might possibly prove hostile; he worked on the principle that he who is not with me is against me. The army was purged, and a number of high noblemen were huddled into the common jail — among them was the distinguished and highly reputable Prince Rangsit, whose house had for many years been a center of cultural activity. Rangsit was the son of one of Chulalongkorn's minor wives, but as his mother had died young, he was brought up by Queen Sawang. He was a member of the innermost circle of the royal circle and Prince Mahidol was a close friend of his. He was universally respected. He had never taken the slightest interest in politics. But Pibul was not running any risks. Rangsit was the kind of man whom a Royalist coup d'etat might raise to prominence. Best be on the safe side. Bangkok was outraged by the news of his arrest. After a token trial he was condemned to death. A number of the prisoners were shot, but Rangsit was among those whose sentence was transmuted to life imprisonment. He was eventually released, and the fact that he was subsequently appointed regent is proof enough that he was innocent. But it is doubtful if even then Pibul considered he had made a mistake. The wise man removes from his path anyone who is capable of becoming a danger if circumstances move a certain way.

It would have been surprising if Pibul did not welcome the outbreak of the European war. Siam declared its neutrality at once, and neutrals usually find wars profitable; an opportunity might well arise of coming in on the winning side and earning a seat at the peace table. As a start towards the new dispensation, the name of Siam was changed to that of Thailand to signalize the surgence of the new voice of freedom. But Pibul's regime was basically fascist. Not much was left of the democratic program with which Pridi had inspired his followers in Left Bank cafés.

Pridi during this time appears to have been content with his secondary position as minister of finance. He had elevated the law school to the dignity of a university — it was known as UMPS (University of Moral and Political Sciences) to which Pibul had retorted by getting himself made dean of the Chulalongkorn University. He was still the mentor to the young intellectuals. He had a happy home life, with six children, most of whom did well scholastically, one of them graduating from London's Royal College of Music. He had not made money out of politics. He does not seem to have been interested in money and often forgot to collect his monthly salary: his wife retorted by serving him indifferent meals. He liked social informality, with friends dropping in on him for a meal and himself preparing it from recipes that he had learned in France. He was in no sense the conventional careerist. He avoided official functions. He never asked himself, "Will it do me good to be seen there?" He was friendly; acquaintances relaxed in his company, but he maintained a reserve. He evaded intimacy.

Rayne Kruger writes of him: "It was this inaccessibility, more than his remarkably luminous eyes or the brilliance of a mind as lucidly expressive in French and English as Siamese, that accounted for the magnetism of his personality." His opponents spoke of him as being devious, stealthily ambitious. But if they were right in thinking that, they must have added that he lacked the sense of timing that is so essential to achievement;

[198]

without which in fact nothing substantial can be achieved. Either Pridi played his cards badly, or he had no basic strategic plan. He was a day-to-day tactician, once he had carried through his first revolutionary campaign. Pibul may have been somewhat jealous of Pridi's popularity with the intellectuals, but the two were not really, so far at any rate, in competition with one another. They wanted different things in life and out of life. And Pridi was essential to the things that Pibul wanted. Pibul wanted power and he wanted money. He needed Pridi's financial wizardry. He needed money for Siam's armaments. Siam must not be unprepared if war reached Southeast Asia. He also needed money for himself.

Pridi at the start of his marriage had been content with a small house in his parents' compound. Later his parents gave him a piece of land on which he built a house; he sold his law books to meet construction costs. That would not have been enough for Pibul. As prime minister he was palatially installed officially. But in addition he had in his large compound near the British embassy three double-storied houses, one for his children, one for his wife, a small one in the middle for himself. He was seemingly a good family man. His sons were devoted to him. His house was furnished expensively but not flamboyantly. Here with the tide running for him, he waited for the moment to arrive.

It came in June of 1940 with France reeling in defeat under the onslaught of Hitler's panzer divisions. Was not this the time to recover those portions of Cambodia and Laos that the French had filched from Thailand? In their hearts the Thais had never ceased to believe that they were entitled to a sovereignty over those lost provinces. And indeed they have as much right to them as France has to Alsace-Lorraine.

The visitor by air to Bangkok today on the way in from Don Muang airport will be confronted by an impressive obelisk set about, high on its base, by four bronze statues of men-at-arms. It is, he will be informed, the monument of Victory and it contains the ashes of those who fell in battle during the Indo-China war. It cannot contain many ashes. The French were in no mood for fighting; moreover the Japanese insisted on acting as mediators. The French were in no position to oppose them. The Thais were awarded a considerable slice of Cambodia; by an ordinance of self-promotion Pibul was raised to the dignity of field marshal, and the pavements of Bangkok accorded to him and his troops their equivalent of a Roman triumph. But he who sups with the devil must needs have a long spoon. The Japanese expected a *douceur*. Pridi foresaw the danger. Pibul had again proclaimed Thailand's neutrality, reminding the world that a million men were under arms and ready to defend it. But that to Pridi was not enough. Could not the premier go further? Could he not enact a law that every Thai, whether at home or overseas, was beholden to defend his country to the death? Pibul was not prepared to argue a case like that. When the time came, he could bow his head to whichever wind was blowing.

He had to exercise his agility sooner than he had expected. On the night of December 7 the Japanese ambassador called on the Thai foreign minister. He requested permission for Japanese troops to pass through Thailand on their way to attack Burma and Malaya; an answer was required by 1 A.M. next morning. Pibul acted prudently. He absented himself. The foreign minister sought for the next senior minister, who was Pridi. Pridi was less prudent. He refused. Next day Pibul reappeared upon the scene, to countermand Pridi's orders, and though fighting continued in the south and the Thais suffered severe losses, Bangkok was entered without the firing of a shot.

It was here, probably, that the coalition between Pridi and Pibul ended. They realized from henceforth that they were on opposite sides of the tracks. Yet there is little doubt that Pibul's decision was the wise one. Opposition could only have brought untold misery to the Thais, and in actual fact the British residents should have felt grateful to Pibul for his submission. They had a far less uncomfortable time as Siamese prisoners than they would have had working, as the residents of Malaya did, on the railroad on Japanese rations, prodded by Japanese bayonets. The Siamese did all they could to make their lot easier; they smuggled in to them the local rice-whiskey-mekong, and visits from girl friends were not prohibited. It may be presumed that the Thais received in exchange checks made out in sterling, which were eventually cashed to their considerable advantage. The Japanese not unnaturally behaved with courtesy, forbearance and sympathy towards their Asian cousins. They were their allies after all, for they had insisted on Siam declaring war against the United States and Great Britain.

As regards the British this allowed the Thais to confiscate a good deal of British property, and there was probably a certain amount of United States property in Thailand, though not a great deal as the country was not then in the American sphere of influence. But in the United States itself Siam's declaration of war was a fiasco, for the simple reason that the state department never received official notice. The Thai minister in Washington happened at that time to be Seni Pramoj, a descendant of Rama II's sixty-first child, a graduate of Oxford University, where he had won as a lawyer the Birkenhead Prize, a man of letters, and at this current time of writing (March 1969) active in Bangkok politics as the leader of the democratic opposition party. Seni simply ignored Bangkok's instructions to declare war on the United States of America. He put the document in a drawer in his desk and locked it, so that officially Siam was not at war with the United States at all — and though when the United States air force had to undertake an air raid against Japanese lines of communication Thailand was not regarded as a neutral, when the war was over it was far simpler for the Americans than it was for the British to resume normal relations with the Thais. In actual fact there was not a great deal of bombing over Thailand. There was not much point in it as the bombs so often dropped in the canals and did no damage. One Thai friend of mine who was then at college told me that she was evacuated from her home in the center of town, to a house built on one of the klongs. She described it as having been a wonderful picnic. She loved splashing about in the water, taking her morning and evening baths in it and cooking on her verandah. It was not surprising, she concluded, that the Thais were such a happy people. The peasantry led a wonderful life on their canals, so gay, so free, so healthy. How different from the city slums of Europe and the United States.

On the whole Bangkok continued its customary life undisturbed during the three and a half years of war. A great many Thais made a great deal of money trading with the Japanese, and the money with which they were paid was never recalled. Large fortunes vanished from public scrutiny. The Thais usually manage to enjoy themselves. In later years Pibul described himself as having been an active member of the resistance movement, but on the surface certainly he filled amply the role that was played so ignominiously by the Norwegian Quisling. He collaborated intensively. The Japanese did not approve of the Asian appearance of their new allies. They pleaded for Westernization. They found Pibul most cooperative. Orders were issued that women should wear gloves, hats and stockings. The Japanese disliked the black teeth that the women acquired through chewing betel nut. Pibul ordered the habit to be discontinued and to ensure that it was, he had all the betel nut trees cut down. This caused considerable anguish to his mother

Air view of life on the river. The Krung Kasem pottery market is in the
lower left foreground

but he was not deterred. The Japanese did not consider that the Thais showed sufficient respect to their wives, and it was decreed that when a man left his house in the morning and returned to it at night, he should bestow a kiss upon her cheek. It was additionally ordered that a tribute should be paid to one's patriotic instincts by the performance of traditional dances at evening parties. Inevitably in wartime, in an Asian country, martial law was in operation; but the National Assembly still held meetings. A newspaper in the English language continued to appear. It was managed by the Japanese. Its slogan ran "One country — Thailand; one leader — Pibul; one aim — Victory." Pibul was delighted with his own success. He remembered how General Taksin, a wartime leader, had been made a king. Why should not under the stress of war a field marshal rise to the same heights? The Japanese did not, however, see eye to eye with him. They had a built-in regard for the divinity of kingship. They did not see Pibul as regal timber. They probably had no great respect for him. He was someone who was useful to them for the moment: to be discarded later when his period of usefulness was over.

That was Pibul's position in 1942. Pridi's was very different. When Pibul had made an alliance with the Japanese in the sacred palace of the Emerald Buddha, Pridi had resigned from the cabinet. He was prepared to concede that Pibul was justified in allowing the Japanese a free passage to Burma and Malaya, since resistance could not have been effective; the country would have been devastated. But to become an ally of the invader had been too much.

Pibul was reluctant to see him go. He was conscious of his popularity and there was a danger that he might become a center of dissident opinion. But it was not necessary to lose Pridi's cooperation altogether. There was a vacancy on the regency council: why should he not fill that? It would keep him within the circumference of the government.

It was for Pridi, for a little while at any rate, a fortunate appointment. The other regent, Prince Aditya, was an agreeable dilettante who was content to leave all the hard work to his colleagues. Even so Pridi was not overworked; but he was aware of what was going on behind the scenes, and in a very short time it had become important for him to know precisely that, since Seni Pramoj in the United States had not contented himself with locking away Thailand's declaration of war in a desk; he had in addition publicly dissociated himself from the actions of the puppet government in Bangkok. He defended himself on the strength of the law which had demanded that every Thai, whether at home or abroad, must defend his country's independence. In a radio speech delivered in San Francisco, he announced that he would form a Free Thai movement, exactly as the exiled European governments had done. The BBC relayed the speech to the Far East and Pridi heard it. It gave him an idea. Why should he not organize a resistance movement within Thailand itself? His post on the regency council gave him the perfect cover for an underground activity.

For the remainder of the war he devoted himself assiduously to the organization of this underground. How effectively he worked can now never be known, for the war ended before the movement — it was called FTM — could go into action. But preliminary steps had been taken; cells had been formed; volunteers had been recruited; contact had been made with Lord Mountbatten and with the American OSS. And perhaps even more important for Bangkok, an opposition to the Pibul government had been built up.

Pibul was conscious of this opposition. He tried to coerce the Assembly, docile as it was, by converting it into a body composed only of nominated members. Prince Adyiha refused to be coerced; he joined Pridi in his official residence on the west bank of the river, and Pridi's naval friends patrolled the river and prevented Pibul from landing a police force there.

Shortly afterwards the fortunes of war in Europe began to change, and Pibul started to wonder whether he had not backed the wrong horse. He devised a scheme for building a capital in the northwest which he could defend against the Japanese, and which could prove a useful base for the British forces who were campaigning in Burma. This was an exceedingly expensive project and the Japanese became suspicious. Their support of Pibul grew lukewarm. In the meantime many members of the Assembly had become members of FTM. They refused to support the building of the northern capital; not only was it costing a large sum of money, but a very, very great number of indented laborers had died through disease in the process of constructing it. Pibul, outvoted and without the sustenance of Japanese bayonets, was driven to resign.

Pridi was now in control, but he had the good sense not to force his claims. It was in his interest and in Siam's interest that he should stay in the background a little longer. He secured the appointment as premier of Kuang Abhaiwongse, who through his control of the department of posts and telegraphs had been so useful at the time of the 1932 revolution. An entertaining and eccentric creature, he was nicknamed "the great comedian." But he had an astute and practical intelligence. Rayne Kruger tells a number of amusing anecdotes about him. A typical one concerns the discovery by the Japanese of what appeared to them to be a secret airfield. "Nonsense," he said, "we're clearing the field to plant chillies." The moment the Japanese had left, he said to his ADC, "Get busy right away and see that there are chilies planted there."

12

Murder Most Foul

ALL this while in neutral Lausanne, King Ananda was awaiting the summons to return to his own country. He continued his studies under his mother's supervision. In addition to the curriculum, she installed a number of tutors; there was a Greek, who became a substitute for a father. He supervised the boys' nursery games, the toy electric train, the white mice and the canaries; he took them on expeditions, on picnics, he taught them to ski and climb. There were sailing, rowing, swimming; there was also a Swiss music teacher, and an Englishwoman recruited from a young ladies' finishing school next door. Their Siamese studies were not neglected. The equivalent of a doctor of theology taught them Siamese and instructed them in the tenets of the Buddhist faith. The family kept very much to itself. There was an informal atmosphere about the home, but the two boys did not invite their school friends back to it.

The two boys were apparently good friends. They shared with their Greek tutor what they called a "club" which consisted of a large packing case at the bottom of the garden. The boys were reminded of their royalty by the guard which the Swiss government placed night and day outside the house. Just before his eighteenth birthday, Ananda spent six months as a weekly boarder at the Ecole Nouvelle. He was an adequate scholar. From this school he was later transferred to the law school of Lausanne, and here at last there was some breaking away from the tight atmosphere of his family life. He made friends with some of his classmates and now and again he invited them to his home. But he was still closely attached within the narrow limits of his family. How very different a life his father had led in Chulalongkorn's court surrounded by half-brothers and half-sisters.

It is easy to understand why the princess mother should have arranged so confined a life for her children. She had no idea what kind of existence awaited her sons after the war. One day the Japanese ambassador called to make a gift of rice. She did not know whether she should receive him as a friend or not. She decided that it would be diplomatic to receive the gift but she sent it to a hospital. She could not be sure who was going to win the war. If the Axis powers won it, would they want to continue the monarchy? If the Axis lost, how would the Allies treat a country that had signed a treaty with Japan? The Americans claimed to be fighting for the four freedoms. They described China and the Soviet Union as democracies. What would they call Thailand? Would they insist on what they called a free election, which with the people not knowing what they were voting for might well result in the establishment of a republic? It was better surely to move with extreme caution. It might well be that she and her children were destined for a life of exile.

Then in 1945 on a September morning, a few days after the dropping of the bomb on Hiroshima, a cable was delivered by her official secretary. It was signed by Pridi. It reminded the king that on September 20, he would celebrate his twentieth birthday, when he was due to fulfill his royal functions in conducting the government of the state. On that day his own regency would terminate and the king was requested to return to the capital as soon as possible.

A week was to pass before Pridi received an answer. It was a noncommittal one. The king was anxious to serve his country, but he felt that he would be better fitted to do so when he had completed his studies. He had, he explained, passed his first examination at the law school in July. Another more difficult one had to be taken in eighteen months. Then he would need another year to prepare the thesis for his doctorate. He hoped that the government would agree with him. He suggested therefore that he should come out for a short visit, and then return to Lausanne.

It was not quite what Pridi wanted, but it was better than nothing. It was to him most important that the presence of the king should emphasize the ending of Pibul's regime. Pibul was in disgrace and was awaiting trial as a collaborator with the Japanese. The name "Thailand" had been replaced by the former Siam, but the 7th Indian Division was in occupation of the city. It was by no means certain that they would be as cordial as the Japanese had been. Siam was an enemy country after all. Bangkok had been less affected by the war than any capital city that had been exposed to bombing. The people were well-nourished. There was plenty of rice. There was work for anyone who needed it. But there were rumors that an indemnity was to be levied in terms of rice for the benefit of those of the belligerent countries who were actually hungry. Some awkward diplomatic problems lay ahead. It was essential that Siam should present itself to the conquerors as a regenerate nation, ready to play its part in a newborn world. Europe was talking of a federation of its separate nations, why should not there be a similar federation of Southeast Asia, with Siam as the locking pin. Moreover Pridi wanted to liberalize the 1932 constitution. The king's presence was essential.

[209]

A food vendor shows her wares along the Mahanak

Pridi's second cable was more insistent. He agreed that the king should continue his studies, but for many reasons it was in the national interest for the king, as had been graciously suggested, to return for a short visit. Certain fundamental issues had to be resolved and he listed the constitutional changes that were proposed: changes that could not be decided without "His Majesty's participation and consent." He added that he hoped to arrange with the British to have an aircraft placed at His Majesty's disposal. He ardently hoped that His Majesty would accede to his invitation.

Ananda could hold out no longer. He accepted but the princess mother's secretary added to the cable of acceptance the proviso that he should leave in the beginning of December and return in the first week of January.

It was not by the great comedian that the king was welcomed but by Seni Pramoj who had returned from Washington as a hero for his work with the FTM. He stood in well with both the Americans and the British, and he was admirably fitted to negotiate a peace treaty with the British. It was not to prove a simple task, and Pridi was irritated with the delays that were involved, even though the treaty was signed as early as the first of January. It was a taut nervous period and during it, the chief figures of the resistance movement were to quarrel among themselves; enmities were to arise between Seni Pramoj, Pridi and the great comedian. First Seni Pramoj resigned the premiership, then the great comedian did. Finally Pridi took it on himself. In retrospect it may seem surprising that he did so, in view of the misfortunes that the premiership was to bring him; he was a man who had always preferred to work in the background, but he was desperately anxious about the new constitution, whose passing had been his chief ambition ever since he had argued into the night in those Left Bank cafés. He did not believe that anyone but himself could navigate its passage through the Assembly. So high a store did he set by this that he persuaded Ananda to prolong his stay until he could place his seal on it.

Behind the scenes there was a considerable measure of dissension, but there were none of the reprisals that were to disfigure the days of liberation in so many other cities. The political prisoners were released but no action was taken against Pibul. The courts decreed that it was illegal to take retrospective action against war criminals and war crimes — a distinction that the Nuremberg War Crimes Tribunal did not accept, and the field marshal retired for the time being into private life: it may be presumed however that he had put aside ample funds to meet just such a contingency. He knew that he had only to await his opportunity. He was not yet fifty. He had plenty of time. Had he been in Pridi's place, he would not have left himself at liberty.

The leaders were quarreling among themselves, but for the city it was a time of high festivity. The war was over. The Japanese had gone; the British and American troops were spending a lot of money, and — what mattered most of all — there was a king in the Grand Palace, in the Barompiman Hall.

Ananda exhibited himself during those months as much as possible. He was subjected to a fixed routine. He would get up at around half past eight, which was late for a man living in tropical Bangkok but would have seemed unreasonably early to his grandfather and his great grandfather. He breakfasted with his brother and his mother, then the official routine started. He would go over state business with his secretary. Then he would study with a lay priest the Siamese language and points of Buddhist doctrine. A little later he would grant audiences to his ministers. Before lunch he would read or write letters or maybe drive a car round the palace grounds. He would lunch at half past twelve with his mother and his brother. Sometimes he would be joined by a relative or a minister. He would rest a while; then a further study of Buddhism or a reception of officials, until it was time for tea — quite often held in the Tortoise Garden. In the late afternoon he might visit his grandmother. He might take exercise of some kind with his brother. Dinner would be at seven. Afterwards there might be visits from a friend or relatives; there might be music, or a film or play. There might be a strolling through the palace grounds; the evening would end early, as evenings tend to do in the tropics. At about ten thirty Ananda would pay a final goodnight visit to his mother in her quarters. One is forced to reflect how much more fun the royal family had in the days of the harem, when Mongkut and Chulalongkorn really enjoyed playing with their children and they with him.

That of course was only the pattern for an average day. There were festal occasions; there was Lord Mountbatten's visit, which lasted for three days. There was a state ball and there were endless ceremonies at which, so the *London Times* reported, "The king displayed great poise, impressing those he met with his intelligence, sincerity and wide reading." He made a number of trips into the country. Every route was crowded. The people would wait for hours in the dusty ditches to proffer their poor gifts of flowers. Pridi and Pibul, Pramoj and the great comedian were not even names to them. This was their King, who brought the rain on which their livelihood depended. He smiled at them and they were happy, reassured in their beliefs. He paid his respects to all the chief monasteries; he paid his tribute to the many Buddhas. He visited government activities, factories and colleges, he endeavored to show appropriate interest. He can have been in no doubt whatsoever that his people loved him. Occasionally at night he made incognito trips about the city; sometimes he was accompanied by Pridi.

He had aimed to return to Switzerland at the beginning of

January, but it was not till the middle of June that the political situation had become sufficiently smoothed out for him to book his passage back to Switzerland. The day chosen was the thirteenth of June. This to a European would have seemed an ill-omened date, but the royal astrologer was consulted. He approved the choice. Public interest in the departure was heightened by the invitations from the American and British governments for a state visit to their countries before the king resumed his studies.

His final days in Bangkok were fully occupied. On June 3 he visited the Chinese quarter of the city, a garish section lit with neon lights, with vast advertisements in front of cinemas, with crowded shops. The Chinese, who were never quite sure of the extent to which they belonged in Bangkok, were hysterical in their enthusiasm. On the sixth of June the annual Oxford and Cambridge dinner was held in one of the royal palaces. A great many Thais have been educated at those two premier universities. I attended the dinner in 1958. It was a very lighthearted occasion when the health of each university was proposed by a member from the rival fount of learning. I shall always remember the speech in praise of Oxford, by the Cantab, that highly gifted poet and controversialist, D. J. Enright. "There," he said, "are your young barbarians all at sea."

On the following evening the king interviewed Pridi. By the new constitution a senate had been created. Pridi's followers had a majority in both houses, but under the constitution Pridi had to resign and secure the approval of both houses. Then the king would invite him to renew his premiership. The signing of the royal proclamation of Pridi's reappointment took place during this meeting. There was also a discussion of the regency during the king's absence abroad. Pridi was in favor of Prajadhipok's widow, but the king preferred his uncle, Prince Rangsit, who had recently been released from prison. It was to be suggested later that this discussion had become an argument.

Next day the king felt ill. He let his brother fulfill the two public functions that were entered in his diary. He experienced waves of nausea; and he was slightly feverish. In the late afternoon the princess mother had a doctor sent for. Ananda's health had never been robust. He often had fits of indigestion. The doctor prescribed both a sleeping pill and one that would lower his temperature. He also ordered an enema. In the morning he must take a dose of castor oil. After the page who was on night duty had prepared him for the night, the queen mother brought him his sleeping pill. He had a bell beside him that he could ring if he wanted anything.

The sequence of events next morning was to be established later in the course of a long investigation. At 6 A.M. the princess mother went to see her son. He was asleep and she had to rouse him. He told her that he had slept well. She gave him the prescribed dose of castor oil and brandy, and afterwards a glass of hot milk. The king rose to brush his teeth, then went back to sleep. At five minutes to seven the two pages, Nai Chit and Butr, began to set out breakfast on the porch. June is one of the worst months climatically. The temperature had scarcely dropped below 80° during the night. The city had already begun its crowded daily life. The streets were noisy with honking car horns. The monks were carrying their begging bowls. In the palace the screen door that opened onto Ananda's dressing room had been left open, so that the page on duty could see when the king woke up. This usually was between eight and eight thirty. He would then go to the bathroom and the page would take him a glass of orange juice and the morning papers. On this morning, as on every other one, Butr made his preparations for the moment when his master woke. At eight the newspapers were brought, and a little later one of the staff brought a book on the royal page service which Ananda had asked for on the previous evening. At about eight thirty Butr, who had been waiting in the corridor, looked into the dressing room and saw the king standing there. The king saw Butr but said nothing. He then went towards his bedroom. Butr followed him with the glass of orange juice. He paused in the doorway. Ananda was lying in his bed with his knees drawn up. He waved Butr away. Butr took up his position in the corridor outside the dressing room.

A quarter of an hour later the other page, Nai Chit, arrived. He was not due to take over from Butr for another two hours, but a box was being made for the royal jewels and he wanted to take their measurements. They were kept in a safe in Ananda's dressing room. Butr explained to him that the king had refused his orange juice and gone back to bed. Nai Chit, not wishing to disturb the king, waited with Butr outside the dressing room.

A little later Prince Bhumibol, who had finished his breakfast, came down the corridor. He asked how his brother was. He was told that everything appeared to be in order, that the king had been to the bathroom, and had gone back to bed without taking his orange juice. The prince went back to his own bedroom. There was silence in the palace; then at about 9:20 the explosion of a shot rang out, and the king was found lying on his back, his legs straight, his arms outside the coverlet, a pistol an inch or two from his left hand and blood trickling from his forehead. A calamity such as this would cause instantaneous panic in any country and at any time. The panic was intensified in the royal palace by the fact that the disaster had befallen a king, and in a country where royalty had been for so long considered sacrosanct. The police chief was for example prevented by Prince Rangsit from examining Ananda's body. Royalty must not be touched by a policeman. It must be remembered that Prince Rangsit's half-sister and his aunt had been drowned, because it would have been improper for the boatmen, who were commoners, to pull them from the water.

An examination of the premises and the staff left the police in no doubt that the king had committed suicide. It would have been impossible for an assassin to have got into the king's bedroom without being seen. The revolver that lay beside the king was fully loaded except for one missing round; a spent cartridge was found upon the floor. The ministers and princes who assembled on the ground floor had no doubt about what had happened, but they were profoundly puzzled as to what the public should be told. The dignity of the throne had to be maintained. Suicide was disgraceful to a Buddhist. It was inconceivable that a king — the incarnation of Vishnu — could perform such an act of sacrilege. On this point Prince Rangsit was insistent. An explanation had to be given to the people. Was there any alternative to a verdict of death by accident?

A communiqué was prepared and read over the radio in the late afternoon. It explained that the king had been suffering for a week from an intestinal complaint which had considerably weakened him. He had not in consequence been able on the eighth of June to attend the royal ceremonies that had been scheduled for him. On the morning of the ninth he had risen at six, taken a dose of castor oil, performed the details of his toilet, then returned to bed. At about nine a shot was heard, and the royal pages found the king lying dead on his bed, covered with blood. Police and medical experts had concluded that the king must have played with his pistol as he was fond of doing; and there had been an accident.

None of the ministers who prepared this communiqué believed it to be true, but they considered that it gave the public a practical presentation of what the facts should have been.

There remained the immemorial ceremonies to be performed. It is the Siamese belief that though the physical body is dead, the astral body remains alive and present for forty-nine more days. The funeral of any Thai is a lengthy business. For royalty the procedure is fantastically ritualistic. First of all the thigh of the corpse has to be injected with preservative. Then follows the ritual bathing.

On the evening of June 9 Pridi had brought the news that a special meeting of the Assembly had instructed him to invite Bhumibol to be the king. Bhumibol accepted. He promised to do his best to lead Siam to a glorious future, and his first duty as king was to preside over this ritual bathing; scented water which had been blessed by the monks and kept in crystal vessels was poured over Ananda's feet. A selected group from that selected body of pages who were allowed to touch the king, draped him in the rich robes that he was to have worn at his coronation. Then he was arranged into a silver urn: seated upright with his legs crossed and pressed close to his body, his hands which held incense sticks and a candle were clasped together, as though in prayer. He was wrapped with white cloth as though he were a mummy. It was a tight fit. The procedure was watched by Bhumibol who put a crown upon his head. The lid of the urn which followed the contoured spine of the crown was locked.

This silver urn was then borne on a palanquin to the Dusit Hall, where it was enclosed in the eight-sectioned golden urn that had been built by Rama I. The white umbrella with its nine silk bands of diminishing circumference was set above it. Now started the official ceremony of the hundred days. The new king spent an hour there each evening. In the morning the monks who had been chanting through the night were fed by princes. The public filed past in the afternoon. There were elaborate ceremonies on the seventh, fiftieth and hundredth days. But although the hundred days were eventually accomplished, there was no talk yet of the cremation. Indeed four years were to pass before Ananda was taken from his golden urn and a great, great deal was to happen during them. The whole direction of the country was to be rerouted by that single shot that was fired on the morning of the ninth of June.

13

The King's Death Case

THE trouble about a lie is that it has loopholes; and the lie that had been issued as a communiqué was pitiably threadbare. There were too many witnesses; too many people who could be asked "Tell me now, what really happened?" There were rumors, there were whispers: Bangkok was dazed, and it was indignant. Was it really true that the king's finger had slipped while he was playing with his revolver? Was that likely? The war was less than a year old. The suspicions and enmities that it had aroused were not yet lulled. The recent political rivalries were still raw. Then suddenly, startlingly, these rumors were confirmed by the doctors and nurses from Chulalongkorn University who had embalmed the body. They had found in the back of the head a hole smaller than that in the forehead. They believed that a bullet makes a greater hole when it leaves a body than when it enters it: from this they deduced that the king had been shot from behind. It was neither suicide nor an accident. It was murder.

The doctors were in point of fact entirely mistaken in believing that a bullet always makes a larger hole at the point of exit than of entry, and in order to prove this, the king's own physician made an experiment with four pigs whom he shot in the compound of police headquarters. These shootings convinced the police that the bullet had entered by the forehead. To substantiate this contention the bullet was later found embedded in the mattress. But once the theory of murder had been started, it was not easily stopped. The assassin had shot the king not from behind but from in front. Who was the murderer?

Bangkok was indignant. Why had nobody been arrested? The police issued another communiqué to the effect that their investigations had found nothing to suggest that there was an alternative to accident. Bangkok was not satisfied. What was Pridi doing? He as prime minister was responsible for the king's safety. Through his carelessness the king had been betrayed. Was not Pridi therefore responsible for the king's death? Maybe he had instigated it himself. Why not? Had he not been in disagreement with the king only a few hours before on the issue of the regency. Rumors multiplied. In a cinema a voice shouted from the darkness: "Pridi killed the king." There was a spate of anonymous telephone calls to embassies and to high officials.

In self-defense Pridi set up a commission of inquiry. He hoped that it would produce a verdict of death by accident. But this it failed to do because of the nature of the pistol that had fired the shot. It was an American .45, which was a very heavy weapon; it was nine inches in length and it weighed nearly three pounds. The bullets were an inch long. It is very powerful. It has a tremendous kick. The safety catch consists of a small panel at the back of the butt, which has to be pressed at the same time that the trigger is pulled. A very strong handhold is required to fire the weapon. It is not in fact the kind of weapon that could be fired by mistake. It is most unlikely that as the police tried to show at the inquiry, the king when playing with it in his bed had let the weapon fall and, grabbing at it, had pressed the trigger and the safety catch simultaneously;

and even if he had, it is scarcely possible that he could have done this at a moment when the barrel was pointing at his head or heart. The betting against this was so great that there was no possibility of doubting that the revolver was pointed at the king's head and the trigger deliberately pulled. It was either suicide or murder. And there was a universal and obstinate reluctance to believe that the king had committed suicide.

Before the commission of enquiry had issued its verdict, a general election had shown that the people as a whole warmly supported Pridi. His party won fifty-seven seats, the Democrats eleven and the Independents seven. Pridi considered that he could now retire from the arena and take up the role of senior statesman, while his friend Admiral Dhamrong formed a new government. He said to Edwin Stanton, who became United States ambassador in June, "It is terrible to have people always whispering against me. I am very tired." He was relying on a verdict of death by accident. The new constitution had been passed. He had done what he had set out to do. Now he wanted peace. But the verdict of the commission precluded the possibility of that. Particularly as the commission had complained that it had been hampered by not knowing whether the police had produced all the evidence. It insisted that it had not done more than carry out a preliminary examination. It reported its doubts "for the benefit of further investigation to find out the truth." The government had only one possible course open, to order a further examination.

This it did; but it was not until December 7 that it did; and it was not until the following June that the police set up an internal committee under a senior officer. And by November no real progress had been made. The dilatory behavior of the police unquestionably intensified the atmosphere of suspicion. If the government had nothing to hide why were they not trying to clean up the mystery of what had come to be known as "The

Small skiffs are a common form of river transportation for one or two persons. The larger boats such as the tourist boat in the background supply mass transit across the Chao Phya River in Bangkok

King's Death Case"? Suspicion of Pridi mounted. Certain awkward questions remained unanswered. There was a Lieutenant Vacharachai who had been ADC to Ananda. The king had sacked him, but he had been made secretary first to Pridi then to Admiral Dhamrong. Then there was the king's secretary in Lausanne, Chaleo, whom the queen had not liked: who had shown disrespect to the throne, who had crossed his legs in the royal presence which had meant the pointing of his toe, a heinous solecism. Had he resigned from the royal service or had he been sacked? Anyhow Pridi had got him into the senate. Then there were the two pages; why had they not been arrested? How could the murderer have entered the king's bedroom without their connivance?

These rumors and counterrumors spread at a time when many were alarmed about the economic condition of the country. The British troops had left and there was no outside impartial authority in control. Asia was hungry; rice was plentiful in Siam. Rice was controlled, but it could be smuggled if the right official received an appropriate *douceur*. A number of men in the government had become rich suddenly. To F. M. Pibul waiting in the wings the moment seemed propitious for a return to public life. In March 1947 he announced that he would lead the "might is right" party, which was composed mainly of military and right wing extremists. He did not however obtain a great deal of support, and Pridi's followers were divided among themselves — Pridi had not the complete support of Seni Pramoj and the great comedian. Moreover Pibul was a very able soldier.

Pridi still lived in his official residence, on the river near to the Grand Palace. On the night of November 7, 1947, he was visited by the prime minister and the chiefs of the armed services and police; he had heard rumors that the army was planning a coup d'etat. Had the proper precautions been taken? He was assured they had been. There was no cause for worry. Admiral Dhamrong was going to a ball. He was already a little late. Might he be excused? Pridi's guests departed. Pridi sat on a low wall by the river, his mind cozily abroad. Abruptly his peace of mind was shattered by the telephone. An urgent personal call. The coup had started. Soldiers were on their way to kill or capture him. When he was still talking on the telephone, tanks were in the roadway. Shots were fired. Axes crashed into woodwork; but by the time the soldiers broke into the house, Pridi had leaped into a sampan and vanished into the far darkness of the river.

Admiral Dhamrong also had been warned. The soldiers who broke into a ballroom found that he had escaped by the back door. All night long the search for the prime minister and the elder statesmen continued through the canals and back streets. Dawn found them still at liberty.

At that moment Pibul was being carried shoulder-high into the ministry of defense. Later Pibul was to deny that he had planned the coup. It was the head of the air force, the commander of the Bangkok garrison — and his son-in-law Police General Pao — who were responsible. But whether or not that was true was immaterial. Pibul was back in power, and the staffwork of the coup had been planned and executed as meticulously as had fifteen years earlier the coup that had surprised King Prajadhipok on his golf course at Hua Hin — "Far from Worries." We may assume that the same hand planned them both.

Pibul had his program ready. The purpose of the coup, he announced, was to clear up the mystery of the King's Death Case. He proposed to Prince Rangsit a new constitution far less liberal than Pridi's. Prince Rangsit can have had no feelings of warmth for the field marshal since it was under Pibul's administration that he had been put in prison on no evidence at all. But he can have had no feelings of warmth for Pridi either, since it was Pridi who had overthrown the power of the royal princes and only very recently had opposed the king's choice of himself as regent, so he signed the document. He pointed out, however, that it was very certain that the Western powers would not recognize an army-inspired revolution. The performance had to be given an appearance of legality. Pibul had his answer ready. He sent for Luang and Seni Pramoj and invited them to form a government. Only three years ago they had been Pibul's bitterest enemies; they had also been Pridi's closest friends. But the whirligig of politics had brought them into different camps. They did not relish serving under Pibul, but it might be better for the country if they, rather than a couple of less competent newcomers, took their portfolios. They could act as a brake upon the wheel. They accepted what seemed to them the lesser of two evils, and certainly Seni Pramoj has "lived to fight another day." At the time of writing, he is the chief spokesman, almost the only spokesman, for the ideals that he held as a young intellectual.

In the meantime the search for Pridi was actively pursued. To justify the coup he was now openly named as the chief conspirator in Ananda's murder. Only a very few people knew where he was. Admiral Dhamrong had after a night-long drive through the alleys of the city, presented himself just after daybreak at the British embassy. The ambassador, Sir Geoffrey Thompson, who had greatly endeared himself both to the British and the Iraqis during his period as councillor in the embassy at Baghdad, offered him asylum but the admiral, with courtly tact, after shaving and breakfasting, escaped again, this time crouched behind the front seat of a car.

During subsequent days along with such of Pridi's followers as had not yet been captured, he plotted a counter-coup. They relied entirely upon Pridi. They were aware that he was with the navy; they knew that Pridi had many sound friends in the navy as a result of his days with the Free Thai movement; the navy had always kept apart from the army's escapades. The navy might have helped them; but neither the navy nor Pridi wanted to involve the country in civil war. This reluctance to shed blood is a distinctive feature of Bangkok's life. A coup is attempted; if it does not succeed at once it is abandoned. If it succeeds during the first attempt, no counter-coup takes place. There has really only been fighting once, during the royalist coup of 1933, when troops were marched in from the provinces and a pitched battle was fought. The Thais are practicing Buddhists. This fact is confirmed at every point of their history. It is one of the very many reasons why as a race they are so beloved by *farangs*.

Pridi was not prepared to sacrifice his countrymen for his own aggrandizement, and in that connection it has to be noticed that Pibul in spite of his vituperative arrests, did not shed blood. Pridi decided that he was doing the navy no good service by remaining with them. He could only be an embarrassment to them. He had clearly to leave the country.

His leaving of it is as dramatic as any incident during that nerve-tossed time. On November 19 the British naval attaché was awakened at 6 A.M. by a Siamese naval officer who said "Ruth is here." The attaché, Captain Stratford Dennis, remembered that "Ruth" had been the code name for Pridi's Free Thai movement. Dennis, a man of fifty, a Cantab — a graduate of St. John's — who had ridden five times in the Grand National, was tough in the way that Rodney, Nelson, Drake were tough. War services had brought him three D.S.C.'s, the Polish Cross of Valor, five mentions in dispatches. He was a Jutland veteran and a commando man. When the Japanese surrendered, he was in Delhi, SEAC's deputy head of combined operations, and it was in this capacity that he had come to Bangkok, to disarm the

Japanese and reform the Siamese navy. He had looked on Pridi, the head of the resistance, as his likeliest ally.

The car that called at Dennis's house in the early morning contained six ruffianly looking figures, armed with bombs and submachine guns. One of them Dennis recognized as Lieutenant Vacharachai, but it took him a little while to acknowledge as his old comrade in arms a heavily moustached man with a big cap, thick spectacles and sunken cheeks. Pridi was not only exhausted by a two-hundred-mile drive over bad roads, but he had further disguised himself by putting his teeth in his pocket.

Once he had identified himself, however, he realized that he was in good hands. Dennis went straight to the British ambassador. Sir Geoffrey acted promptly. He telephoned the United States ambassador, Edwin Stanton, who was later to provide a valuable commentary on the situation in his book *Brief Authority*. Stanton was as ready as Thompson to help a wartime comrade. Neither of them considered it conceivable that Pridi could have plotted against the king. The American naval attaché was summoned; so was the Shell Company's local chief who as a prisoner of war had worked on the Burma Railroad and cherished no warm feelings for Pibul, the collaborator. The oil man was able to inform their excellencies that a tanker bound for Singapore was at the mouth of the Menam, waiting for the tide. While plans to get Pridi upon this tanker were being prepared, one of Pibul's princely supporters presented himself at the door. He had heard rumors, he explained, that Pridi was in Bangkok planning to escape by river. Could Dennis confirm these rumors? Yes, Dennis could. He had heard on excellent authority that Pridi was planning to leave for his home in Ayudhya from a jetty on the other side of the city. A search along this false trail gave Pridi the time he needed.

It was to prove a hazardous journey. Dennis drove a jeep; beside him was the Siamese naval officer who had driven Pridi to his house that morning. The remainder of the party followed in a saloon. They were stopped at several barricades, but the sentries had been given instructions to avoid clashes with the navy, so they allowed the European officer with his Siamese naval escort to pass unquestioned and unsearched. At the main docks a launch was waiting. It belonged to "Skeats" Gardas, the American naval attaché. It was an ex-submarine chaser with twin propellers. Gardas had taken the precaution of giving his Siamese crew a holiday. He and his nineteen-year-old sister would conduct the operation. Pridi and his companions were put on board and with the Stars and Stripes flying, the launch set out on its twenty-mile journey down the river.

Dennis and the oil man returned to the British embassy. No sooner had they arrived than the United States military attaché rang up to report that there appeared to be an ominous measure of military activity around the embassy. He had no arms. Could Dennis help him? Dennis could. He conveyed to him in diplomatic bags the arsenal that Pridi had left behind. They were not needed but the Americans were glad to have them.

There was nothing now for Dennis to do but wait. It was a long, slow-passing afternoon. At last at 6 P.M. a telephone message came through from the master of the tanker that "after a short stop due to engine trouble the vessel was running smoothly." This was the prearranged code signal to indicate success. Paradoxically enough, no sooner had Gardas delivered his passengers than he did have real engine trouble, ran into a sandbank and did not return till the following morning. It was a question of minutes. Had the engine trouble developed a little earlier, the tanker would have sailed without its controversial cargo.

The behavior of the two ambassadors was not conventionally diplomatic, but Ernest Bevin, Britain's foreign secretary, cabled his approval, and Thompson with Stanton's agreement wrote a letter to the great comedian, explaining that the two of them could not resist the appeal for assistance from a wartime comrade. They also expressed the hope that Pridi's absence would facilitate the restoration of law and order.

But though Britain had condoned the action of its representative, there was no doubt that Pridi's presence in British territory was awkward, while the King's Death Case was still under review. Unable to stay on in Singapore, he left for China. Before he did so he wrote to Britain's special commissioner in Southeast Asia: "I hereby deny that I was in any way implicated in the death of his late Majesty King Ananda, which I most sincerely deplore. I further declare that to the best of my knowledge and belief no member of my present entourage was implicated in that unhappy event." It was now up to Pibul to prove that he was. If that could be established, Pridi could present no threat to the new regime. Pibul set to his task.

Three men had been arrested. The two pages Nai Chit and Butr, and the ex-secretary Chaleo. These were small fry and the real purpose of the trial was to implicate Pridi and Vacharachai.

The trial opened in September 1948. The court met three times a week. It was not until May 1951 that the defense closed its case. During the two and a half years that the trial lasted, 161 witnesses were examined. Finally on September 27 the court met to deliver judgment.

The trial was conducted throughout in a competent, workmanlike way. It was very far from being a fixed trial, such as those that were staged in Russia under Stalin and Germany under Hitler. There was a sincere attempt to get at the truth. At the same time the whole process was confused by the reluctance of either side to admit the possibility of suicide. The court in its judgment dismissed this possibility at the very start.

A traffic tie-up slows progress at the floating market on Klong Puant

It based its decision on the fact that there were traces of rust inside the barrel of the revolver that lay beside Ananda's hand; this was held to prove that the revolver had not been fired for four days before the shooting. Moreover the bullet that was found inside the mattress was not indented as it should have been if it had passed through a human skull. The judge believed that the bullet had been "planted" and that the fatal shot had been fired from a different revolver. Elaborate ballistic experiments were made to establish this contention, but the defense does not seem to have attacked the witnesses with nearly enough vigor on this point. No one wanted to believe that the king had committed suicide. The idea was repugnant to a Buddhist Thai.

The first theory of an accident had been ruled out. There was therefore for the average Thai, no welcome alternative to assassination. The defense concentrated on trying to prove that the three accused men had had no hand in the assassination, and this was a hard task because it would seem impossible for a murderer to have introduced himself into the royal bedroom and escaped after firing the shot without the connivance of one or other of the pages. In a sense the two sides were working with different objectives. While the defense was trying to prove the innocence of the three defendants, the prosecution was trying to establish the existence of a plot in which Pridi and Vacharachai were involved.

The story of the trial is told at length and most dramatically by Rayne Kruger in *The Devil's Discus*. Every detail of the king's last days is examined with minute care. Witness after witness testified to the existence of bad feelings between the king and Pridi. Why, it was asked, should Pridi have promoted Chaleo and Vacharachai after they had left the king's service, unless he hoped that they would further his fell designs? It was reported that Chaleo had conducted himself improperly in the royal presence, that he had once gone as far as to cross his legs. Several witnesses said that they had seen Vacharachai near the palace on the fatal day. One of them testified that there was blood on the sleeve of his coat. There were many who believed that Pridi was guilty in the way that Henry II was of the murder of Thomas à Becket, that he had said, "If only the king were out of the way," and that Vacharachai had taken him at his word. The royalists, it must be remembered, were against Pridi because of his leading part in the coup d'etat that had broken the power of the royal family in 1932. It was also held against him by his detractors that he had proposed in the days of "Mr. Constitution" a communist solution for the country's financial problems.

Rayne Kruger defends very effectively his case for the king's having committed suicide. The king, he argues, was in the mood to do so. He was ill, he was oppressed by the responsibilities that awaited him. He had contracted a fondness for a Swiss girl whom he would never be allowed to marry. Soon he would be seeing her in Switzerland. The meeting could not fail to be unhappy. The revolver at his side offered him an easy exit. That is Kruger's argument but suicide was not a solution that either side was ready to admit. And if suicide was not accepted, there was little chance of the pages whose duty it was to protect the king escaping conviction.

The prosecution made no real attempt to prove how the murder had been committed or by whom. It was only concerned to show that there had been a conspiracy and subsequently an assassination. There was no reason why Pridi should have wanted the king murdered. He had everything to lose and nothing to gain by such a deed. It was very hard to believe that a bullet had been planted in the mattress. It was very hard to see how a murderer could have been introduced into the royal bedroom. It was harder to see how after a shot had been fired the murderer could have been hustled out of the bedroom. But that was irrelevant. There had been a murder: therefore there must have been a murderer. It was as simple as all that. And since that was the way it was, that murderer could not have achieved his purpose without the connivance of one or both of the pages.

The reading of the final judgment took five hours, each judge reading a part of it in turn. The prosecution had asked for a verdict of guilty not only against the three accused but also against Pridi and Lieutenant Vacharachai. The court ruled however that since Pridi and Vacharachai were not being prosecuted and had not been able to defend themselves, it would only consider such evidence relating to them as was essential for decision on the facts at issue. This meant that their names might remain uncleared. As indeed it subsequently transpired.

The judgment had been prepared with the greatest care. It first of all decided that the king had been assassinated, that the revolver found by his bed was not the weapon that had been used, and that the bullet in the mattress had been planted there, as had the cartridge case that had been found on the floor. Since it was the page Nai Chit who had produced the cartridge case and found the bullet, it had to be assumed that he was responsible for the planting. A number of ballistic experts had given their opinion on the issue of the revolver, but it is Rayne Kruger's opinion that those experts would not have been able to maintain their theory in a Western court if cross-examined by a competent counsel. For the court in deciding that the .45 found by Ananda's bed had not been fired on the morning of his death ignored the assertion of accepted Western authorities that it was impossible to fix the date of the discharge of a firearm with any scientific accuracy after the lapse of a few hours. And it was not till three days after Ananda's death that the firearm in question was examined. But the judges accepted the reasoning of their own experts. They were resolved to maintain that there was no question of suicide. In consequence they ruled that the page Nai Chit, who was responsible for the planting of the revolver and the bullet and had tried to create an appearance of suicide, had connived at the murder. He therefore was condemned to death. There seemed however to be no evidence against Butr, the other page. He appeared a rather stupid fellow. The conspiracy would have been limited to as few people as possible: there was no reason why he should have been included. He was therefore acquitted: so was Chaleo against whom no conclusive evidence had been brought. His close association with Pridi was not a proof of guilt.

That however did not end the case. Nai Chit appealed against his conviction and the prosecution appealed against the acquittal of Chaleo and Butr. The evidence given in the trial had to be reviewed. It was not until December 1953 that the appeal court gave its judgment. The reading of this judgment lasted fourteen hours. It decided that Butr must have been privy to the plot. How could the plot have succeeded without his cooperation? It is indeed hard to see how Butr could have been acquitted by the first court. He would surely have interfered at some point. Chaleo, however, was still considered innocent. There were to be further appeals, however, both by the defense and prosecution: this time to the Dika, the highest court in the kingdom. There was a delay of ten months before this court gave its verdict. It was a short verdict. The Dika confirmed the sentence of death that had been passed on the two pages, but this time it included Chaleo. His conduct in the royal service was considered so disrespectful as to have betrayed a treasonable attitude towards the throne. Rayne Kruger comments that "it is unlikely that a judicial tribunal had ever in history sentenced a man to death for sitting with his legs crossed."

On the seventeenth of February 1955 the three men were executed. They had been arrested in November 1947. During all this time Nai Chit, and during most of it Butr and Chaleo, had been kept in prison heavily chained. They had been ceaselessly interrogated, they had been roughly handled, they had been given "truth drugs." But they had, all the time, firmly maintained their innocence.

14

Dictatorship Takes Over

At the end of the First World War when the morale of the French army was low, the military authorities insisted, so it was rumored, on the prolongation of the trial of Landru — the multiple wife murderer — because the daily account of it amused the troops and kept their minds off their dangers and discomforts. And it is probable that on this principle Pibul welcomed the dilatory procedure of the courts because it kept the public entertained and occupied, so that he could concentrate on his own concerns without irksome interference. And actually a great deal was going on in Bangkok during the six and a half years that the three men were in custody. Pibul was not long in making himself a complete dictator.

For a few months, so that the new government should be recognized by the Western powers, he had allowed Kuang, the great comedian, to remain in office; but as soon as he felt that his position was safe, he sent four army officers to call on Kuang and suggest that the time had come for his retirement. Kuang accepted the suggestion. So that within three years of his arrest as a collaborator, Pibul was once more prime minister.

He had the army firmly on his side. The navy was hostile, but he could afford to ignore that, since the general in charge of the police, Pao, was his loyal henchman. Prudently Pibul set about the creation of a police state; within a short time Bangkok could muster one policeman for every hundred and fifty citizens. Pibul was not only head of the government but minister of finance, so that there was no lack of funds for what amounted to a private army. He had good reasons for strengthening the police force. Wars are usually followed by lawlessness, and countries that are occupied by enemy troops are forced to rely on illegality for the necessities of livelihood. In France the pursuance of System D, a black market operation for the outwitting of the Germans, was the conduct of a patriot. The Thais had taken similar advantage of the Japanese. The trouble, however, about a System D is that when it is continued after the war, it throws the economy out of gear.

There was a great deal of smuggling in operation — opium, jewels, rice. Gasoline was reexported. There were illicit factories for cigarettes, morphine, fake pharmaceutical drugs. There were a great many robberies. And at first the public approved of the strict measures that were taken. The extent of the corruption that was practiced was not realized, and it has to be remembered that bribery had always been an essential element of the Thai way of life. A strict censorship was imposed. Newspapers which criticized the government were banned, and their editors beaten up. Siam is basically a rich country; there was enough money to go around. And soon Pibul was given an excuse for exercising further vigilance.

On the night of February 26, 1949, Lady Thompson returned from a concert in a state of high perturbation. A coup was going on, she said. She had been held up for half an hour at a barricade. A marine had pushed a tommy gun through the window and kept her covered throughout the entire delay. During the night there was the sound of firing.

Next morning the ambassador learned what had happened.

Pridi, disguised as a naval warrant officer with a neat moustache, had entered the University of Moral and Political Sciences. Two dozen armed men had joined him. A little later Lieutenant Vacharachai led these men to the Grand Palace, which was only a few yards off. Without much effort they surprised and overpowered the guards. Pridi arrived soon after midnight. Another group captured the radio station in the public relations building and announced over its network that a provisional government had installed a new prime minister who would restore a democratic constitution. Pridi was confident that the navy would now move in to his support.

Unfortunately for him the coup had not been planned with the thoroughness that had marked his and Pibul's plan in 1932. He had not taken the precaution of seizing the leaders of the establishment. Pibul was free and Pibul acted with his customary efficiency and speed. Within a couple of hours he had surrounded the Grand Palace with artillery and tanks. Pridi had expected the navy to intervene before the army could move. It failed to do so. And once again with the traditional reluctance to shed Siamese blood, Pridi decided that he and Vacharachai would be wise to return to China. There were a few skirmishes between soldiers and sailors; there were some casualties; but by ten o'clock next morning the whole affair was over, and Pibul was given an admirable excuse for announcing a state of emergency.

He had previously changed the name of Siam back to Thailand, and he now launched a nationalist campaign. He also posed as the foe of communism. Chiang Kai-chek had recently been flung off the Chinese mainland. And the West in general and the United States in particular were delighted to picture Thailand as the bastion against communism in Southeast Asia. General Pao had now a special riot police force a thousand strong, and anyone hostile to the regime could be conveniently liquidated. In the meantime the public attention could be distracted not only by the drama of the trial, but the return to Bangkok of King Bhumibol with the beautiful eighteen-year-old Sirikit to whom he had become engaged in Switzerland. Bangkok could now indulge to the full its love of pageantry not only with the marriage and coronation of the king, but the cremation of Ananda.

At the end of March 1950 the great golden urn that had been constructed for Rama I was hoisted onto the royal catafalque nearly forty feet high. It was, so Rayne Kruger describes it, "a spired pavilion upon a boat-shaped structure upon wheels, drawn by a hundred marines. Its sides were built up in red and gold ornamental tiers inlaid with green glass mosaic and so richly carved was it with scarlet-tongued dragons and praying angels and geometric designs that, slowly though it moved, the spectators could take in little detail."

At the crematorium, another but larger-spired pavilion was reached by four flights of steps, to which the urn was carried. In the late afternoon the king in the uniform of the Royal Guards mounted the steps and lighted a candle that was placed before the urn. He then descended to listen to a sermon from the prince-patriarch. Then once again he mounted the steps, this time to prostrate himself before his brother's remains. Then he lit the pyre with a taper, a symbolic act; three volleys were fired and the last post was sounded. Members of the royal family and court officials mounted to the dais in their turn. A vast crowd had assembled since dawn to watch the ceremonies. It is not surprising that a people whose daily life was enriched by such pageantry should be indifferent to the vicissitudes of Mr. Constitution.

The cremation was a solemn occasion but it was not a tragic one. To a Buddhist death is not the end. The spirit of Ananda reborn in another body would continue the work that he had

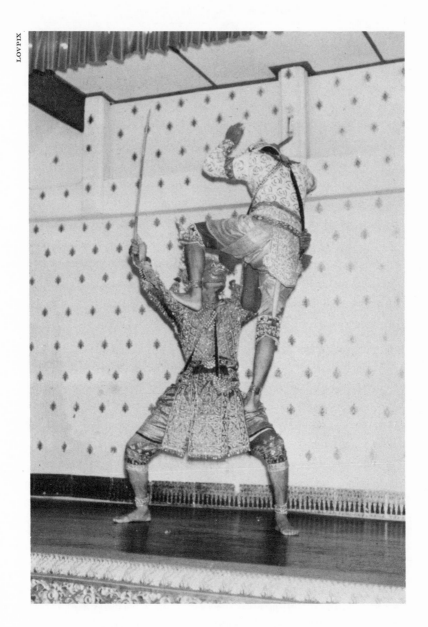

Thai dancers perform the ceremonial sword dance

done in this terrestial manifestation, until after many lives it could achieve perfection and merge in the eternal.

The rites following the cremation lasted for several weeks. Then the people of Bangkok surrendered to the festivities that would attend the coronation and the king's marriage to the exquisite Sirikit who by her beauty, her grace, her charm had quickly endeared herself to the entire nation.

The actual wedding was a private and simple occasion. It always is in Buddhist countries, because perfection cannot be achieved until a human being has rid himself of physical desires. Marriage is not for a Buddhist as it is for a Christian a state of grace. It is rather a recognition of the frailties and imperfections of the human body and the acceptance of a compromise that will permit those frailties and imperfections to be exercised with dignity.

The wedding ceremony in a well-to-do Bangkok family is a very simple matter. In the morning the couple sign the marriage register. The priest comes to the house and blesses it. In the afternoon they receive the elders and their parents' friends. There is a room near the entrance where guests leave presents. The young couple are seated. They lean forward; they rest their elbows on a cushion. They clasp their hands. Roses are arranged under their hands. Each has a crown made out of cord. The crowns are joined. The guests queue up to pour lustral water on the hands of the bride and bridegroom. Each guest on leaving is given a small souvenir, a handkerchief bearing the bridal names or a pencil that opens like an umbrella. Guests sign their names as they go out.

For King Bhumibol and his bride the ceremony was no more elaborate. There was the signing of the marriage register, and the pouring of lustral waters over their hands by the royal grandmother. This took place in the house of the royal grandmother, the mother of Prince Mahidol, and in the morning.

Later in the day, in the royal palace, the king announced the fact of his marriage and there was more pouring of lustral water. The young couple then left for a few days' honeymoon in Hua Hin.

The coronation was a very different matter. It lasted for twelve hours, it cost over $120,000, and to the populace it was worth twice as much. There was a sacramental bath during which the royal astrologer sounded the Victory Gong. Then in his golden coronation robes the king sat on a throne that was shut off from the gaze of any foreigner. Eight deputies of the Assembly presented themselves as the Gods of the Eight Directions; they brought lustral water that had been collected from rivers in the eight directions of the compass. This water was held by the king in a golden conch. The nine-tiered umbrella was handed to him by the Chief Brahmin. Soldiers presented arms. The band played the national anthem. The king then moved into the throne room, to which foreigners were admitted. He sat on a different throne under the nine-tiered umbrella. The Chief Brahmin invoked the presence of the gods. Then twenty pieces of regalia were presented to the king. Each article represented a quality or possession of his kingship. By this ceremony the land, the water and sky of Siam and the life of every human being and every creature in it was entrusted to him. He set on his head the diamond-studded golden crown. It weighed seven kilograms. Priests chanted blessings; a hundred and one guns saluted him. In every monastery in the country gongs were beaten. In just this way had his grandfather, his great-grandfather, and the first of the Chakris been installed in power. In face of this pomp and circumstance what significance had a coup d'etat? Nothing had really changed.

The prince-patriarch blew out the victory candle. There was a royal distribution of gold and silver flowers to the monks. Silver trees were offered to the image of the Emerald Buddha.

There were more speeches, more processions. The chief of the royal scriptures division of the government declared that the king's wife was queen. In honor of the occasion princes were raised in rank, convicted prisoners were forgiven. The king might be powerless to check the ravages of Pibul and his police general — those two robber barons — but in the hearts of his people he ruled supreme, as dear to them as ever Mongkut and Chulalongkorn had been.

On May the ninth the defense in the regicide trial closed its case. For the next month the two sides summed up their arguments, but that was far from being the most important event in Bangkok during May and June. Pridi had been anxious to have the mouth of the Menam dredged so that larger vessels could sail up to Bangkok. He had had neither the time nor resources to implement this project, but Pibul had. And to further his ambition the United States gave to Thailand a dredger called the *Manhattan.* A ceremony was arranged to take place on a royal jetty near the Grand Palace. An impressive group of diplomats, officials and royal personages assembled with their wives to honor the occasion. The occasion was however denied the dignity that had been intended for it, for when Field Marshal Pibul stepped forward to accept the presentation at the hands of the American ambassador, he found himself confronted by the muzzle of a revolver. The revolver was held by a young naval officer who invited Pibul to step into a launch that was waiting by the jetty. At the same time a party of sailors covered the party with rifles and machine guns. In their alarm many of the guests, in their elegant and flimsy dresses, their starched collars and striped trousers, prostrated themselves upon the ground. In mid-stream a Siamese battleship was moored. Pibul was hurried towards it, and there locked in a cabin.

This was a far more ambitious coup d'etat than the one

which had fizzled out in a few hours two years before. The conspirators had ensured that the field marshal should not be left at liberty. With the dictator held in hostage, in the same way that the royal princes had been in 1932, surely a change of regime could be achieved without bloodshed? But the conspirators had not been as thorough as the promoters. Those earlier revolutionaries had captured every single leader who might have offered powerful resistance. They also through the great comedian assumed control of communications. Perhaps it was simpler in 1932 when the city was smaller and the leaders lived within close distance of each other. At any rate this time the navy had left at liberty Police General Pao with his thousand-man-strong riot squad. Pao could contact the army and the air force. Pao was as capable in a crisis as Pibul had been. He closed the Chakri memorial bridge, thus cutting off the battleship from the naval bases and the open sea. The air force then announced that unless Pibul were released, it would bomb the battleship in spite of Pibul's presence in it. In the meantime there was a good deal of firing along the riverbank. It was generally believed that a stalemate had been created. But next morning, to everyone's surprise, the air force began to bomb the battleship. It scored a number of direct hits and the ship went down. Pibul was not, however, in it. When his captors realized that the air force was prepared to carry out its threat, they decided to give their prisoner a sporting chance. They unlocked the cabin and invited him to swim for it. He made the shore and within thirty-six hours of his capture, he was back in full command; this was his fourth lucky escape. Three attempted murders, now a kidnapping.

It had been, however, the most destructive of all the coups, successful or unsuccessful, except for the royalist attempt in 1933 which ended in a pitched battle. Six hundred and three civilians were wounded, one hundred and three fatally. The figures among the soldiers and marines have never been given. The navy's failure on this occasion makes one suspect that the navy was a less efficient force than the army. Perhaps that is to be expected. Thailand had no long based maritime tradition, but the Thais had been warriors from the start.

It was rumored that Pridi took part in the attempted coup: there is no real evidence that he did, but there is little doubt that he encouraged and inspired it. His association with the navy was always close. But it cannot have been easy to organize a revolution from a base in Peking.

The attempt certainly strengthened Pibul's position. It gave him an excuse for purging the navy, and the precautions of Pao's police force could be doubled. Pibul's position was further strengthened by the final verdict of the regicide trial. It did not exonerate Pridi; and Chaleo, one of Pridi's henchmen, had been convicted of conspiracy. Pibul could now claim that his stealing of power and position had been justified. He had ousted a murderer. He was further helped by Pridi's presence in Peking. China was the new enemy. He could present Pridi as a communist, who had tried to introduce a communistic budget the instant he was put in power. The years had sent him further and further to the left.

Pibul was an astute tactician. The West was ready to welcome Thailand as a bulwark against the spread of communism. The Vietnam war had not yet warned the United States against involvement in Far Eastern politics. John Foster Dulles had the ear of Eisenhower. Pibul set out on a world tour to enlist the foreign aid that would support his corrupt and excessively militarized economy. He preached the need to withstand communism. Did we want a Third World War? We must be on our guard against a second Munich. The Free World must stand united. He had an effective personality. His audiences were delighted and Eisenhower presented him with the Legion of

LOVPIX

Ceremonial dancers demonstrate Thai classical dancing

Merit. Few men in the world can have faced the immediate future with greater confidence than Pibul did in 1955. Yet for him too the bell was about to toll. The success of his foreign tour turned his head. Since his early days in Paris he had scarcely been outside Thailand. Now he was acclaimed across the Western continents as the defender of the Free World in Southeast Asia. How many English writers have not lost their sense of proportion under the stimulus of their first welcome in the United States? Pibul like so many others committed the sin that the Greeks labeled *hubris*. He incurred the envy of the gods. On his trip to England he had been inspired by the speakers' soapboxes in Hyde Park. This, he felt, was true democracy. Was he not the champion of liberty and free speech? He decided to institute a speaker's corner in Bangkok.

It seems incredible that he should have done so. For years he had imposed the strictest censorship in Bangkok. There had never been free speech in Thailand. In the days of the absolute monarchy criticism of the throng had been *lèse majesté*. "Mr. Constitution" had ruled for a bare four months. Then there had been the Japanese occupation; a couple of years of Pridi, then a military dictatorship. The Thais were not ready for speaker's corner. But that did not mean that the citizens of Bangkok did not ardently welcome the opportunity to air their grievances. It was a new game for them. They called their corner "Hyde Park." Loudspeakers were permitted and crowds of 10,000 assembled. The meetings were vociferous. There was a certain amount of violence. Before long Hyde Park had to be closed down. But the damage had been done. The reputations of Pibul and Pao had been irretrievably damaged. They had been not only criticized in public but insulted. People who had been afraid to voice their opinions found that many others shared their views. Things could never be the same again.

It may seem strange that Pibul should have made this rash

experiment, but Pibul was an uncomplicated man: he had, as the astrologer had told him, a rare ability to see wrong as right. He was an opportunist. He took a short view. He did what seemed to be in his own interests at the moment. He compromised with each new situation. His conduct during the Japanese occupation was typical. If he needed money, he raised it by the method that happened to be most convenient. Yet even so he had as a very young man listened to the mentor in Paris cafés. He was a democrat at heart. He was no doubt sincerely impressed by the soapboxes in Hyde Park. This is how a country should be run. Let the people get things off their chests — how salutary an experience for the rulers! They could discover how the people really felt. Surely this was what Bangkok needed. Perhaps it was. But it was unfortunate for Pibul and Pao that Bangkok should have been given it. There was now no going back. The meetings had been discontinued, but the discontent remained. Pibul recognized that something had to be done.

Pibul had up till now retained his control of the Assembly by the presence there of nominated members, but he had given his promise that the system of nominated members would be ended in 1962. He felt that it was desirable that an election should be held now, as a trial of strength, to prove to the country that the majority of voters were on his side. The chief opposition was the democratic party headed by Kuang. Electioneering started in the autumn of 1956 for an election that was to be held in the following February. Never had there been so much tension over a campaign. The public had had its appetite for free speech whetted. The elections resulted in a narrow victory for Pibul, but it was a victory that undermined his power more than a defeat would have done. The public was convinced that the election had been rigged. There was talk of the "dirty election": for a while the government persisted in its denials; but the temper of the protests mounted. There were marches and public demonstrations. Students raised their banners on the lawns of Pibul's official palace. In the end Pibul was forced to admit that there had been irregularities. The admission came too late. The marches and the demonstrations continued with greater vehemence. The moment had come for a dramatic intervention and waiting in the wings was the man capable of producing it.

For a long time a Lao named Sarit, an army officer of character and distinction who was now head of the army and garrison commander in Bangkok, had been watching Pao's behavior with mounting fury. The time had come for him to move. He summoned Pibul to his presence. As head of the army he could issue orders even to a dictator. He informed Pibul that things had gone far enough. It was time for him to go, and for Pao as well. Pibul had no alternative to acceptance. He was out of the country within hours. It was an effortless revolution. There were no summary arrests, no capture of communications. The army just took over. There was no need for executions. Pibul lived for a while in California; he spent some months in a monastery in India; then made a home for himself in Japan. He made no attempt to return to Thailand. He had as a soldier the good sense to recognize when a battle had been lost. Pao, too, knew when the field was lost and it is probable that he had taken even more ample precautions against his ultimate dismissal. But if rumor is true, he did not profit for long from his defalcations. He died in Switzerland in 1960, it is reported, of delirium tremens, with his money irretrievably consigned to a numbered account.

Sarit was to rule Thailand as a dictator until his death in 1963. At the start he tried to rule constitutionally through the Assembly. The election which was held in the following December was watched by foreign observers, and everyone was agreed that it was completely honest. Unfortunately the Assembly that emerged from this election was incapable of government. It was divided into contending splinter factions, and Sarit's health was so bad that he had to go to the United States for a major operation. A succession of bad reports reached him during his convalescence. No progress was being made and there appeared to be a genuine danger of a communist revolution. He decided to return to Bangkok.

On his arrival the premier — an army general and a close friend of Sarit's — resigned and Field Marshal Sarit proclaimed a revolution. His party, which had the support of the armed forces and a certain number of civilians, was known as the Revolutionary Party. In its declaration after the usual preamble about respecting human rights, the independence of the courts and the country's international obligations, it asserted that it would adhere strictly to the principle that the sovereign and the Thai nation are one and the same inseparable entity. Thai history is founded on the conception that the sovereign is the symbol of the nation and the palladium of the Thai people. The Revolutionary Party would do all in its power to uphold and cherish this institution and to see to it that the sovereign is held in the deepest veneration and that no sacrilege is perpetrated on the sovereign, the royal family and the royal traditions.

His Majesty expressed appropriately gracious approval of this declaration and appointed the field marshal as his premier. A provisional constitution was proclaimed and members of a constituent assembly were appointed. It was several years before there was any talk of an election. Sarit's dictatorship was complete.

Sarit was a dashing figure. He was handsome, with thick dark hair. He was plump but he was not fat. He was agile. He loved life; he was avid in his appreciation of female beauty. The Thais did not grudge him his successes nor his extravagance.

His weaknesses were those which Thais are readiest to condone. He was a genuine patriot. He was out for himself, but then who in public life is not? The Thais knew that he had their interests as well as his own at heart. Moreover he was prepared to work.

His public image outside Bangkok was marred by the discovery after his death of the extent to which he had appropriated public funds. A great deal went to women and a certain amount of this was recovered. But the Thais themselves were neither indignant nor surprised. Bribery is accepted as a perquisite of public service. And Sarit did effect a number of needed changes. He cleaned up the town, both physically and morally. He sent brothels and blue cinemas underground. He put down opium smoking. It had been the custom for Chinese merchants at the end of the year to balance their budgets by burning down their homes and factories and collecting the insurance. Sarit made arson a capital offense. When I was there in December 1958, there were a number of executions, and excursions were made to see the bullet marks in the white wall of the old city. A great many Thais were shocked by such ruthless treatment. It scarcely accorded with the Buddhist philosophy. But it did stop the spread of arson. He also, in Rayne Kruger's opinion, "restored some measure of dignity to Siam's national life and international status by his personal bearing, his ready cooperation with United Nations agencies and his support of extensive schemes for economic and social progress." It is probable that Thailand was better ruled by Sarit than it had been since the death of Chulalongkorn.

Sarit continued to fill the role of Southeast Asia's buckler against communism. He would have been very foolish if he had not. That was the way to get foreign aid out of the United States; he possibly overrated the menace that communism presented to Thailand, but it is probable that there is a danger. Half of the population of Bangkok is Chinese, and one hears many stories of the way in which arms are being smuggled into the country — stories of a coffin that contains not a corpse but rifles. Vietnam is not far away, and diplomatic relations between Thailand and Cambodia are constantly breaking down.

Sarit's death did not alter the political and administrative pattern. Power passed into the hands of another general and dictatorship continued, with the new premier's task being made considerably easier by the escalation of the war in Vietnam. Dollars poured into the country. Thailand supplied the bases from which United States bombers took off for North Vietnam. Troops and construction companies had to be housed and fed. There was employment for anyone who cared to work. A great deal of the foreign aid went into private pockets, but a great deal of it improved the general economy of the country.

15

A Millionaire Vanishes

Tʜᴇʀᴇ was yet another admirable provider of foreign currency, the silk industry. During World War II, an American
army officer, James H. W. Thompson, had been attached to the
OSS, in which capacity he was engaged in surreptitious operations against the Japanese forces occupying Thailand. He had
special reasons to be interested in the country since his grandfather, James Harrison Wilson, a Civil War general in the
Union Army, had held a diplomatic post in Bangkok.

Thailand in general fascinated Thompson. It reminded him,
he told a reporter, of the Delaware of his boyhood. "As a boy I
always had the feeling when I was in the country, that the
world around me was full of surprises. That's the way I feel
about Thailand now." Bangkok appealed to him even more
than Thailand had. He was an amiable and easygoing man and
the surprises that he found were always happy ones. He felt
himself in tune with the lighthearted, pleasure-loving Thais. He
wondered if it might not be possible for him to stay on. During
his trips into the country he had become interested in the silk
weavers he had found scattered over the country. There were
some two hundred of them, working on ancient handlooms.

The Thai art of weaving silk was intricate and painstaking,

passed from one generation to another. The silk was hand-woven and dyed in cottages. But the younger urban Thais scorned the brilliant colors that their parents and grandparents had worn. They wanted to look like Europeans. Thompson wondered, however, whether there might be an export future for these silks that would compensate for the lessening demand in Thailand itself. Had not these silks a vividness that those of India and China lacked?

He started to collect samples and in 1947 returned to New York with a bulging suitcase. He took them to the editor of *Vogue*, Edna Woolman Chase. "She took one look," Thompson was to recount, "stepped back dramatically and issued a command that no one was to leave the office without seeing them." The green light flickered. He returned to Bangkok with a capital of $700 to restore and rejuvenate a dying craft.

Within two years he had founded the Thai Silk Company. It had thirty-three backers, thirty of whom were Thais. He sought out the surviving weavers. He helped them to set up looms in their own homes. He supplied them with Swiss dyes and taught them how to use them. He searched the National Museum for designs that could be block printed. His success was worldwide and instantaneous. By 1966 he was employing 4,000 weavers and his company shipped $1.5 million worth of silk. Nor by now was he alone in the field. He had a number of competitors who provided work for thousands and enriched the treasury with foreign currency.

Thompson himself had become a legend. He was much more than "just another American tycoon who had hit the jackpot." He was in his way a philanthropist. His employees were not only well paid and in receipt of annual bonuses, but they drew their share of the profits. He was also a collector, avid in his search for antiques. He acquired seven original Siamese teak houses, moved them to Bangkok and established on the banks

Priests at Wat Po relax in the Crocodile Garden of the temple

of a canal a home that became speedily a museum, decorated with Burmese, Khmer and Siamese Buddha images, some of which dated back to the twelfth century. He had red and gold Balinese lions, Ming dynasty rosewood screens, Thai paintings and Oriental porcelains. So renowned was this collection that he decided to open it twice a week to visitors. The admission fees at $1.25 a head went to the Bangkok School for the Blind. A visit to his house was an essential feature of every city tour. It still is; though under sadly different circumstances.

Against the background of the Thai silk industry there has been enacted one of the most perplexing mysteries of our modern day. On April 7, 1967, *Time* magazine, under the heading "Thailand," printed a series of paragraphs entitled "A Walk in the Jungle." It described how James Thompson had visited the Cameron Highlands of Malaysia, a popular health resort, a hundred and forty miles north of Kuala Lumpur and 5,000 feet above sea level. He had gone there for a holiday as the guest of two Singapore friends, Dr. and Mrs. T. G. Ling, in their country home, "Moonlight Bungalow." One afternoon when his host and hostess were enjoying a siesta he took a stroll in the jungle. It was a practice of his to take such strolls. He enjoyed searching among ruins. His hosts were not surprised at his going out without leaving any message, but they became alarmed when dusk fell and he had not returned.

They alerted the police and a manhunt was set in motion, with three hundred soldiers and with policemen using tracker dogs. Helicopters flew low over the trees. A group of aboriginal tribesmen joined the search. In Bangkok a Portuguese Jesuit brother who was reputed to be clairvoyant examined a map and indicated a spot where Thompson was likely to be. A United States brigadier flew off to Malaysia with the map. A Thai witch doctor did his best. Local bandits had quite often captured Chinese merchants and extracted ransom for them, and

Thompson's friends hoped that this was what had happened. They offered substantial rewards, printing the offers in local newspapers. A cook in a Lutheran mission reported that she had seen him standing on a nearby plateau for half an hour. "Then suddenly," she said, "he disappeared." But no other clue was found.

Four weeks later *Time* printed another series of paragraphs under the heading "Thailand." This time the series was titled "Air of Intrigue." The plot, it said, had begun to thicken. No trace of Thompson had been found, although the search had continued. No rumors had come down from the villages. There had been no congregation of vultures. Two curious facts were noted. Thompson was a chain cigarette smoker, but he had left the house without his cigarettes. He also had trouble with his gall bladder and he invariably carried a phial of pills. He had left his pills behind. His friends had begun to wonder whether he was not the victim of some international intrigue. An offer of $25,000 was made for proof of his death. The services of Peter Hurkos were requisitioned.

Peter Hurkos is one of the more fabulous characters of our unlikely age. During his early years he was a house painter in the Netherlands, obscure, industrious; then he had the luck to fall one day from a scaffolding and land upon his head. He emerged from his stupor with the mystic ability to visualize people and places many miles away, to recall incidents from the past of which he could not have been informed, and to foresee the future. He was not invariably correct in his prognostications. Few people can be so consistent as to be always right. He failed, for instance, to extricate the Boston Strangler, but he is reputed to have hit the nail upon the head nine times in ten, and his series of successes now finance a sumptuous apartment in Hollywood that is redolent of incense and decked with

[258]

gaudy Oriental rugs. The police of several countries are grateful to him.

When he came out to "Moonlight Bungalow" he was at first treated with contemptuous skepticism by certain of the attendant journalists, but he quickly settled their hash by reminding a photographer whom he had never seen before that his wife had a scar on the left side of her stomach. He stood pensive on the verandah, then delivered himself of a monologue that was recorded on a tape. "He was sitting in the chair . . . right here . . . I see trucks . . . ah, trucks about from here to the road . . . he walks down the road . . . somebody woke him up, he was sitting, staring outside there, and somebody came in here . . . a friend of his . . . Bebe or Prebe . . . Pridi had, has his own army, no bandits, he walks about exactly a half mile, with Bebe or Prebe . . . got morphine . . . morphine, sleep in truck."

To the Malaysian police Hurkos maintained that after being drugged Thompson was flown to a neighboring country, but he insisted that publication would entail Thompson's death. A Buddhist monk with clairvoyant capacities named independently the same town in that foreign country. Hurkos offered to lead a rescue party, but for diplomatic reasons such a foray could not be attempted. Hurkos was relieved to be able to return to his apartment in Hollywood. He considered that his own life was now in danger.

Thompson's friends, so the *Time* paragraph continued, were inclined to agree with Hurkos. They were ready to admit that he might have been kidnapped for the sake of a ransom which had not yet been demanded, but they were readier to believe that he had been abducted for political motives. He might well be the prisoner of the communists. He had known a number of Ho Chi Minh's agents when he was working against the Japanese. He might know too much. Or the communists might want to use him as an intermediary.

Two suspicious incidents that had not been noticed at the time were now recalled. On the way up to his friends' home in the highlands, the driver of Thompson's taxi was suddenly changed. The taxi had then stopped at a garage for repairs; here Thompson and his traveling companion were asked to move into another taxi. It already contained two passengers. Thompson refused to share the ride with strangers; he would wait, he said, until his own taxi had been repaired. Was this a first attempt at an abduction?

It was also remembered that on the day of Thompson's disappearance, a caravan of five cars was seen going up the road leading to the highlands. That road was usually free of traffic. Three hours later, almost immediately after Thompson had disappeared, the cars were seen coming down the road. Had Thompson been in that caravan?

A few weeks later the plot was to thicken further. Thompson's sister, Mrs. Katherine Thompson Wood, was murdered in her American home. She had been the daughter-in-law of the late Major General Wood, who had been Governor General of the Philippines and had been considered as a Republican candidate. Her marriage was not a successful one. Her husband, an Army lieutenant in the Philippines, had conducted by cable such successful stock market speculations that there was talk of a congressional investigation. He left the service, went with his wife to Europe, and lost all his money at the gaming tables. His wife divorced him. She never remarried, even when her husband — who after working in a coal mine had restored his fortunes and risen to the rank of adjutant general of New Mexico's National Guard — died in 1950. One experiment in matrimony was enough for Mrs. Wood; in this she resembled her brother. James Thompson's one marriage was a brief and fruitless one.

He was divorced in 1946, and his name was never linked with anyone's in Bangkok. Rumor did not touch him. One would be tempted to surmise that "that side of life" meant very little either to the brother or the sister.

Though Mrs. Wood's husband had run through his own fortune at the gaming tables, hers remained intact. She had summer homes in Maine and on the Delaware shore. She also had a mansion in the Du Pont country. Her two passions were fox hunting and gardening. But she lived unextravagantly, in relative seclusion. She had been worried, of course, by her brother's disappearance, but she was confident that he would arrive at her house in the United States for dinner on Labor Day, as had been his custom for several years.

Four days before Labor Day, however, the morning maid heard whines from the two large dogs who shared Mrs. Wood's bedroom. When she opened the door to release the dogs, she saw Mrs. Wood, in her nightdress, dead among her pillows. She had been bludgeoned to death. Her private papers were scattered on the floor and across the desks, but nothing of value had been taken. It was clear that Mrs. Wood herself had put up a desperate defense, but there was no sign of the dogs having tried to rescue her, nor did they seem to have been drugged. Her grandfather's Civil War revolver had not been touched.

The murder seemed completely pointless. Was there any connection between it and Thompson's disappearance? Peter Hurkos was convinced there was. "I am very worried now about her sister, Mrs. Douglas," he told a *Life* correspondent. "She is in grave danger. She should have protection."

Life magazine had now come to consider that the matter was worth full treatment and in *Life* it soon appeared under the title "Murder Compounds." The story began: "Recipe for a classic mystery." *The Ingredients* were "One distinguished-looking art-collecting American millionaire bachelor, with a past embracing espionage in the Orient where he continues to live. One socially prominent sister of the millionaire dwelling quietly in a rambling mansion on a fourteen-acre estate near Wilmington, Delaware, where she keeps a .38 revolver at her bedside and maintains two much-feared dogs. Another socially prominent sister of millionaire, married to a former high civilian in the American defense hierarchy. One sybaritic Dutch seer with an impressive but fallible record in solving mysteries psychically. Assorted Asian princes, Buddhist mystics, American generals, an aborigine witch doctor, diplomats and intelligence agents, Malaysian and Thai police officials and a dash of communist operatives (to taste)." Then came *Preparation:* "Place American millionaire in a cool, high remote Asian bungalow; surround with luxury and jungle. Then with a flick of the wrist make him vanish. Stir in Dutch seer, Buddhist mystics, Malaysian and Thai police, assorted Americans, etc. Spice with suggestion of internationally important political intrigue. Bring to boil, then lower the flame. As mixture simmers, add mysterious murder of first sister in her secluded American mansion. Now add Dutch seer's visions linking brother's disappearance and sister's murder, followed quickly by seer's warning that another sister is in grave danger. Dilute with several dashes of chilled water supplied by skeptics."

It was "the works" as *Life* understands that word. The article was written by Henry Moscow. The information had been gathered by Time, Inc.'s bureau chief in Bangkok, and *Life*'s special correspondents in Los Angeles, Boston, Singapore, Philadelphia, Paris, Chicago and Washington. Stephany Couftney, who accompanied Peter Hurkos, provided the tape on which the seer's musings were recorded. The data was collated by Susan Costello.

It was a seven-page article. After setting out the story with appropriate verve, it records the various explanations that have been suggested. Thompson's brother Henry dismissed the possibility that there could be any connection between his sister's murder and his brother's disappearance. "Forget about it. There is no connection whatsoever. My sister didn't have an enemy in the world." The other sister, Mrs. Douglas, was in agreement, but Mrs. Wood's son Harrison was not. He suggested that Thai communists resented the prosperity that the silk industry had brought to the country and murdered his mother in revenge. A Philadelphia journalist produced a solution that was even more fantastic. He believed that Thompson did visit his sister in Delaware, pursued to her house by the assassins who had forced him to disappear. Once again he eluded them, but the assassins killed Mrs. Wood to prevent her appearing as a witness. As the Duke of Wellington said on a different occasion, "If you believe that, sir, you would believe anything."

The *Life* article concluded with a return to the Dutch house painter. He still believed that Thompson was alive and in the hands of the communists. They had tried to make him denounce over the radio the Americans in Thailand. When he refused, they threatened to kill his sister. When he still refused, they made good their threat. They then showed him the press clippings. "You have another sister," they said. "Do you want her to remain alive?"

Two years have passed, and the sister is still alive. No clue to the mystery has been found; but there are still many who hold that this mystery is another installment of the Pridi saga. After all, Thompson and Pridi were friends in the days of the resistance. Unlikelier things have happened.

In the meantime, his house in Bangkok remains one of the chief exhibits on the tourist itinerary. It and its treasures have been left to his family in the United States, but the will cannot be cleared until it has been proved that Thompson is no longer alive. He was sixty-one when he disappeared; many years will have to pass before his death can be assumed. When that time does come the Thai government may well object to the removal of national heirlooms. It is probable that the Thompson house will remain as it is, untouched, a permanent museum.

Epilogue

As I have already told, I first visited Bangkok in September 1926. I did not enjoy myself. The heat was stupefying. There was no air conditioning and the mosquitoes were triumphantly voracious. I presumed that I had come at the wrong time of year. But September, I was to learn later, is far from being "the cruellest month." That privileged distinction is reserved for May. Indeed, the climate of Bangkok is, for the Westerner, one of the most trying in the world. The sea is ten miles away and no breezes blow from it. If you motor to Pattaya, which is on the sea to the southeast and some three hours away, you will notice a marked change of atmosphere when you have got halfway.

There are three seasons — the summer, which runs from February to May, the rainy season from May to October, the winter from November to February. December and January are the only two months when you can be certain to have no rain. The average maximum temperature during the hot season is 103.7 Fahrenheit (39.85 Centigrade), but during the rainy and cool seasons it can reach 98.1 Fahrenheit (36.7 C). The humidity is constant, vacillating between 71.9 percent in the driest month and 83.2 in the wettest. It is the lack of variety in temperature that makes Bangkok so exhausting. April is not in the rainy season but it has more thunderstorms than June, July, August and October.

The thunderstorms are very violent. Great leaden clouds build up in the northeast. Thunder rumbles. About midday lights are turned on in office buildings. A long breathless pause is followed by great wind rushing through the treetops. It is like a large sea swell. There is no preliminary shower. Just a solid cascade of water for half an hour. Winter is the season of the northeast monsoon.

May is considered the most trying month, but in consolation that is the period when the most luscious fruits are at their best — the mangosteen, the mango and the dourian, which the elegant often decline to eat because of its cloying smell. The pineapple comes as a reward in the hot season. The papaya is available all the year round. The lychee is in season in October; so are the sack fruit and the rambutan.

Bangkok is less trying now with air conditioning and the mosquitoes partially controlled. But even so I have been careful to time my later visits in terms of the calendar.

I have made four such visits since 1957. My last one was in November 1968, when I was in search of the material that would round off this book.

I set out that last time with some misgivings. Everyone assured me that Bangkok was spoiled. The jet age had filled it with tourists. The Vietnam war had turned it into a rest and recreation center. The traffic was impossibly congested, the klongs had been filled in and the trees felled so that the streets might be broadened. Consequently the climate had changed, through the lack of shade and with the heat refracted from the pavements and the vast concrete hotels that lined every avenue. The city, I was told, had lost its special, its distinctive charm. It was, in fact, no longer Bangkok. I was prepared to be disenchanted.

I arrived at sunset and it was completely dark by the time I was in my taxi. The road from the airport runs through dead level country, past rice fields and small houses. It was the crowded hour. I could see nothing but neon signs and the headlights of approaching cars. There was no familiar landmark that I could expect to recognize. It was one straight road after another.

At last the succession of straight streets, leading into one another, was cut across at right angles by the road that is still called "New" although it is the oldest road in Bangkok. We turned to the right, then down to the left. My heart contracted. Whatever else had changed, I prayed that the Oriental would be the same.

My prayer was granted. No first class hotel has a less prepossessing exterior. Its entrance is no more than a lighted door on the flank of a crowded car park, but there was the same uniformed head porter to supervise its traffic; inside there was the smiling welcome of the receptionist, Ankara, every bit as elegant as she had been eleven years before; instead of the conventional hotel lobby there was the same Japanese garden with the red bridge across its water, the same passage led between the short row of shops to the garden and the swimming pool. Within a few minutes I was looking down from a third floor window on to the green lawn, the palm trees and the old two storied façade with the words Oriental Hotel in antique lettering.

At the back of it rose the tall rectangular block that had gone up early in 1958; but in front of it were the two classical statues carrying lamps, just as they had been when Maugham suffered from the fever which he described in *A Gentleman in the Parlour*. Eleven years before, when I had stayed in the old wing, I had had a broad balcony with long chairs and a desk at which I had done my writing. The large bare bedroom at the back had

The Buddha in Petchaburi Cave, 113 miles south of Bangkok

wire netting across the windows — the mosquitoes were so insistent that I could not sit on the balcony after dusk. At the back of the bedroom was a bathroom that may have contained a shower, but as far as I recall was furnished with a large water tub from which I splashed myself with a dipper. I cannot remember if there was hot running water. Before air conditioning one did not expect or need hot water in the tropics. I believe that the room I had then is now refurbished as a luxury suite, with Thai silk hangings. Yet the feel of the Oriental is still the same. "There is a barbecue tonight," Ankara told me. "Shall I book a table for you?"

The barbecue was staged on a new broad terrace running along the waterfront. "You needn't worry about mosquitoes," Ankara told me. "We've got that problem settled." I remembered how eleven years ago, on solitary evenings when I had had an aquavit, a chicken sandwich and a glass of beer under the colonnade behind the lawn, I had soon found myself driven by the mosquitoes to the security of my screen-protected bedroom. But tonight there were coils of smoldering disinfectant underneath each table. My ankles did not itch.

There were at least a hundred guests at the barbecue. Most of them seemed *farangs*. But here was a fair sprinkling of Thais. Nobody was wearing a dinner jacket; most of the men wore ties, and shirts that buttoned at the wrist. None of them seemed warriors from the jungles. There is an unmistakable atmosphere about the man on leave.

Next morning I called on my travel agent. His office was in the Narai Hotel, in Silom Road. I had to cross New Road to get to it. *Samlors* are prohibited now in Bangkok and the tramlines had been taken up. Here at any rate the traffic problem had been improved. Eleven years ago Silom Road had been for me full of familiar landmarks. I was taking a course of weekly penicillin injections to counteract the effects of a bronchial attack with which a particularly damp English summer had afflicted me. My doctor's clinic was a mile or so down the road. His home was a few doors from it. His wife, Maudie, was a good friend of mine and usually after my injection I would call on her for a cup of coffee. She was one of the people I was most looking forward to meeting again. A letter from her had awaited my arrival at the hotel. She had changed her address, it told me. She was now living in the suburbs. I was soon to understand why she had moved. The imposing façade of the Narai Hotel occupied the site of her charming, rambling two-storied house. The Narai is an impressive building. It adds dignity to the broadened thoroughfare. But I missed the little klong that ran along its sidewalk, and the trees that had shaded it and the rickety wooden bridge by which I had crossed over into Maudie's garden.

Shortly before starting on this trip, I had met a friend who had recently taken one of Kuoni's package tours of the Far East. His tour had included Bangkok. How was it, I asked. "I'd never been there before," he said. "It was the highlight of the trip. Fantastic. All those temples. At the same time four days is quite enough."

On my first lengthy visit in 1957 I had stayed four weeks and had left reluctantly with a sense of unfinished business, resolved to return as soon as possible, which I did in the following November, to stay ten weeks and leave genuinely regretful that the conditions of my nomad life did not allow me to put down roots. But I could see what my friend meant. Within four days a package tour could show you all that is special and different in Bangkok — the klongs, the floating market, the Royal Palace, the Emerald Buddha, the recumbent Buddha, the Gold Buddha that had been hidden in cement, the Temple of the Dawn, the silk factories; there were also the special attractions of Thai dancing and Thai boxing.

I had seen all these before, during previous visits; but I had not seen them as part of a conducted tour. I had seen them at my leisure, being escorted there by Thais at times when such special objects as the Emerald Buddha were not open to the public. I am not sure indeed to what extent conducted tours were organized in 1957 — it is my impression that the boom in tourism began a little later with the opening of jet travel. But this time I put myself down for all the tours, so as to refresh my memory and also to judge the effect of the tourist boom upon the city.

During the course of these tours I came to realize what people had meant when they told me that Bangkok had been spoiled.

Perhaps my staying at the Oriental made these tours more exhausting for me than for the others, because as the Oriental is on the river, the excursions began and ended there; and as the cars had to go around the town picking up and depositing tourists, each trip was preceded by and concluded by a half-hour's drive through drab, dreary and congested streets. In some cities an attempt has been made to draw a green belt of parkland around the commercial center. In Bangkok the core of attractive buildings that lie along the river are cut off from the suburban countryside by a belt of noisy squalor.

The tours themselves are well arranged, the guides informative and amusing, but there is such a congestion of tourists now that it is very hard to see the various exhibits. Somebody's head is always in the way. Moreover the guides are convinced — perhaps with justice — that the two main objects of the tourist are to take photographs and make purchases. In consequence a great deal of each tour is occupied with visits to shops and pauses at photogenic points.

Tourism has its distinct credit side, and facilities are provided by which the visitor can quickly get an idea of the life of the community. No one would seriously argue that Tahiti has been improved by the arrival of the jet, yet when I was there in 1959 I saw on the island of Moorea far better dancing in the traditional manner than I had thirty years earlier in the "unspoiled" days. Teams of dancers had been collected and trained, and the result was exquisite. I saw the real Tahiti that Captain Bligh's mariners had disturbed. It was to meet the demands of tourists that there has been this restoration of classic dancing.

In the same spirit, Bangkok has created a museum, halfway to the airport, which provides the visitor with a valuable insight into the traditional life and habits of the Thais. Under the name of Timland — Thailand in miniature — it presents within a twenty acre park an assemblage of the various local industries. In microcosm you are shown the life of the country, with the buffalo at work upon the plow, the rice industry, the transplanting, the threshing, the husking and the polishing by hand. The spinning of the silk from the cocoons is shown. There are silk weavers, gem cutters and wood weavers. There is a demonstration of elephants at work with teak logs. The use of the fisherman's windmill and waterlift is explained. There is an aquarium, a snake house and an efflorescence of orchids. There is a display of dancing. Finally there is a gymkhana, for Thai boxing and Thai fencing, with clubs and sticks. There is cockfighting, and a master of snakes demonstrates his skill. Every aspect of the Thai way of life is there. In fact in the five days that are allotted to him, the tourist can see not only what the city itself has to offer, but he can get an accurate impression of the life of the countryside and its people.

Bangkok is today one of the great tourist attractions of the world. Five days are as much as the contemporary tourist can devote to any place, and there is a greater variety in Bangkok than in any city that I know. There is moreover the unfailing charm and friendliness of the Thais themselves. Their country has never been enslaved. In consequence they can meet the visitor with self-confidence and pride. They have no chips upon their shoulders. For the contemporary world traveler Bangkok is a must. And yet, I fancy that a great many of the tourists who send off postcards to their friends, and flash the photographic souvenirs of their trip upon their drawing-room screens, with the warm assertion "Yes, Bangkok *was* the high spot," will add as an afterthought, "But I'm not sure that I should like to live there."

They will add that afterthought because of the exhausting nature of that gray belt of squalor that divides the riverside palaces and temples from the countryside. Traffic is a problem in every city in the world today. In Bangkok, it is intensified by the heat. Before I arrived, I had written to the representative of the British Council, inviting him and his wife to lunch with me. He replied that much as he would have liked to, his office was too far from the Oriental. We changed lunch to dinner, but his inability to lunch was symptomatic of the change in Bangkok during the last few years. In 1958, even in 1964, members of the British Council and the Embassy staff made no difficulties about lunching at the Oriental.

The British Council's representative lived in an accessible part of the city, by no means in the suburbs; but the journey when I lunched there took twenty-five minutes in a taxi. He told me that during the rush hours it needed forty minutes to reach his office. In addition to that he frequently had to go to the embassy for conferences. Not many cars are air conditioned; the heat was a constant drain upon his energy.

It may be that the Vietnam war is responsible in part for the rapid increase in traffic congestion; and the war is blamed for the blocking up of the klongs and the cutting down of the trees; their removal has certainly robbed the city of a great deal of its charm. Bangkok can no longer be called "The Venice of Asia," but probably even if there had been no war, the klongs would have had to go sooner or later. The city had to be modernized.

I had expected that the presence of United States troops would have made more difference to the city than the cutting down of the trees and the filling in of the klongs, particularly the presence of Negro troops. A twelfth of the American soldiers serving in Vietnam are Negroes. But this is not the case. I was not aware that a foreign army was using Bangkok as a rest and recreation center. When I stayed at Pattaya, I was surrounded by men on leave. Apart from the hotel staff, I should not have known that I was in Asia; but in Bangkok itself, I hardly saw a serviceman.

Men on leave keep to themselves, with Negro and white soldiers having their own separate nightclub areas. I went there one evening and was surprised to find how orderly it all was. There were plenty of pretty girls for the GIs to dance with. Most of them were drinking the mild local beer. It has been agreed everywhere that the troops have behaved extremely well. The war had indeed had far less effect than I had expected. When I heard people say "Bangkok is spoiled" I remembered how often I have heard my contemporaries and immediate juniors say "London — or New York or Rome or Paris — is impossible today." And indeed I do find that getting about in London or New York imposes a heavy strain upon my waning powers. But then I ask myself, whether I do not feel this way simply because those powers *are* waning and because my friends and I are fifteen years further down the course. Perhaps the trouble is that we are trying to live in London and New York with the social techniques that we acquired in the '30s and the '40s. My children do not find London impossible today. I think that is how it is with Bangkok.

The ten weeks that I spent there at the end of 1958 were as good as any I have known. I loved my first-floor room in the Oriental. I was working on a novel, and the difficult early stage was past. I breakfasted as soon as it was light, and by seven o'clock as soon as the balcony was clear of mosquitoes I was at my desk. I stopped writing round about eleven. By then I had done fifteen hundred words. There was no swimming pool then in the hotel, but several of my friends had pools. And those that had not, were members of the country club. Most days I got a swim. Most days I had a lunch or dinner date, or I had guests coming to me at the Oriental. There were picnics over the weekend. I had a number of friends, Thai, British and American. It was a varied, lively social life, with the four hours that I had spent at my desk each morning giving the day poise and balance. I do not see any reason why I should not in the future, in this new changed Bangkok, spend two equally contented months working upon a novel, spending my leisure hours among friends.

Very few of the British and American friends that I made in 1957 and 1958 are still in residence — with the exception of two professors at Chulalongkorn university; the turnover in official appointments is fairly swift, and ten years is a long stretch even for someone employed by a business corporation, but their replacements are invariably gregarious and from one decade to the next the same type of Briton and American looks for an overseas posting. On the other hand, my Thai friends were leading the same kind of life, most of them in the same houses. My doctor had moved out into the suburbs, half an hour's drive away, but his wife still had a flat near his clinic in Silom Road. Her "boutique" was in the same side street. I have had the good fortune to become a close friend of Prince Phya

Rangsit, to whose father I have previously referred. The only change in his house was the organization of an air-cooled room on the first floor, where we sat after dinner and which was perhaps used as a guest's bedroom. Prince Chula died at a wistfully early age in 1963, but his palace is still maintained by Captain Bisdar and his family, with the prince's widow visiting Bangkok, usually with her daughter, every year. During my visit her birthday was being celebrated and I was invited to the ceremony. It was a small and intimate occasion; there were three *farangs* in addition to myself, two American ladies and a Swedish silk merchant. Maudie, the doctor's wife, drove us out there.

It was a half hour's drive through the familiar dreary streets. We could have got there by river in half the time. We arrived at half past ten. The ceremony had already started. On a raised platform seven priests were seated with crossed legs, chanting a series of prayers. They were joined by a piece of thick string which symbolized unity, and which they held between their hands. They were arranged along a corner of the wall, at right angles, four of them on one side, three on the other. A kind of altar-throne had been fixed at one end of the platform; in front of it was a framed photograph of the princess. Facing the platform was a row of chairs on which the guests were seated: every so often there was a pause in the chanting. The priests would sip from a glass of orange juice. Each had a bowl beside him into which, if he wanted, he could spit. Eventually the head priest made a sign that he would like the photograph of the princess brought forward. He sprinkled it with lustral water. Then he sprinkled the guests. The stretch of string which had symbolized the unity of the priests was rolled back on to its ball. The ceremony was ended. The priests were at liberty to proceed to the dining room. It was eleven o'clock. Beneath each chair at the table was a bowl. Now that the habit of chewing betel nut has been largely abandoned, there is little need for these bowls. But tradition decrees their presence.

The family and guests walked across the lawn to the terrace that looked over the river. Facing us was a broad tributary stream that was crowded with launches and small craft. It was the stream by which a week earlier, after a guided trip to the floating market, I had emerged into the main river. We had made a big circle among the klongs and I was not quite certain where I was. I had suspected that Prince Chula's palace must be somewhere across the water, but I failed to recognize it.

We were served a choice between orange juice or gin and tonic. The tributary river was filled now with the kind of launch in which I had been carried to the floating market two Saturdays before. The two Bangkoks were in fact facing one another, the tourist Bangkok with the launches piled with the packages that had been bought in the floating market, and that had brought into the country the hard currency that its economy so urgently needed, and the traditional Bangkok of the saffron-robed priests who were paying tribute to the widow of a royal personage. Neither was aware of the existence of the other, yet each was complimentary to the other.

The priests had finished their meal. Midday was close at hand; after which they must take no nourishment until the following morning. There remained the ritual of the gifts. The priests resumed their places on the platform. The family and guests resumed the chairs facing them. To each of the priests in turn was handed a plate laden with joss sticks, lotus flowers, fruit and an envelope that contained money. The four *farangs* were given the opportunity of presenting a plate. If the plate was presented by a man the priest could take it with his own hands; if by a woman, he placed a cloth in front of him and the plate was put upon it. He could then take the plate and put its contents into the bag which every priest carries over his right shoulder. When the last gift had been handed over, the priests rose and took their leave, with the family bent down on their knees before them. In that ceremony lay for me the reassurance that the Bangkok that I loved would remain itself, in essence.

I asked Prince Rangsit whether the Second War, with its Japanese occupation, had really altered the life of the city. He hesitated. "I suppose there must have been a blackout." But it did not seem to have made very much impression on him. There had been a resistance movement of which his future brother-in-law had been a member. His father-in-law had died during the war, and the son had not been able because of his membership to attend the funeral. But he had cycled in and watched the procession from the pavement. The bombing had been tiresome; and Princess Rangsit's library — her father had been a poet of high distinction — had been destroyed. Maudie was at college then. She had gone to live across the river, in a house on one of the klongs. The Allies were unlikely to drop bombs there, and if they did, only a direct hit would do much damage. She had rather enjoyed herself, she said.

No place remains the same forever. But Bangkok has been so loved because it is the expression of the Thais themselves, of their lightheartedness, their love of beauty, their reverence for tradition, their sense of freedom, their extravagance, their devotion to their creeds — to characteristics that are constant and continuing in themselves. Bangkok has always been that: I think that it will stay that way. I do not believe it can be spoiled.

Bibliography

ALL books are listed chronologically, in relation to the periods they cover.

Lords of Life: A History of the Kings of Thailand, by H.R.H. Prince Chula Chakrabongse, with a preface by H. R. Trevor-Roper. Alvin Redman, London, 1960.

The Twain Have Met, by H.R.H. Prince Chula Chakrabongse. Foulis, London, 1956.

A History of Siam, by W.A.R. Wood. Unwin, London, 1926.

Thailand, by Noel F. Busch. Van Nostrand Co., Inc., 1959.

Siamese White, by Maurice Collis. Faber & Faber, London, 1936.

Description du Rayaume Thai du Siam, by Monseigneur Pallegoix. Vialat, Paris, 1854.

A Journal of an Embassy from the Governor General of India to the Courts of Siam and Cochin China, by John Crawfurd. London, 1828.

The Kingdom and Peoples of Siam, by Sir John Bowring. Parker Sons, London, 1857.

The English Governess at the Siamese Court, by Anna Leonowens. Boston, 1870.

Anna and the King of Siam, by Margaret Landon. London, 1945.

Fanny and the Regent of Siam, by R. J. Minney. World Press, Cleveland, 1962.

The Pearl of Asia, by Jacob T. Child. Donohue, Chicago, 1892.

A Physician at the Court of Siam, by Dr. Malcolm Smith. Country Life, London, 1943.

The Gentleman in the Parlour, by Somerset Maugham. Heinemann, London, 1930.

Siam in Transition, by K. P. Landon. Oxford University Press, London, 1939.

Siam at the Cross Roads, by Sir Joseph Crosby. Hollis-Carter, London, 1945.

Opium Venture, by Gerald Sparrow. Robert Hale, London, 1957.

The Star Sapphires, by Gerald Sparrow. Jarrolds, London, 1958.

The Devil's Discus, by Rayne Kruger. Cassell, London, 1954.

Bangkok Editor, by Alexander MacDonald. Macmillan, New York, 1949.

[281]

Inside Asia, by John Gunther. Harper's, New York, 1939; revised edition, 1942.

Siam, Land of Temples, by John Audrig. Robert Hale, London, 1962.

Front Line Diplomat, by Sir Geoffrey Thompson. Hutchinson, London, 1959.

Thailand, by Wendell Blanchard. H.R.A.F. Press, New Haven, 1957.

Brief Authority, by Edwin Stanton. Harper's, New York, 1956.

The Mask of Siam, by David Garnett. Robert Hale, London, 1959.

Land of the Lotus Eaters, by Norman Bartlett. Jarrolds, London, 1959.

The Bangkok *Mail*, June-December 1932. Articles by St. Clair McKelway.

Time magazine. April 7, 1967.

"*Murder Compounds: The Thompson Case.*" Article in *Time*, 1967.